LOUIS AUCHINCLOSS

Literature and Life: American Writers

Selected list of titles:

SAUL BELLOW	*Brigitte Scheer-Schäzler*
TRUMAN CAPOTE	*Helen S. Garson*
RACHEL CARSON	*Carol B. Gartner*
THEODORE DREISER	*James Lundquist*
WILLIAM FAULKNER	*Alan Warren Friedman*
F. SCOTT FITZGERALD	*Rose Adrienne Gallo*
ROBERT FROST	*Elaine Barry*
LILLIAN HELLMAN	*Doris V. Falk*
ERNEST HEMINGWAY	*Samuel Shaw*
JOHN IRVING	*Gabriel Miller*
THE NOVELS OF HENRY JAMES	*Edward Wagenknecht*
THE TALES OF HENRY JAMES	*Edward Wagenknecht*
KEN KESEY	*Barry H. Leeds*
MARY MCCARTHY	*Willene Schaefer Hardy*
JAMES A. MICHENER	*George J. Becker*
ANAÏS NIN	*Bettina L. Knapp*
JOHN O'HARA	*Robert Emmet Long*
THE PLAYS OF EUGENE O'NEILL	*Virginia Floyd*
EDGAR ALLAN POE	*Bettina L. Knapp*
J. D. SALINGER	*James Lundquist*
JOHN STEINBECK	*Paul McCarthy*
LIONEL TRILLING	*Edward Joseph Shoben, Jr.*
MARK TWAIN	*Robert Keith Miller*
NATHANAEL WEST	*Robert Emmet Long*
EDMUND WILSON	*David Castronovo*
RICHARD WRIGHT	*David Bakish*

Complete list of titles in the series available from publisher on request. Some titles are also in paperback.

LOUIS AUCHINCLOSS

Christopher C. Dahl

UNGAR • NEW YORK

Acknowledgments

The author gratefully acknowledges the work of Donna Wessel Walker, who made the index. He would also like to thank Professors Claude J. Summers and Curtis Dahl for reading the manuscript at several stages and for making many helpful suggestions.

1986
The Ungar Publishing Company
370 Lexington Avenue
New York, N.Y. 10017

Printed in the United States of America

Library of Congress Cataloging-in-Publication Data

Dahl, Christopher C.
    Louis Auchincloss.

    (Literature and life series)
    Bibliography: p.
    Includes index.
    1. Auchincloss, Louis — Criticism and interpretation.
I. Title.
PS3501.U25Z62   1986   813'.54   86-11253
ISBN 0-8044-2123-4

For E.C.D., A.K.D., and especially Ruth

*For E.C.D., A.K.D., and
especially Ruth*

Contents

Chronology

1917	Louis Stanton Auchincloss is born 27 September in Lawrence, Long Island, son of Joseph Howland and Priscilla Stanton Auchincloss.
1923–29	Attends Bovee School for Boys on Fifth Avenue in New York.
1929	Enters Groton School (Massachusetts); influenced by headmaster, the Rev. Endicott Peabody and young English teacher, Malcolm Strachan; graduates in 1935.
1935–38	Attends Yale College, where he studies English and French literature and history. He serves as an editor of the *Yale Literary Magazine* and writes a novel in his junior year.
1938	Leaves Yale without graduating when his attempted novel is rejected by Scribner's.
1938–41	Attends University of Virginia Law School.
1941	After graduation from law school, he enters firm of Sullivan & Cromwell as an associate. Admitted to New York State Bar.
1941–45	Serves in US Navy as a naval intelligence officer in Panama, an LST officer during the invasion of France,

1965   He is elected to the National Institute of
        Arts and Letters.
1966   *The Embezzler* is published.
1967   He becomes President of the Museum of
        the City of New York.
1971   *Edith Wharton: A Woman in Her Time*
        is published.
1972   *I Come As a Thief*, his twelfth novel, is
        published.
1974   His autobiography, *A Writer's Capital*,
        is published. He receives an honorary
        Doctor of Letters degree from New York
        University.
1975   *Reading Henry James* is published.
1980   *The House of the Prophet*, his fifteenth
        novel, is published.
1982   *Watchfires*, his seventeenth novel, is
        published.
1985   *Honorable Men*, his twentieth novel, is
        published.
1986   He receives further recognition for his
        work when he is awarded an honorary
        degree from the University of the South.

1

A Life in Law
and Letters: A
Biographical Sketch

"People ask me how I manage to write and practice. Sometimes I think it is the only thing about me that interests them," Louis Auchincloss has written. "All I can say is that a great step was taken when I ceased to think of myself as a 'lawyer' or a 'writer.' I simply was doing what I was doing when I did it. But mine is a career I should not recommend to a young man starting out. It is a peculiar shell that over the years I have managed to manufacture for myself."[1] Auchincloss is a unique figure in contemporary American letters: he has continued to be a practicing attorney in a major Wall Street law firm while publishing more than thirty works of fiction, literary criticism, and biography. Since the publication of his first novel in 1947, he has resolutely gone his own way as a novelist. Refusing to bow to contemporary fashions in fiction, he has followed in the tradition of the novel of manners as practiced by Henry James and Edith Wharton, modifying that tradition with his own insights and infusing it with a thoroughly modern skepticism. The most literary of contemporary novelists, he has at the same time always appealed to a popular audience. Though he is the very opposite of a confessional writer, his life has influenced his work at practically every turn. He has written that "all a novelist's characters are himself," and gracefully told the story of how he became an author in his memoir, *A Writer's Capital*.

Louis Stanton Auchincloss was born on September 27, 1917, in Lawrence, New York, the second son of Joseph Howland Auchincloss and Priscilla Dixon Stanton.[2] Both his parents were members of prominent New York families who had lived in the city for several generations, and Auchincloss grew up in a world filled with grandparents, aunts and uncles, and countless cousins. The first Auchincloss to come to this country had arrived in New York from Scotland in 1803 — relatively late by old New York standards — and he had come to set up a branch of the family's dry-goods business. He prospered, and by the end of the century the family was securely connected by marriage to such older families as the Russells and the Howlands. Although there never was any single large family fortune, Auchincloss observes that "each generation of Auchincloss men either made or married its own money." Auchincloss's mother came on one side from an old family, the Dixons, very much like several that appear in his novels, who "were bound together by tight tribal loyalties that had not altogether disintegrated in the nineteen twenties" when he was growing up.

Auchincloss was brought up in comfort on the upper East Side of New York, in a country house on Long Island, and at a large shingled summer cottage in Bar Harbor. Though his parents held themselves apart from the more frivolous aspects of fashionable society, Auchincloss as a boy — much to their horror — was fascinated by the dramas of wealth and greed, divorce and infidelity, that he saw played out in the world around him. Always an observer, he recalls that he began at an early age "to see my family and their friends in terms of stories."

As is often not the case with many writers, Auchincloss's family was a happy one. His parents were devoted to each other. His father, a lawyer who specialized in corporate trust indentures, was a popular, gregarious man who loved sports and music and spent most of his time and energy outside the office on his family. He spent his entire professional career in the law firm now known as Davis Polk & Wardwell. For him the firm was almost a club. He especially relished his daily contacts with partners and associates, and the spirit of camaraderie he found at work. Auchincloss's mother was the dominant figure in the household. She was a capable manager of the family's various establishments, an omnivorous reader with incisive literary opinions, and a woman with a genuine gift for friendship. But she was troubled by a strong, almost neurotic sense of duty, which she passed on to her children. Her son early drew a sharp distinction between the world of people and books in which his mother seemed to live and the grim masculine world that he, as a male, would eventually be expected to enter. "I came to think of women," he recalls, "as a privileged, happy lot, with the right to sit home all day on sofas and telephone, and of men as poor slaves doomed to go downtown and do dull, soul-breaking things to support their families." Years later, Auchincloss's boyish premonitions seemed confirmed when his father suffered a nervous breakdown said to be connected with worry over an error he had made in a trust indenture.

Auchincloss began his education at the Bovee School for Boys, a private day school that admitted a larger range of students and had a rather more relaxed atmosphere than similar schools in the city. Following family tradition, he was sent at the age of twelve to Groton School in Massachusetts. At the time Groton was presided over by the impressive figure of its founding headmaster, the Reverend Endicott Peabody, then in his mid-seventies. Auchincloss was at first miserable at Groton because he was unpopular and a poor athlete, but by his second or third year he found a niche for himself as a hardworking student and editor of the school literary magazine, to which he contributed a number of stories and articles. Under Peabody's influence, he went through a brief but intense religious phase. In his English classes, he was introduced to Victorian novels and, although at first he read mostly for grades, he came to know the works of Dickens and the Brontës and discovered the *Rubáiyát of Omar Khayyám*. From the teaching of Malcolm Strachan, a remarkable young master, he became aware of the joys to be gained from literature. Groton was later to become the model for Justin Martyr School in Auchincloss's novel *The Rector of Justin*.

At Yale College, which he entered in 1935, Auchincloss studied English and French literature and history. There too he became an editor of the *Yale Literary Magazine*. As he had been in childhood, he was fascinated by society and attended more than his share of debutante parties in college, primarily as an observer: "I 'collected' parties. I would go to one where I knew nobody at all, simply because it was given in a house or club that I wanted to see or because something interested me about my host or hostess." In his junior year, he wrote a novel about a young school teacher who married her way into society. Intended as a determinist novel — Auchincloss's own version of *Madame Bovary* — the book was politely rejected by Scribner's. Yet the process of writing the novel was a revelation. For the first time, Auchincloss intensely enjoyed writing. The novel was not an exercise like all his earlier stories, but "a part of *me*."

The rejection of the novel led directly to Auchincloss's decision to leave Yale a year early and go to law school. His action was a kind of expiation of the sin of frivolity. Deeply influenced by his mother's sense of duty, he believed "that a man born to the responsibilities of a brownstone bourgeois world could only be an artist or writer if he were a genius, that he should not kick over the traces unless a resounding artistic success, uni-

versally recognized, should justify his otherwise ridiculous deviation." Auchincloss went off to the University of Virginia Law School to devote himself to the
serious career, downtown, that men of his background
were expected to follow.

Law school turned out to be a far pleasanter experience than Auchincloss had anticipated. He enjoyed the
countryside around Charlottesville and came to enjoy the
study of law. He was elected an editor, and later one of
the managing editors, of the law review, taking pleasure
not only in legal writing but in the fellowship of the congenial friends who managed the journal. He was reas-
sured to find "that here was the real world, a man's
world, and that I was part of it and liked being part of
it." Though he finished a second abortive novel during
the summer following his first year in law school, he
"neither read nor wrote any fiction" for the remainder
of his time as a student. After his graduation in 1941 he
was hired by the large Wall Street firm of Sullivan &
Cromwell, where he was first introduced to estates and
trusts, which became his legal specialty.

The coming of World War II interrupted his career at Sullivan & Cromwell. Receiving a commission
in naval intelligence in 1942, he was sent to Panama. As
an intelligence officer in the headquarters of the Fifteenth Naval District in Balboa he experienced the absurdity of military bureaucracy, which he would later
describe in his first novel, *The Indifferent Children*. In
Panama and in his later service as an LST officer in
Europe and the Pacific, Auchincloss read constantly —
Henry James, the Victorian novelists (especially Trollope
and Thackeray), and the complete plays of Shakespeare
and Marlowe, which he read aloud with fellow officers.
More than a way of keeping his sanity, this wartime
reading shaped his sensibility and was an influence on
his later writings.

While in the Pacific during the last year of the war

Auchincloss began to feel confident enough to write
again. At the end of the war, before returning to Sullivan
& Cromwell, he took a long vacation and finished *The
Indifferent Children*, which was accepted for publication by Prentice-Hall in 1947. Despite this acceptance,
Auchincloss was still ambivalent about becoming a writer.
Both his parents discouraged publication — his mother
because she thought that he could write a better book,
his father because he thought a single novel would do
him no good in his career at Sullivan & Cromwell — but
the novel ultimately appeared, under the pseudonym
"Andrew Lee," borrowed with bitter irony, Auchincloss
said, from the name of "a clerical ancestor of Mother's
who was supposed to have cursed any of his descendants who should smoke or drink." Though *The Indifferent Children* received mixed reviews, one comment
confirmed Auchincloss's resolve to become a writer. The
novelist William McFee, reviewing the book in the *New
York Sun*, hailed him as "a novelist of the caliber of the
Henry James who wrote *Washington Square* and *The
Portrait of a Lady* rather than of the author of *The Ambassadors*. It is James alive to our times, aware of things
and people James himself never even sensed, but with
the psychological alertness and a mastery of English the
master would have enjoyed very much indeed."[3] Though
this praise struck so devoted a Jamesian as Auchincloss
as heresy, it encouraged him to write more. Two of his
short stories were accepted by the *Atlantic Monthly*, and
his first collection of stories, *The Injustice Collectors*, appeared in 1950, to generally favorable reviews. By the
time his next novel, *Sybil*, followed in 1952, he began
to be known as a writer.

　　While these books were being written, Auchincloss
was still working full time as an associate at Sullivan &
Cromwell. He began to worry that he was slighting his
literary talent by writing only in spare moments and on
weekends and evenings. But he also realized that he en-

joyed his work and shared his father's enthusiastic interest in the life of the firm. His dilemma was compounded because at the time he felt no burning desire for the responsibilities of partnership and conventional professional success. At the end of 1951, he resigned from Sullivan & Cromwell to devote all his time to writing. Though his father did not approve of his decision, he generously supported the experiment.

During two years away from the firm, Auchincloss not only wrote *A Law for the Lion* and the stories collected in *The Romantic Egoists* but also had time to be psychoanalyzed by Dr. John M. Cotton, who showed him how to free himself from the oppressive expectations he had set for himself. As he comments in *A Writer's Capital*, analysis "confirmed my suspicion that a man's background is largely of his own creating." During that period, he also met a number of other writers, including Norman Mailer, Gore Vidal, William Styron, and Frederick Buechner. By the end of 1953, however, Auchincloss realized that the experiment with a purely literary life had been a failure and that he missed the law. The years away from law "added nothing to my stature as a writer," he has commented. "My writing hours increased, but both the quantity and quality of my writing remained the same."

Auchincloss could not return to Sullivan & Cromwell, but through the kind offices of a member of his old firm, he found an ideal position at the firm of Hawkins, Delafield & Wood and began work in the spring of 1954. In 1957 he married Adele Lawrence, herself the descendant of two prominent New York families, the Vanderbilts and the Sloanes. His three sons were born in 1958, 1960, and 1963. In 1958 he became a partner in his firm.

At the age of thirty-six, when he returned to the practice of law, the essential pattern of his life was finally set, and the conflict between the worlds of his mother and father resolved. Since then he has continued to work

at Hawkins, Delafield & Wood, and he has continued
to write at a steady pace, publishing some thirty more
books. Though the pattern of his activity has not changed,
Auchincloss has steadily grown as a writer, and his critical reputation has seen several revolutions in taste and
popularity.[4] Auchincloss's reputation as a novelist of manners was firmly established by *Sybil* and *A Law for the
Lion*. Though some critics complained about paleness or
lack of warmth in the central characters, few denied
Auchincloss's sympathetic grasp of their situations. The
short stories in the first two collections were also praised
for their urbanity and precision, and for a Jamesian
psychological acuity, but they too were sometimes criticized for their lack of intensity.

With the publication of *The Great World and Timothy Colt* in 1956, Auchincloss shifted to a consideration of men in the downtown world of law and finance.
Elizabeth Bowen praised the novel as "his masterpiece,
genuine and exciting."[5] Though Auchincloss has almost
invariably been singled out for the authenticity and authority of his descriptions of lawyers in large firms, here
and in subsequent novels and stories, most critics felt that
he had not yet achieved the major novel he was capable
of. Many of the same complaints were raised against
Venus in Sparta in 1958, but again several critics called
it the best novel Auchincloss had yet written. Both Auchincloss's critical reputation and his popularity were
enhanced by the publication of *The House of Five Talents* in 1960 and *Portrait in Brownstone* in 1962. In these
two works, Auchincloss's long-standing interest in "the
story of money — how it was made, inherited, lost, spent"
finally found fruition, and his essentially historical sensibility found a suitable vehicle of expression.

The House of Five Talents marks Auchincloss's ar-
rival at the maturity of his powers as a novelist; after the
appearance of *Portrait in Brownstone*, J. Donald Adams
argued in his column in the *New York Times Book Re-*

view that Auchincloss might well be "the best living American novelist."[6] Though most critics did not subscribe to this extraordinarily high opinion of Auchincloss, it was echoed by at least two well-known reviewers when *The Rector of Justin* was published in 1964. At its publication Auchincloss's most popular work — it remained on the *New York Times* best-seller list for thirty-seven weeks — and still his most respected achievement, the novel was praised for its portrait of the rector and for its subtle analysis of significant moral issues. Since the mid-1960s — and especially during the late 1960s and early 1970s — Auchincloss's fiction has received generally less favorable comment, though individual critics have praised particular works. *The Embezzler* (1966) had a number of admirers, but most critics found *A World of Profit* (1968) and *I Come as a Thief* (1972) disappointing.

Many critics in the 1960s and 1970s excoriated Auchincloss for the alleged irrelevance of his subject matter and settings, but his recent novels have been treated more kindly as the 1970s have given way to the more conservative 1980s. *The House of the Prophet* was greeted in 1980 with high praise by Kenneth S. Lynn, who claimed that "the powerful literary portrait" Auchincloss had previously produced in *The Rector of Justin* had "been surpassed both in psychological sublety and in moral significance."[7] Such recent novels as *Watchfires* and *Honorable Men* have also received respectful attention.

During the 1970s, too, important reevaluations of Auchincloss's work also appeared. In 1972, in a major study of the novel of manners in America, James W. Tuttleton argued that Auchincloss was "the rightful heir of the tradition [of the novel of manners] as it has been handed down through the great European and American practitioners of the form," and suggested that his fiction should be more highly valued because "he keeps alive a lively tradition in novels that are themselves vital proof of his considerable talent."[8] And in 1974 Gore Vidal, writing in the *New York Review of Books*, defended Auchincloss against the unfair criticism of book reviewers who automatically dismissed him as irrelevant because he did not write about the common man and of academic writers who ignored him because he was not technically innovative.[9] Though there has been little scholarly writing on Auchincloss, critics seem gradually to be recognizing the substantial though specialized role that Auchincloss has played in American fiction since World War II; and in 1980, Benjamin DeMott, in the past not an uncritical admirer of Auchincloss, published a review in the *New York Times* entitled "In Praise of Louis Auchincloss."[10] In 1985 Susan Cheever hailed him as "the most underrated writer in America."[11]

While Auchincloss has continued his steady output of novels and stories, seemingly oblivious to the vicissitudes of critical fashion, he has also been active as a literary critic and biographer. In 1961, he published *Reflections of a Jacobite*, a collection of critical and historical essays, some of which had previously appeared in such journals as *The Partisan Review* and *The Nation*. *Reflections of A Jacobite* was followed in 1965 by *Pioneers and Caretakers*, a critical study of American women novelists; by a study of Shakespeare, *Motiveless Malignity*, in 1970; and by *Reading Henry James* in 1975. In the last decade or so, Auchincloss has also become very interested in biography, having produced a pictorial life of Edith Wharton and studies of Cardinal Richelieu and Queen Victoria's Court. Most recently, his essays and criticism have appeared in *The New York Review of Books*. As biographer and critic, he has emulated the Victorian man of letters, a generalist at home in his own profession, but able to write intelligently and gracefully for a wide audience on a variety of topics and in several genres.

Auchincloss's regard for biography stems from a broader interest in history that is reflected in many of his novels. Since the 1960s he has been active not only as a writer but also as a trustee and President of the Museum of the City of New York in attempting to preserve the heritage of that earlier New York he depicts so fondly in *Portrait in Brownstone* and elsewhere. In recent years, the historical dimension of his fiction has become even more evident. At the time of the United States bicentennial, he published *The Winthrop Covenant*, a collection of interrelated stories that explores the persistence of the Puritan spirit over three hundred years of American life. *The Cat and the King*, published in 1981, takes a look at life in the court of Louis XIV through the eyes of the memoirist St. Simon. *Watchfires*, which appeared a year later, is concerned with the American Civil War. And even *The House of the Prophet*, a less explicitly historical work, attempts not only to define the character of a journalist very much like the late Walter Lippmann but also to distill American history from World War I to the Vietnam war.

In the past two decades, Auchincloss has also been accorded increasing public recognition as a writer and New York civic leader. In 1965 he was elected to the National Institute of Arts and Letters, and he received honorary degrees from New York University in 1974 and Pace University in 1979. Despite this public recognition, the verdict is not yet in on Louis Auchincloss. He is still writing and still practicing law. It seems likely, however, that the best of Auchincloss's novels will still be valued in the future for their elegant style, their acute grasp of human psychology, and their authentic portrayal of a changing, perhaps vanishing world. As James Tuttleton has pointed out, Auchincloss is "our most important living novelist of manners."[12] To say this is not to say that he is a major novelist on the scale of Melville or James, but the range of his work and the substance and clarity of his vision make him a significant figure in the enduring tradition of American literature.

2

nnnnnnnnnnnnnnnnnnnnnnnnnnnnnn

The Complexities
of Character:
The Rector of Justin

Even two decades after its publication in 1964, *The Rec-tor of Justin* remains Auchincloss's best known work. An immediate best-seller when it appeared, it has also re-mained his most popular work. Its themes, settings, and narrative technique are thoroughly representative, and in many respects it is Auchincloss's finest novel.

Reviewers have often taken Auchincloss to task for writing almost exclusively about the "little world" of "the well-to-do and the well bred," as Granville Hicks once put it. While praising the authority and precision with which the people and settings in his novels are portrayed, Hicks and other critics have frequently gone on to com-plain that Auchincloss seems to be unaware of any other world beyond the one he depicts.[1] Such complaints, of course, might also be lodged against Jane Austen and Henry James — and indeed they have been. But at first glance *The Rector of Justin* seems particularly suscepti-ble to such criticism. It is set in an exclusive boarding school for boys, Justin Martyr School, and its central character is the eighty-year-old headmaster and founder of the school, the Reverend Francis Prescott, an Episco-pal priest and descendant of an old Boston family, who is about to retire from the post he has held for more than fifty years. Though Auchincloss's hero is hardly Everyman and his school is a world set apart from everyday experience, *The Rector of Justin* transcends the apparent limitations of its setting. In this, his most ambitious work, Auchincloss is concerned with the complexities of human character and the ways in which we perceive it, and he depicts the inevitable corruption of human institutions and the problems of faith in an age of doubt.

The sort of criticism that automatically dismisses a novel as irrelevant because it deals with only a small segment of society has always puzzled Auchincloss. In his memoir, *A Writer's Capital*, he recalls a conversation with the director Sidney Lumet shortly after *The Rector of Justin* was published. Lumet, he says, "brilliantly" told him everything he had had in mind in writing the novel: "Never have I had the feeling of being so perfectly understood. But when he added, by way of underlining his own perspicacity, 'And my background is one hundred percent the opposite of yours,' I failed to see the relevance. There is nothing in *The Rector of Justin* which requires a special background to be understood."

While Auchincloss is correct in reminding his readers that *The Rector of Justin* — as well as his other novels — is ultimately concerned with questions about human actions and motives that apply to everyone, it is also true that he is very much an artist who draws from life. *The Rector of Justin* is no exception in this regard. Indeed, the novel caused consternation among many people from Auchincloss's "special background" — graduates of Groton School, which he attended and from which he drew many of the details in the novel — who were annoyed because they were convinced that his hero was an unfair portrait of Endicott Peabody, Rector of Groton from 1884 to 1940.[2] Although there are important similarities between Peabody and Francis Prescott, Auchincloss's rector is a fictional creation, and in *The Rector of Justin*, as in any good novel, tracing biographical equivalents is no substitute for examining the work itself. Like his master in the art of fiction, Henry James, Auchincloss often begins with a character or event from his own experience and uses it as the "germ" for a novel. Francis Prescott is not Endicott Peabody, but Peabody's situation as one of the last surviving members of his generation of headmasters in Episcopal boarding schools did provide Auchincloss with the central problem for his novel, and Peabody's friendship with a young English teacher gave him the idea for the distinctive narrative structure he employs in this and several later novels.[3]

The Rector of Justin is cast in the form of a journal kept by Brian Aspinwall, a young teacher who comes to Justin Martyr shortly before Prescott's retirement. Brian admires the headmaster and eventually decides to write his biography. Though he leaves for divinity school when Prescott retires, he keeps close track of his mentor while he is away, and after his ordination he returns to Justin Martyr as a teacher and assistant chaplain. His journal is at once an account of the developing friendship between the two men and a chronicle of his quest for some sense of the rector's true character. Since Brian's personal knowledge is confined to the last seven years of Prescott's life, Auchincloss supplies information about his boyhood and early years as headmaster by skillfully weaving into the novel five memoirs that come into Brian's possession in the course of his biographical investigations. Thus we see the rector at various periods in his life from the vantage points of his oldest friend, one of his daughters, the chairman of the school's board of trustees, and several former students. Since the interpolated narratives are arranged in chronological order, the plot of the novel advances simultaneously on two planes. As the reader learns about Prescott's final years, he also catches glimpses of his development from an earnest, athletic schoolboy to a great headmaster. The effect of Auchincloss's technique is kaleidoscopic, for the reader sees the many different facets of Prescott's character from constantly shifting perspectives and it is often difficult to resolve the discrepancies among the several accounts. At the end of the novel, Auchincloss leaves us with a richly ambiguous but predominantly favorable impression of the rector.

Brian, nonetheless, is plainly the central consciousness through which the reader sees Francis Prescott. His journal holds all the other narratives together because it introduces their authors and supplies us with background information. His relation with the rector — which ultimately becomes his relationship with the subject of his biography — is the heart of the novel. In many ways Brian is the total opposite of Prescott. He is weak rather than strong, vacillating rather than decisive, shy and introspective rather than outgoing and athletic. Yet in spite of the great difference in their ages the two men are drawn to each other by their common faith. Unlike most of the other people at the school, they are motivated by ideals of selfless Christian service. Like many virtuous characters, however, Brian is at points a somewhat unappealing figure. He is often priggish, and his boyish enthusiasm is prissy rather than endearing. Auchincloss has conceded that Brian is a weak character in some ways, but his prime virtue in the economy of the novel is his essential honesty. One may be put off by the way he describes himself at the beginning of his journal, but he is believable: "I am shy and lack force of personality, and my stature is small. I stammer when I am nervous, and my appearance is boyish rather than manly. All this will be against me. But I am not afraid to say what I mean, and I think in a real crisis I can be counted on to stand up for the right, if only because I have such a fear of letting God down." Brian acts decisively when he must, but by nature he is an observer rather than an actor. Though not a forceful character, he makes an admirable narrator.

In the opening chapters of the novel, which consist

of entries from Brian's journal, Auchincloss lays the groundwork for the subsequent action. As Brian slowly and painfully learns his duties as a master at Justin Martyr, the reader is introduced to the school and its headmaster. Brian proves to be a poor disciplinarian and Dr. Prescott must show him how to restore order in his dormitory; he tries to avoid coaching football, but Prescott forces him to learn the game. Initially, Brian is dismayed by the rector, but he is immediately charmed by his wife. A lively Boston intellectual of the old school, Mrs. Prescott shares Brian's literary interests and asks him to read Henry James to her during her final illness. Out of Brian's intimacy with Mrs. Prescott develops a close friendship with the rector. Brian is appointed assistant to the headmaster, and when Prescott announces his retirement shortly after the death of his wife, Brian has become his closest confidant.

Prescott's decision to retire is precipitated by a visit from his oldest friend, Horace Havistock, who, after fifty years as an expatriate in Paris, has been driven back to America by the Nazi invasion of France. As an aesthete and epicure, and a friend of writers and artists from James to Fitzgerald and from Redon to Braque, Havistock contrasts strikingly with Francis Prescott. From his unpublished memoir "The Art of Friendship" the reader learns of Prescott's schooldays in New Hampshire, his career at Balliol College, Oxford, and the two years he spent working for the New York Central Railroad before deciding to go to divinity school. As an aesthete who prides himself on having led a "non-useful" life and a person with little religious faith, Havistock seems an odd source for most of the information Auchincloss gives us about Prescott's business career and decision to enter the ministry. Yet like Brian he is an observer; his very detachment makes him reliable. From the beginning Prescott dominates their relationship. At one point Havistock compares it to "that of a strong, single-minded husband

and a clever, realistic wife." Havistock is shy and easily
wounded, while Prescott is athletic and at times insensitive. All Havistock can do to express his gratitude for
Prescott's protection from the school bully is to help him
with his French and introduce him to New York and
Newport society, but (very much like Brian later on in
the novel) at a crucial moment he rises to decisive action,
breaking up Prescott's engagement because he knows his
fiancée will never make a good headmaster's wife.

The next document to fall into Brian's hands comes
from David Griscam. As an early graduate and longtime
trustee of the school, Griscam himself had hoped to write
the life of Francis Prescott, but Prescott refuses to
cooperate with him and he decides to give his notes to
Brian. Griscam is a successful Wall Street lawyer, who
describes himself at the beginning of his memoir as a
man absolutely without prejudices. He entered Justin
Martyr only five years after its founding, when the school
was still an intimate institution. His relationship with
Prescott as a student was intensely filial — perhaps the
most important relationship in his life. Yet in spite of his
continuing connection with the school over several
decades, he is never able to recapture the sense of com-
munion with Prescott he felt as a boy. As trustee and
fund-raiser, he is responsible for the dramatic expansion
of Justin Martyr just before World War I.

When he receives the notes from Griscam, Brian
believes that he may have been called to write a biography of Prescott. Left alone on the deserted campus of Justin Martyr in the summer after Prescott's retirement, he becomes depressed and begins to doubt his
larger calling — that to the ministry. Since he cannot face
entering divinity school in the fall, he goes to work for
Griscam in New York. Griscam encourages him to interview Cordelia Turnbull, the rector's youngest daughter, whose recollections provide the third major account
of Prescott's character. Brian's encounters with Cordelia

(which end when she attempts to seduce him) lead to a loss of faith and an emotional crisis that brings on a severe case of pneumonia. The rector comes down from his retirement home near the campus to nurse Brian in his illness and manages to put him back on the path to seminary.

As Cordelia tells Brian, her life as the daughter of two strong parents has not been particularly happy. At seventeen she had eloped with a man who represented "the reverse in every respect of what Pa would have wanted a graduate of Justin to be." Without divorcing her husband, she lived in Paris with Charley Strong, one of her father's "golden boys," who was badly wounded in World War I and had become a member of the lost generation. Prescott rescues Charley from disillusionment and despair but at the same time breaks up his relationship with Cordelia. Cordelia's second marriage to a newly rich businessman named Guy Turnbull is almost as unsuccessful as her first. She is physically attracted to Guy, but like her first husband he appeals to her because he differs so strikingly from the typical graduate of Justin. As a husband, he proves to be brutal and unfaithful, but even before the divorce is granted, her father has taken him over and converted him into a benefactor of the school.

The two remaining documents introduced in the novel are written by students who knew Prescott in the years after the expansion of the school. The first is a brief chapter from the stream-of-consciousness memoir Charley Strong wrote while he was in Paris with Cordelia. It is the most remarkable stylistic achievement in the novel. As Prescott suggests to Brian when he offers him the manuscript during his illness, it reveals a guilty obsession with sex, but it also depicts the rector as a gigantic father figure and judge that Charley cannot get out of his mind. The other document is a memoir written by Jules Griscam, son of the chairman of the trustees

and the rector's "greatest failure." Like Charley's manuscript, this account, written for a French psychiatrist
shortly before Jules's death in a suicidal automobile accident, presents Prescott as a larger-than-life figure, but
for Jules the rector is a demon rather than a demigod.
Even after he enters college, Jules lashes back at Prescott
in an elaborate plot to destroy a painting and a stained
glass window in the chapel at Justin. Jules's resentment
is pathological, but it is exacerbated by Prescott's earlier
mistakes in handling the boy in his career at Justin.

Jules Griscam's memoir is introduced in the novel
just before Brian returns to Justin Martyr from theological seminary. It serves as a reminder of the destructive
effects of one side of Prescott's character — a certain hardness and intolerance mentioned earlier by both Horace
Havistock and David Griscam. It also sets the stage for
the final episode in the novel, in which Prescott is tempted to throw the weight of his influence behind a group
of dissident faculty members who wish to destroy his successor Duncan Moore because they dislike his innova-
tions. Restrained by the timely intervention of Brian and
David Griscam, Prescott resists the temptation to speak
out against Moore's policies. Much to the surprise of the
dissidents, he graciously praises Moore at the school's diamond anniversary celebration, thereby averting a crisis
which might well have destroyed the school. This re-
sistance to an egotistical desire to keep control of the institution he has created is the last major event in Prescott's life, and perhaps his finest moment, yet when he
dies of lung cancer several months later he is still troubled by what the incident has revealed about his character and about the school. As the novel ends, Brian
closes his journal, and sits down to write his biography
of the rector.

Looking back on *The Rector of Justin* five years after it
was published, Auchincloss decided that in the character

of Francis Prescott he had succeeded in one of his early schemes for the novel: to portray a man who was a saint in some significant sense of the word. "It still seems to me," he wrote in 1969, "that the shifting points of view are effective in keeping constantly open the question of good or evil in the headmaster's relationships. What to me is not meant to be open is the central fact of his faith and sincerity."[4] Even granting that central fact, however, one might add that a number of widely divergent conclusions might follow about Prescott himself and the variety of sainthood he represents. This is one of the central strengths of the novel, and in fact Auchincloss seems almost to go out of his way to present the negative as well as positive aspects of Prescott's character.

Even Brian Aspinwall, who virtually comes to idolize the rector in the course of the novel, is keenly aware of his flaws. He disapproves of his emphasis upon the brutal combat of football as a means of building character, and he sees that, like other headmasters of his generation, Prescott is a perfectionist and something of a martinet, concerned with the smallest details of discipline within the school and willing to expel boys for relatively small infractions of the rules. At several points in Brian's journal, Auchincloss describes incidents that reveal the rector's goodness and spiritual strength, only to follow each of them immediately with an instance of his pettiness or meanness. At the end of the novel, Brian endorses Horace Havistock and David Griscam's idea that there was excessive hardness in Prescott's conduct during the middle years of his life.

All of these faults, except the hardness of heart, are relatively minor. What is more important in the novel, however, is Prescott's effect on members of his family. More fully than any other twentieth-century novelist, Auchincloss reminds us of a fundamental truth grasped by some of the Victorians: the costs of Christian altruism and self-sacrifice apparently paid by a good man are often borne in large measure by the people around him. This is true to some extent in the lives of Horace Havistock and Prescott's longtime assistant Mr. Ives, but it is most sharply demonstrated in Auchincloss's portraits of Mrs. Prescott and Cordelia Turnbull. As Mrs. Prescott reaches the end of her life, all her anger at having sacrificed so much of herself to her husband's school begins to surface. As Mr. Ives explains, "Few husbands, Brian, can have been loved as much as that man has been. And yet she must have known, as *I* have always known, that for every grain of love that comes back from Francis Prescott, a pound goes to the school."

Mrs. Prescott's anger and the contrast between her character and that of her husband are admirably delineated in a series of deft allusions to Henry James at the end of the first chapter. Brian has been reading *The Ambassadors* (one of Auchincloss's favorite novels) to Mrs. Prescott, but she significantly tells him to skip the chapter in which Strether, the middle-aged hero of the novel, warns his young friend Little Bilham not to waste his life as he has done. In her angry state, Strether's advice to Bilham to "live, live all you can" would be bitter gall for Mrs. Prescott. When Dr. Prescott enters the room and begins to poke fun at James ("one cannot read James properly without bearing in mind that for every three parts genius he is one part ass"), she loses her patience, and the ensuing argument about James's highly refined late novels defines their respective positions in life. For her, as for James, living is in large part a matter of achieving intense aesthetic discriminations; for the rector, life is primarily action. Here, as is often the case in Auchincloss's work, debates about art or literature serve as a means of presenting ethical issues.

Cordelia Turnbull, on the other hand, is an interesting study of the embittered child of strong parents. Though she is one of the less reliable narrators in the novel, her attitude toward her father is revealing. She even regards her name as her father's sardonic revenge on her for not being the son he wanted. Like Cordelia in *King Lear*, she is the youngest of three daughters. She considers herself rejected by her father, as Cordelia was at the beginning of Shakespeare's play, but for her there is no possibility of happy reunion with her parent. When Dr. Prescott breaks up her relationship with Charley Strong, she envisions herself as a Cordelia who has been not only banished from the realm but deprived of the consolation Shakespeare's heroine found in her marriage to the Duke of Burgundy. She regards her plight as worse than that of Cordelia in the play, but ironically she does not accept her lot with any of the charity and forbearance displayed by her namesake. For her, Justin Martyr School is "a monster of red brick and Romanesque arches, of varnished, carpetless halls and dreary stained glass windows" created by her father so that "he could transfer an egotism that must in his youth have been even worse than mine." Cordelia's tragedy is not merely that her love for her father cannot be fully reciprocated because so much of his emotional energy goes to the school, but also that any hope for individual achievement as an artist or aesthete is snuffed out by her mother's superior knowledge and sensitivity.

Though one must obviously discount Cordelia's views, there is at least some truth in her theory of her father's conduct in regard to the two men she is closest to, Charley Strong and Guy Turnbull. Prescott's intense need to influence the lives of younger men puts him "in basic competition" with his daughter. Admittedly his rescue of Charley Strong in Paris is an extension of his role as headmaster, but when Cordelia marries Guy Turnbull, who has no connection to the world of Justin Martyr, her father takes him over, too. Guy admires Dr. Prescott's business sense, and Prescott in turn flatters him by inviting him to address the older students. As Cordelia points out, the rector's mixed feelings of admi-

ration and contempt for the crudest sort of businessman
are characteristic: "wealthy men who gloried in the bitter competition of the marketplace and in a creed that
put the profit motive ahead of all intrigued him. Perhaps, he felt that like soldiers, they were nearer the basic
male than himself." Even after Cordelia divorces Guy,
her parents remain friendly to him, and, in an oddly
ironic burst of generosity, he donates a building to the
school as a memorial to Charley Strong, her former para-
mour. As Cordelia wryly observes, Guy and Charley
"had more in common at last than the physical possession of Cordelia."

The indignant picture of personal loss that Cordelia presents should not be allowed to obscure the more
positive aspects of Prescott's character. For good or ill,
Prescott remains an idealist. In *The Rector of Justin*
Prescott's life and the history of his school are inextricably intertwined. To see the origins of his character and
the basis of the school one must consider his childhood
and family background. His concept of an all-encom-
passing school community was a reaction to the disorder
of the school he himself attended. As Horace Havistock
tells us, St. Andrew's School in the 1870s became "a
model of all that Frank Prescott thought a school should
not be." There were no organized activities outside of
classes and no coached team sports; hazing was rampant;
boys were permitted to form cruel cliques; hygiene was
nonexistent. Add to this picture the fact that Prescott was
an orphan, and the tightly controlled community — a sort
of extended family — that Justin represents is a logical
development.

Prescott's ideal for Justin Martyr also is a direct
outgrowth of the post–Civil War America in which he
grew up. According to Havistock, young Prescott "passionately believed that an age of heroes had died with
his father," who had been lost in the battle of Chancel-
lorsville, "and that a generation of jackals now gorged

itself on the bloated carcass of valor." To bring moral purity to the sons of this corrupt generation and from them "to raise up new leaders of men" were his chief goals, even when he first conceived the idea for his school while still at St. Andrew's. Both he and Havistock went to Balliol College, Oxford. There, however, he lost his faith, abandoning his dream of being a schoolmaster. Yet religion still attracted him while he was beginning a promising career in the offices of the New York Central Railroad. It is no accident that he regains his faith after having a vision of his father. His new faith is centered in a concept of Christ which emphasizes "divinely assured selflessness," and it forms the basis on which he founds Justin in 1886. As he tells Brian: "I tried to put God into every book and sport at Justin. That was my ideal, to spread a sense of his presence so that it would not be confined to prayers and sacred studies and to spread it in such a way as to make the school *joyful*."

This high ideal perhaps came closest to being realized in the early days of the school — or so one is led to believe by David Griscam's account of student life at Justin in the early 1890s. The school really did function as "a large happy family," with Prescott as teacher, coach, and chaplain, as well as headmaster, and with his wife ministering to the emotional needs of the boys. Images of paradise, of the Garden of Eden before the Fall, occur several times in Griscam's narrative. Yet for David Griscam this Eden is threatened from the beginning, on two levels: first, a bully destroys his boyish happiness by reminding him of his father's failure in business, and then the inevitable separation of graduation means that he must leave the garden. Never again will he know the intense feeling of belonging that he felt as a school prefect under the rector. Griscam's experiences of loss, however, are really precursors of a more general fall from innocence involving Prescott and the school as a whole.

As a member of the Board of Trustees, Griscam is an agent in this fall, even as he works to build up the school. He proposes that the enrollment be doubled and that a massive fund-raising campaign be waged to get the money needed for new buildings and additional faculty and endowment. Prescott rather reluctantly acquiesces in the scheme, knowing full well that the expansion will destroy the original character of the institution. His support for Griscam's plan actually represents a yielding to the ambitious side of his nature. As Mrs. Prescott tells David, "Frank is ambitious, you know. For himself *and* the school, though they're sometimes confused. But don't imagine he'll admit it."

If we are to believe Mrs. Prescott, her husband's concealed ambition is coupled with a refusal to recognize the actual dishonesty connected with the fund-raising campaign. On the verge of its completion, Griscam solicits a large gift for the new chapel from Shelley Tanager, a Chicago meat-packer with a son at Justin. Just as the gift is about to come in, Tanager's boy is caught using a "trot" to do his Latin translations. With what Griscam perceives as "a hint of something almost akin to triumph in his eye," Prescott announces that Tanager will be expelled. Griscam manages, however, to wring a confession from Max Totten, the scholarship student who rooms with Tanager, and one month later the elder Tanager's pledge comes in for exactly double the amount requested. The campaign is complete, and the chapel the rector had dreamed of is built, along with a dozen other new buildings. "By 1910 Justin Martyr had assumed very much the external appearance it wears today," Griscam writes, "and Francis Prescott took a long stride towards the deanship of New England headmasters." But all this was built on a lie. Max Totten had deliberately taken the blame, as Griscam finds out just before Totten leaves campus. In a sinister handshake, Totten and Griscam agree to keep the truth secret. Later, Totten, who has risen to become president of Tanager's firm because he covered up his roommate's indiscretion, becomes one of Griscam's most valued clients.

The various ironies in the situation and the unexpected twists of plot in the episode are thoroughly typical of Auchincloss's treatment of the legal and financial worlds in other novels. In the world of *The Rector of Justin*, Griscam's deal with Max Totten is nothing less than a symbolic pact with the devil that leads to the virtual destruction of the school as it was originally conceived and foreshadows Prescott's final disillusionment. Rumors about the episode surface shortly before the death of the younger Tanager. Does Prescott know the true story? The reader never finds out. But Mrs. Prescott's comments to David Griscam are significant: "Well, I don't know what Frank thought. I suspect he didn't really face it. In fact, I wonder if he didn't turn his back on it."

As Mrs. Prescott goes on to observe — and as Auchincloss presumably would have the reader believe — "every man has his moments of evasion." Yet, in the climactic scene of the novel, Prescott must face what has become of his school. Again, David Griscam is the agent of his disillusionment. He brings together three trustees — all of them graduates of Justin — for a discussion of the school's future with Prescott on the eve of the diamond jubilee. In their complaints about the policies of Prescott's successor, they reveal their snobbery, materialism, and bigotry. Prescott abandons his plan to criticize his successor and realizes how greatly he has failed in creating the school he had envisioned. Justin has become "another tap for the world's materialism." In the spotlight of adulation in which he has moved in his years as Rector of Justin, he has failed to see the darkness around him. Having founded a church school to train leaders to reform a corrupt society, he discovers that in reality his school has been a servant of that very corruption. At the end of his life Prescott considers himself a failure.

In the scene with the trustees, Auchincloss brings

the three main strands of the novel together: the drama
of Prescott's disillusionment, the story of the school's fall
from innocence, and the development of Brian Aspinwall's character. In rejecting the role of an anguished
Lear howling against his successor, Prescott attains a
degree of heroism, though, as always in Auchincloss,
that heroism is founded on a paradox: it consists in *not*
acting, in refusing to speak against Duncan Moore; and
it is brought about by the resolutely practical machinations of a clever lawyer. In his final humility, however,
Prescott does resemble the chastened Lear at the end of
Shakespeare's play. Auchincloss's view of the fall of the
institution is at once critical and cautiously conservative.
As in several of his other novels, a golden age of innocence and virtue has been irretrievably lost. Justin
Martyr has declined from an ideal state, and in the world
in which Brian writes, a heroic figure like Prescott is no
longer even conceivable as a headmaster. But as Auchincloss implies, there remains some good in a flawed institution like Justin Martyr, and it is better to support the
mild reforms of a decent but unheroic man like Duncan
Moore than to abandon the battle altogether.

Prescott considers himself a failure, but the development of Brian Aspinwall's character is one of his greatest
successes. When he first comes to Justin, Brian is an ineffectual teacher, unsure of himself and doubtful about
his calling to the ministry. Prescott helps him as a teacher
and inspires him as a minister. By the example of his own
faith and by his active concern during Brian's illness, he
rescues him from doubt and shows him that he can be
the full person he longs to be. As Auchincloss has pointed
out, the rector's faith and sincerity are not meant to be
questioned, but often they are unconvincingly manifested. This is not so much a failure on Auchincloss's
part as the result of his technique of leaving many questions of character open. One is meant to see, for example, that there is an element of theatricality in Prescott's

manner of conducting chapel services, as both Horace Havistock and Jules Griscam rather uncharitably point out. But Prescott's theatricality is part of his effective appeal to the students to whom he ministers.

In the episode with Brian, Prescott comes closest to revealing the basis of his faith. He advises Brian to enter seminary in spite of his doubts about being ready. "You will never be ready if you wait," he says. "With you and me faith will always be a matter of exercise. But the faith you work for is just as fine as the faith that is conferred." For Prescott the cycle of faith always includes phases of doubt. The key to faith is acceptance. "I used to worry that I did not sufficiently love my daughters," he confides to Brian. "But now I see that loving them inadequately was part of me and part of the condition into which they were born. God did not expect me to love them more. I couldn't. He expected me to tend them devotedly." This counsel gives Brian the strength to accept his own weak nature, and when he returns to Justin after his ordination he has the ability to act decisively. He is responsible for setting in motion the series of events that prevents the rebellion against the new headmaster, and he persuades David Griscam to give a new library and infirmary to the school. Both these deeds are worthy of a Frank Prescott, though they are performed by a man who remains his opposite in most respects.

How, finally, is Prescott to be judged? Auchincloss's multiple perspectives do not permit us to define his essential self. As James W. Tuttleton has commented, "It might well be asked whether there was any 'real' Prescott behind his various masks. The answer is yes, but we can never know him except as a composite of the limited points of view of his various biographers."[5] This is true, but Prescott's character is perhaps best judged on the basis of his effect on other people. The very pervasiveness of the Prescott legend among those who have known him indicates the strength of his influence. "In respect to Dr.

Prescott most of his graduates had never grown up,"
Brian concludes. "He did not seem to dwindle as childhood figures usually do." Looming over the now dimin-
ished school, the rector presented an even more formi-
dable figure to returning graduates: "The Prescott they
had remembered, by God, was the *real* Prescott."

The last two memoirs included in the novel both
portray Prescott as just such a larger-than-life figure,
though each takes a radically different view of that figure. That we are meant to accept the more benign picture of the rector presented by Charley Strong is suggested not only by Brian's remarks in the concluding
entry of his journal but also by Auchincloss's placement
of Strong's manuscript immediately after the episode in
which the rector helps Brian to regain his faith. As he
did with Horace Havistock and David Griscam in their
school days, the rector reaches out to Charley and Brian
at turning points in their lives and truly saves them. That
Auchincloss places Jules Griscam's memoir last is also
significant, for it suggests Prescott's uncompromising
honesty. As a condition of letting him see the memoir,
Prescott insists that Brian incorporate the story of his
failure with Jules in anything he might publish. Prescott's
desire to make his greatest failure known reflects his fundamental humility, but it also reminds us of another
heroic trait: his self-knowledge. Though he is a complex
and imperfect man, Prescott combines the Christian
ideal of service with the classical ideal expressed in
Socrates' phrase, "know thyself." One is finally inclined
to agree with Brian that "Dr. Prescott was greater than
the school which he created and by which he was ultimately disillusioned."

At the end of the novel, of course, the biography of
Dr. Prescott remains unwritten. One does not know if
Brian will ever finish it. But that is part of the novel's
point. Like Browning, Auchincloss believes that views
of human character are limited and biased: even the best

of biographers may not be able to capture the true self. But the mystery and complexity of human character remain, and the partial, refracted images of Francis Prescott presented in *The Rector of Justin* are Auchincloss's affirmation of the final integrity and importance of human character.

The Rector of Justin was Auchincloss's ninth novel. In many ways it is his most complex and ambitious work. Though in its central preoccupation with the identity of Francis Prescott it is a novel of character, it also displays Auchincloss's extraordinary abilities as a novelist of manners. Cordelia's brief sketch of her family's social position presents a brilliant example of Auchincloss's powers as an analyst of the individual's place in a particular social setting.

Pa and Mother, of course, were supreme at Justin, but from the beginning we knew that Justin was not the real world. The real world was a summer world, seen on trips to Europe or at the Cape, and although it treated Pa and Mother with respect, it was the kind of respect that people might pay to the sovereigns of a small Pacific Island kingdom, more exotic than powerful, not quite to be taken seriously, perhaps even a bit ridiculous. I thought I could sense as a child among the graduates and the parents of the boys that curious half paternal, half protective, almost at times half contemptuous, attitude of men of affairs for academics, and I was determined that I should lead my own life in such a way as to be able ultimately to bring a plague on both kinds of houses. I would be neither sneered upon nor a sneerer. I would be an actress, a poet, a great artist and return to Justin only when Pa begged me, as a special treat, to come back and perform to the dazzled boys. (*Rector of Justin*, p. 179)

In less than a paragraph, not only does Auchincloss show the Prescotts' place in the social hierarchy, the relation between Justin and the larger world, and the ambiguous position of the academic among men of affairs, but he

also manages to locate Cordelia quite precisely in the
emotional matrix of her family.

Auchincloss's control of descriptive detail in *The
Rector of Justin* is also masterful. Physical objects almost
invariably serve to underline aspects of character or
theme. Brian's description of Mrs. Prescott's room in the
first chapter of the novel aptly sums up her personality
and her relation to the rector and the school. A later
description of the objects in Prescott's office suggests his
authority as headmaster and indicates his theological
position. In commenting on the Griscam family's
attitude toward their father's wealth, Auchincloss makes
every detail tell:

> They didn't need, or in the least want, the big solid stone house,
> the shiny town car with the spoked wheels, the thick glass-
> grilled doors, the pompous porte-cochere, all the external
> paraphernalia of wealth without which men of Mr. Griscam's
> generation couldn't quite believe it existed. Poor Mr. Griscam,
> he had provided all the things that nobody wanted because,
> as the child of a bankrupt, he couldn't even take in the fact
> that everybody did not need, like himself, the constant con-
> solation of marble pillars! (*Rector of Justin*, p. 304)

The passage deftly sketches David Griscam's feelings
about wealth while at the same time suggesting the general shift in attitudes toward conspicuous consumption
between 1900 and 1940.

Yet, brilliant as so much of *The Rector of Justin* is,
the novel is not without technical flaws. Sometimes
Auchincloss's dialogue falters. The scene in which Cordelia Turnbull, in an elaborate parody of Fielding's
Joseph Andrews, attempts to seduce Brian Aspinwall is
unconvincing and almost painful to read. Similarly,
Auchincloss does not quite succeed in differentiating the
styles of the various narratives in the novel. Everyone
from Brian to Cordelia to Charley Strong sounds at
points like Louis Auchincloss. Auchincloss is a fine prose
stylist, but like Henry James he is a monolithic one.

Although several critics objected to the complexity of Auchincloss's narrative when *The Rector of Justin* first appeared, the narrative structure is one of the great strengths of the novel. Each section has unity and shape of its own, and the novel as a whole is held together by an intricate pattern of thematic and stylistic connections among its various sections and the characters who appear in them. Like a talented conjuror Auchincloss leads the reader on from section to section by creating an almost voyeuristic interest in the successive revelations of Prescott's character. The complexity of the narrative is, above all, functional. It is part of Auchincloss's affirmation of the richness of human character.

In the final analysis, however, *The Rector of Justin* is an important novel, not only because of its author's technical skill, but because of what it says about individuals and the institutions they create. Auchincloss's work is unique because it combines a detached but sympathetic portrait of a remarkable man from a particular era with a balanced analysis of the universal forces that bring his era to a close. It is also unique because, unlike many preparatory school novels, it focuses directly on the headmaster as a human being and deals carefully with the institutional politics of the school. Furthermore, few if any contemporary novelists other than Auchincloss seem capable of portraying businessmen and lawyers such as David Griscam so convincingly, and in a manner that is at once sympathetic and objective. *The Rector of Justin* has been called "almost certainly the finest work ever written about an American preparatory school."[6] As such, it deserves a place of honor in a tradition of distinguished novels about school life that stretches back to Thomas Hughes's famous portrait of Francis Prescott's nineteenth-century British predecessor, Dr. Arnold of Rugby, in *Tom Brown's School Days*.

3

∿∿∿∿∿∿∿∿∿∿∿∿∿∿∿∿∿∿∿∿∿∿∿∿

Quests for a Limited Identity: The Early Novels

Insofar as most of its action takes place outside of New York City, *The Rector of Justin* is an exception among Auchincloss's novels. Far more typical are *Sybil* and *A Law for the Lion*, the first novels Auchincloss published under his own name and two of the works that established his reputation in the early 1950s. Both are set in the world of New York society, and both show Auchincloss's expert command of the rituals and behavior of the milieu's inhabitants. In these and practically all his works, Auchincloss has profitably heeded the advice Henry James gave Edith Wharton when he wrote her sister-in-law that she "must remain tethered in native pastures, even if it reduces her to a backyard in New York."[1] Following James's advice, however, has not prevented Auchincloss from exploring the timeless forces of human motivation, nor has it precluded cool, detached, and searching scrutiny of the people and customs of his native realm.

Because *Sybil* and *A Law for the Lion* precisely delineate the customs, manners, conventions, and habits of a certain social class at a particular time and place, and because the relationship between self and society is a central concern in both works, they are good examples of the novel of manners. At the same time, however, they are also stories of young women in quest of personal identity. Like many of his predecessors in the tradition of the novel of manners, Auchincloss shows how each of his heroines is shaped by the social environment in which she must live, but he also asserts in no uncertain terms that other forces are at work molding the individual. Sybil Hilliard and Eloise Dilworth, the respective central characters of the novels, are shy, immature women who have been crippled emotionally by unsatisfactory relationships with their mothers and who marry domineering older men at an early age, before they have formed a clear concept of who they are or what they want. In each novel, Auchincloss sketches the painful process by which the heroine achieves a belated and somewhat limited sense of her own identity within the context of the tightly confined society in which she has been placed.

Sybil and *A Law for the Lion* were preceded in 1947 by another novel, *The Indifferent Children*, which was published under a pseudonym. As Auchincloss later explained, his decision to use a pseudonym was motivated not only by parental pressure but also by his own feeling that the book "had failed in its basic purpose."[2] Like many first novels, *The Indifferent Children* attempts too much. Auchincloss places the protagonist, Beverly Stregelinus (whom he later called "the most absurd young man I could imagine"), in three disparate settings: New York society, the US Naval bureaucracy in Panama, and the officers' mess on board a converted yacht pressed into service in the Caribbean during World War II. The various elements of the book, taken from Auchincloss's wartime experiences and from the two unpublished novels he produced in college and law school, never quite coalesce into a satisfying whole. In the course of his experiences, Beverly was supposed "to see his own absurdity in the absurdity of his fellow bureaucrats" and thus "be redeemed and emerge as a serious person." Unfortunately, as Auchincloss tells it, "he simply refused ever quite to do as he was told, and in the end I threw a bomb at him," killing him off in the final episode.

Though it remains an apprentice piece, *The Indifferent Children* is by no means a total failure. Auchincloss's satire of the naval bureaucracy is amusing and sharp, and his portrait of Beverly, for the most part, lively and honest. The novel is primarily important, however, because it served as a kind of seedbed for much of Auchincloss's subsequent fictions. Situations and characters from the military settings reappear in short stories in Auchincloss's first two collections, and Beverly's fiancée, Sylvia Tremaine, is the first in a series of shy, often eccentric female characters that includes the protagonists of the next two novels. Even the novel's central flaw, the failure to portray a convincing change in the protagonist, points ahead to the novels that follow. In telling the story of Beverly Stregelinus, Auchincloss worked his way toward the more successful and fully realized quests for identity portrayed in *Sybil* and *A Law for the Lion*.

Sybil

Published in early 1952, a year after the appearance of Auchincloss's first collection of short stories, *Sybil* is much more tightly organized than *The Indifferent Children*. Jane Austen once observed that "three or four families in a country village is the very thing to work on," and Auchincloss might well be said to have applied her dictum to the novel in twentieth-century America. *Sybil* involves only two families, the Hilliards and the Rodmans. Rather than sprawling over three continents as *The Indifferent Children* had done, the events of the novel take place almost entirely in Manhattan and on Long Island, and, indeed, even its city setting becomes a kind of village because most of its characters have known each other since childhood. *Sybil* begins at a subscription dance following a small dinner party given in honor of its heroine's twenty-first birthday and ends in another dinner party, given by the same aunt on the occasion of Sybil's eighth wedding anniversary. Auchincloss's portrayal of New York society in the novel is more acute than in *The Indifferent Children* because it is less exaggerated, and the work as a whole, if less richly varied than its predecessor, is more satisfying, both because Auchincloss has mastered the technical demands of his form and because he successfully conveys the growth and psychological development of his central character.

The novel follows the relationship between Sybil Rodman and Philip Hilliard from courtship to marriage and from separation to reconciliation. Sybil, a painfully shy, almost reclusive girl who had decided to stay at home rather than go to college and whose only experience in the world beyond her home has been limited to serving as social secretary to her aunt, meets Philip at the dance that begins the novel. A handsome, outgoing law-school classmate of her brother Teddy, he is intrigued by her intense combination of shyness and candor. Even though he insensitively rates her in his diary as "a third-class marriage possibility," he continues to pursue her and proposes only a few months later.

Their marriage succeeds at first because Sybil devotes heself totally to becoming the perfect wife of Philip Hilliard. But when Philip is away for several years in the navy, she grows more independent and begins to question their relationship. At the same time, Philip reverts to the customary pattern followed by males in his family and has an affair with the wife of another naval officer in San Francisco. After the war, Philip returns to the family real estate business rather than becoming the crusading lawyer he had told Sybil he wanted to be when he asked her to marry him. Sybil is disappointed but still content with their life together. Soon, however, Philip takes up with his old girlfriend,

Julia Anderton, and asks for a divorce. Sybil initially accepts the idea, until Julia brashly pressures her to speed
up the process. Seeing how vigorously his wife is willing to fight to save him — and how crudely Julia is capable of behaving — Philip changes his mind and asks for
a reconciliation. Sybil agrees, but after a few weeks asks
for a separation herself.

After the separation Sybil goes through an identity
crisis. Unable to explain her decision even to herself,
she loses faith in herself. She seeks out her old friend
Howard Plimpton, who has left his wife and conventional job to live above a garage and be a painter. Sybil
idealizes Howard's surly independence and seeming honesty, but rejects his sexual advances until she hears that
the Hilliards are having her watched. Then, in a fit of
rage, she sleeps with Howard. This, her first and only
liaison, is of course duly reported to Philip by his mother, who had hired the detective. Paradoxically, the news
of Sybil's infidelity leads Philip, after a few angry scenes,
to request another reconciliation. Sybil accepts, and at
the end of the novel she finds herself again in the bosom
of the Hilliard family — this time to stay. All seems well
on the surface, but the reader is left with significant
doubts about the extent of Sybil's happiness.

Sybil's difficulties with Philip stem not only from
the differences between their personalities but also from
the contrast between their two families. Early in the
novel, Auchincloss places their marriage in a detailed
social context. The Rodmans and the Hilliards represent distinctly different subgroups in the same class.
Sybil's mother, Esther Delafield, the child of an old
family whose fortune was virtually gone, had married
George Rodman, the son of a clergyman from upstate
New York. Though he has high hopes, George never
makes anything of himself. His family is in effect supported by Esther's sister, Jo Cummings, who had managed to marry more successfully and whose husband

Stafford Cummings gives George a job in the family bank of which he is president. Sybil's Uncle Stafford is a rich man, but the Hilliards are very rich: "They had the impregnability that comes from being born with money, of having married money, of scarcely being able, as far as they could peer through the branches of their family tree, to spot a twig unendowed with its independent competency." Whereas Sybil's mother and aunt are earnest and ever mindful of "the responsibilities of being born who they are," the Hilliards entertain constantly and worry very little about the world beyond their own: "They liked animals and people who liked animals and prided themselves on a tweedy, rustic toughness of mind and manner." Sybil is rudely introduced to the world of the Hilliards at a dinner party at which Philip's overbearing mother, Lucy Hilliard, baits her until she flees in abject terror to an upstairs bedroom. Yet, despite her hard exterior and occasional cruelty, Mrs. Hilliard is an appealing character. After she has given up her attempt to prevent her son's marriage, she becomes fond of Sybil and even takes her side when Philip wants to leave her for Julia Anderton.

Though he is keenly interested in the social context in which his characters move, Auchincloss repeatedly stresses that Sybil's problems are ultimately caused, not by society at large, but by forces at work in her own family. George Rodman is an uncongenial as well as ineffectual parent, and Esther, who might be expected to be closer to her daughter, openly prefers Teddy to Sybil. Because of her "maternal egotism," she is the chief negative influence on Sybil. She worries constantly about her children, but they both learn early in life that "what preoccupied and absorbed Esther was the proper fulfillment of her own functions as a parent rather than the happiness and welfare of her children." By a subtle process of manipulation, she turns them into "acolytes in what seemed the never ending ceremonial of [her] dreary

task of doing right." Esther can neither rejoice in Sybil's marriage nor offer any real comfort when the marriage goes sour.

Given parents like Esther and George Rodman, it
is not remarkable that Sybil regards her marriage to
Philip as an escape. As she dances with Philip at their
wedding reception, she thinks, with consternation and
almost for the first time, "I'm actually, actually happy."
Yet the influence of her family also helps explain her
fear and insecurity whenever she is with Philip before
her marriage and her feeling, which persists well into
marriage, that if people really knew her they would
not like her. It is this deeply rooted anxiety, as much as
her pain and anger at Philip, that accounts for her refusal to return to him after his affair with Julia Anderton. "It was a relief," Auchincloss writes, for Sybil "to
feel the door so firmly closed to redemption" after she
had rejected Lucy Hilliard's kind appeal for her to return.

She had always been afraid that her mother-in-law, who had
been in recent years so extraordinarily kind to her, would
have been less kind had she known more about her. Lucy's character, like Philip's, was lacking in subtlety, and Sybil couldn't
but feel that if she had been accepted at all, it was because she
had concealed a large part of her true nature. Now there was
no need to fear. To Lucy she must have seemed indeed con-
temptible. (*Sybil*, p. 206)

The anxiety and low opinion of herself engendered by
her mother's attitudes are also in large measure responsible for Sybil's other self-destructive actions, such as
the abortive affair with Howard Plimpton, which, on
one level, is little more than an anguished attempt to
demonstrate that she is as bad as she thinks other people find her to be.

In its broadest outline, however, the action of the
novel traces a twofold process of enlightenment by which

Sybil sheds many of her romantic notions about life and achieves a limited sense of self-esteem. Even before her husband's affair with Julia Anderton, her romantic expectations about love and marriage have been undercut: soon after Philip returns from the Pacific, she realizes that there was very little basis for their relationship at all, and that she must in effect rebuild her marriage by trying to change herself. And after the separation, the information that Philip's family is having her watched comes as merely "another step in the process of her adult education." The final blow is dealt to her romanticism when she sleeps with Howard Plimpton. Desiring the total consummation and oblivion of a Wagnerian *Liebestod*, she manages instead to become involved in an experience in which both she and Howard remain essentially apart, and she then recognizes that "she had no one to blame but herself." Arriving at her aunt's house in the early morning after her encounter with Howard, she realizes that she no longer has any firm sense of who she is. The familiar objects around her "had ceased to be referents" and "she was nowhere."

From this disillusionment springs the ambiguous decision to return to Philip. Yet, while her romantic illusions are gradually evaporating, she is also gaining self-confidence. The turning point in this latter process is her refusal to cave in to Julia Anderton's demands, but in that moment of assertion she is still impelled by a desire to save Philip. Not until she separates from Philip does she act on her own behalf — and even then her actions contain a troubling self-destructive streak. Like the gradual "process of her adult education," her journey to a firm, unencumbered sense of identity is sombre and frustratingly imcomplete.

Despite the bleak way in which Sybil's development is presented, the novel is tempered at frequent points with a good deal of comedy. There is something larger than life about Lucy Hilliard, for example, even though

she is a major character to whom Auchincloss gives realistic motives and multidimensional depth. Her conversation is marked by the pungent wit of a thoroughly
cynical woman who does not need to worry about pleas-
ing other people and who has the sense to see when she
is wrong. The Hilliard aunts — two maiden ladies who
behave almost like a married couple, who damn Mr.
Roosevelt and take scandalized delight in detecting the
moral shortcomings of the younger generation — are brilliant comic creations, and several of their encounters
with Sybil yield considerable humor as well as pathos.
Even in describing totally "serious" or sympathetic figures, however, Auchincloss keeps his distance, examining their conduct with a satirist's eye for unflattering
detail. This cool detachment, perhaps, is the most striking aspect of his characterizations. As Philip Hilliard
berates his mother for having insulted Sybil, for example, Auchincloss meticulously notes the reactions of Mr.
Hilliard and one of Philip's sisters, who "watch them
with the satisfaction that other members of a family
watch a rift between the two closest." The detail is not
essential to the scene but it underlines what might be
called the politics of family rivalry.

Auchincloss analyzes Philip's motives for marrying
Sybil with the same surgical precision. "Philip was not
a creature of impulse," he dryly informs us, although
he possessed "his own share of the universal craving for
affection." Before proposing, he asks Teddy about Sybil's problems, measures the intensity of his attraction
for her, and calculates how many classes he can afford
to cut in order to travel to New York to ask the question.

Passionately literal, he had always yearned for a disinterested
love that he could clearly recognize and classify as such. What
had made him select Sybil, almost unhesitatingly, from the
large number of more obviously attractive girls of his acquaintance was his strong sense, derived as early as their second
meeting, of her devotion to him. When he thought of her, he

thought of her brown brooding eyes and the pale intensity of her gaze. He felt, and felt correctly, that even her brusqueness was only the shell over her emotion. There was an enormous reassurance to Philip in this sense of a devotion that in no way depended on his future or even on his good character. With Sybil he could relax and be himself and still be loved. (*Sybil*, p. 103)

This is only one instance — and a relatively bland one, at that — of sardonic authorial analyses in the novel. Auchincloss views Philip's later, less appealing actions with the same cool gaze.

As the central figure in the novel, Sybil is judged more sympathetically, but even she is not exempt from critical scrutiny. Her romanticism is naive, and her shyness produces a snappishness that Auchincloss duly notes. Bearing in mind the unfavorable portrait of Philip, one may indeed wonder why Sybil returns to him at all. The question is crucial, for it is the key to the final meaning of the novel. None of the reasons offered by other characters adequately explains Sybil's actions. She does not return, as Philip thinks, because of his generous letter asking her forgiveness. Though she fully recognizes the sincerity of the letter, she is equally aware of its essential prosiness and senses the complacent self-satisfaction with which it was written. The theory proposed by Teddy and by Philip's sister Arlina that the affair with Howard was really impelled by frustrated love for Philip, though it appeals powerfully to Philip's amour propre and leads him to write the letter, does not really account for Sybil's conduct either. The reality Auchincloss portrays is less noble and dramatic. Sybil decides to return permanently because she has no real alternative. Even the possibility of some grand idealistic gesture does not exist. All Sybil can ask for in her life is simplicity and greater order. She returns to Philip, knowing that she is no longer in love and conscious that she must employ dissimulation for the first time in her marriage: "She would go along with the generally accepted theory that, however strangely she might have behaved, she still adored him."

Sybil's decision is encouraged, finally, by the combined pressure of all the relatives on both sides, by what Auchincloss, following Edith Wharton, calls "the tribe." When she realizes that even Teddy, the person closest to her, subscribes to the generally accepted theory of her conduct, "the crazy picture of her summer fell suddenly into place, and she knew at last what it was really like to be alone." And at the dinner party that closes the novel, she acknowledges the anniversary toasts as if she were thinking only of the pleasure of the occasion rather than "how funny it was to find herself, after the years of self-consciousness, without fear, without even embarrassment, in the presence of the assembled tribe." Looked at from one angle, this conclusion is a happy one for Sybil: she has found her place, she has accepted her role, she has learned how to live in society. Yet, from another perspective, the ending of the novel reminds one of the overpowering ability of the social group, the tribe, to defeat the individual. Sybil has found out who she is, but that person is someone whose alternatives, whose very individuality, are significantly limited.

Unlike Jane Austen, whose heroines often end up marrying a man who is not only the best match socially and financially but also the person with the finest moral character in the novel, Auchincloss does not reconcile the social and moral scales in *Sybil*. Philip, despite his social and financial attractions, still has grave flaws. Though Auchincloss points this out clearly, he does not bemoan this. The limitations imposed on Sybil are onerous, but they simply reflect the way things are. Because she holds fast to the romantic notion that there can only be one great love in any woman's life, Sybil finally cannot conceive of any alternative to life with Philip. Auchincloss himself seems to share this notion, and that may be one reason why Sybil is ultimately not a very appealing figure and the novel as a whole lacks a convincing resolution.

A Law for the Lion

Auchincloss wrote *A Law for the Lion* during his extended sabbatical from legal practice in 1952 and 1953. Though the novel covers much of the same ground as *Sybil*, Auchincloss focuses more clearly on the institution of marriage, inviting the reader to consider the unsuccessful marriage of Eloise Dilworth, the central character, in the light of two other relationships that develop in the work. Though Auchincloss's descriptions of social gatherings are as brilliant as usual, he is less immediately concerned with the forms and rituals of polite society and for the first time takes a look at the organizational politics of a large law firm. At the end of the novel, Eloise Dilworth begins to construct a life of her own rather than return to her husband and a fixed place in a tightly knit society. Though Auchincloss recognizes the limitations on individuality, the open-ended structure of the novel — whether inadvertently or by design — implies some small hope that Eloise will happily establish her independence.

Like Sybil Hilliard, Eloise Dilworth was raised in an unsympathetic environment. Her father died when she was a year old, and her mother roamed Europe with a series of husbands while Eloise was brought up by "an aunt whose fussiness was meant to make up for love and an uncle whose decorous politeness was meted out to her exactly as it was to everyone else." Although she went to Barnard College, she continued to live at home. Immediately after graduation, she married George Dilworth, a rising young partner in her uncle's law firm and a widower who asks her "to come and look after" him and his seven-year-old daughter. Though Eloise

does not share Sybil's romantic illusions, she and George
— fourteen years older, very domineering and stuffy, and
interested only in his career — are as ill-matched as the
Hilliards.

Eloise's mother, Irene Bleecker, is marked by her
own variety of maternal egotism. All during Eloise's
childhood, she "had been less a mother" to Eloise "than
a rare and somewhat exotic possession of which she had
to take particular care." Growing up "virtually without parents" has the same ill effect on Eloise that Mrs.
Rodman's destructive worrying had on Sybil. Plagued
by shyness and a sense of inadequacy, she entertains a
recurrent fantasy that "she was brought out on a deck,
a captured princess on a pirate ship, and stripped and
whipped before a jeering crew." In the most distasteful
scene in the novel, this fantasy comes true. Spurred on
by loneliness and George's harsh treatment of her mother, Eloise has an affair with a young novelist. Detectives hired by one of George's partners break into the
novelist's apartment and take pictures of the couple in
bed. A bitter divorce case follows, in which George is
given custody of his and Eloise's children.

The intrusion of the detectives exorcises Eloise's
masochistic fantasies and represents a turning point in
her quest for independence. When George gives her back
the children and asks her to consider remarriage, she
has the strength to refuse him. In rejecting his offer of
alimony, she frees herself from "his last act of possession." It is not clear how well she will support herself
from her earnings as a publisher's reader, but at last she
has achieved autonomy as a person.

A *Law for the Lion* ends, not with the prospect of
a new life for Eloise, but with the engagement of her
stepdaughter Hilda Dilworth to Bobbie Chapin, the lawyer who had represented Eloise in the divorce proceedings. The final scene, which brings the two young people together again in slightly tipsy euphoria after a long

separation, might be read as a hopeful conclusion. In returning to Bobbie, Hilda has shed the stuffiness she learned from her father, and the two young people will marry for love rather than out of the grim sense of duty that made Eloise accept George's proposal. But the seeming happiness of the scene is undercut by the reader's awareness of Eloise's terrible experiences with George and knowledge of the sharp differences in personality between Hilda and Bobbie. Neither this relationship nor the marriage between Eloise's mother and Arthur Irwin that takes place earlier in the novel provides a firm basis for optimism. Irene marries the most important client of her brother's law firm purely for convenience, and Bobbie and Hilda's decision is impulsive enough to raise the suspicion that their marriage will have severe problems. Taken together, the three relationships in the novel seem to urge a realistic view of the limitations on human happiness, but the final scene remains confusing. Because it seems designed to provide a happy ending, it cannot finally be regarded as an ironic commentary, but because Auchincloss veers away from his central character Eloise Dilworth and fails to prepare us adequately for the scene, it is not a convincing happy ending either. The novel as a whole therefore suffers.

Auchincloss took his title *A Law for the Lion* from the final proverb in Blake's *Marriage of Heaven and Hell*: "One Law for the Lion and Ox is Oppression." Blake's proverb, which appears as the epigraph to the book, at once underscores the differences between George and Eloise and points to another important aspect of the novel. *A Law for the Lion* is a powerful reminder of the injustice that results from inflexible laws such as the divorce statutes of New York State under which Eloise's case is tried. Not only do the laws permit George and his partner Harry Hamilton crudely to attack Eloise's character in the courtroom, but they also assign custody of the children to the less suitable parent because Eloise refuses to compromise her intellectual position in answering a purely hypothetical question posed at the trial.

Though Auchincloss may well have favored the reform of New York's antiquated divorce laws, the novel is not a political pamphlet. If anything, Auchincloss is more interested in the law as a sphere of human behavior, as a social institution with its own hierarchy and rituals. That Bobbie Chapin comes from an "uptown" law firm rather than Livermore and Hunt, the old Wall Street firm for which George Dilworth and Eloise's uncle work, tells us something significant about him. Because George and Harry Hamilton turn the divorce case into a messy scandal, they are forced by Eloise's uncle to resign from Livermore and Hunt. As senior partner in the firm, Gerald Hunt has long wanted to get rid of Harry Hamilton; but even though he is upset about the possibility his niece will be dragged into the mire of publicity, he does not try to punish George and Harry until the trial is well under way, and he waits until he has ascertained, through a wonderful piece of veiled negotiation that takes place at a wedding reception, that the firm's largest client, Arthur Irwin, would not take his business away if George were to leave. Business and personal relations become inextricably intertwined in this episode not just because Gerald Hunt is Eloise's uncle but because Arthur Irwin is enamored of Irene Bleecker. The latter connection counts for more, and when George Dilworth sees the announcement of Irene and Arthur's wedding he realizes why his resignation was so willingly accepted.

Auchincloss manages this complex tangle of personal and professional relationships deftly, expertly bringing them together in a narrative that carefully balances different scenes and groups of characters. His portrait of Eloise is sensitive, but, as in *Sybil*, he never sentimentalizes or lets his sympathy prevent him from dryly noting the immaturity and naiveté of his central character. Although *A Law for the Lion* holds out a modest hope that an intelligent woman such as Eloise might find fulfillment and independence, the general pattern of action in the novel is less encouraging. Eloise's marriage, her friendship with the young novelist Landik, and all the turmoil connected with her divorce have merely taken her back to the point where she started. "I want to find out first what I am," she tells George near the end of the novel. "I want to be satisfied with myself as a human being and not only as a daughter or a niece or a wife. I want to go back to where I was when I graduated from college and first met you." Though Eloise may find the answers to her questions, she is starting late, and the whole burden of her experience suggests the limitations to any identity she may find.

Though flawed in some ways, *Sybil* and *A Law for the Lion* display Auchincloss's increasing command of the novelist's craft. They fall short of the standards set by his mature work, but they are considerably more than apprentice pieces. Though Eloise Dilworth in *A Law for the Lion* is a more successfully realized character than Sybil Hilliard, both novels combine sensitivity with ironic distance in their portraits of female characters. In both works Auchincloss establishes his enduring interest in the shy but tenacious woman whose reticence and lack of flashy beauty make her girlhood painful, but who develops in the course of a difficult marriage into a strong person. And in Lucy Hilliard in the earlier novel he effectively portrays the hard but sympathetic middle-aged woman whose vivid grasp of the ways of the world sets her apart from all other characters, male or female, in the novel in which she appears. The major male characters, Philip Hilliard and George Dilworth, are rather less successful, though George may be said to be an effective portrait of the legal technician who lives exclusively for his profession and is insecure outside the realm of his work. Not until his novels of the late 1950s, however, does Auchincloss effectively present male protagonists.

Sybil and *A Law for the Lion* did much to establish Auchincloss's reputation by the mid 1950s as a significant novelist of manners — as an authoritative portrayer of the New York upper classes and the *haute bourgeoisie* of large Manhattan law firms. Yet seen in the perspective of Auchincloss's development, the two works remain most important as psychological novels. Though Eloise Dilworth is far more successful than Sybil Hilliard in her attempts to find out who she is, both novels reveal Auchincloss's early and abiding interest in questions of feminine character and identity. Both novels remain somewhat unsatisfying, nonetheless. In order to find more satisfying and fully realized quests for feminine identity one must turn to Auchincloss's novels at the end of the decade, *The House of Five Talents* and *Portrait in Brownstone*.

4

**New York
Then and Now:
*The House of
Five Talents*
and *Portrait
in Brownstone***

The House of Five Talents and *Portrait in Brownstone*
are Auchincloss's finest novels of manners and rank
among his best works. They invite consideration together
because of the similarity in their settings and central
characters. In both novels, Auchincloss returns to the sort
of shy heroine he had portrayed a decade earlier in *Sybil*
and *A Law for the Lion*, but the later novels have considerably greater depth and complexity. Instead of leaving the question of the central character's identity in
doubt at the end of the novel, he shows in each of the
later works how an initially timid woman develops into
a strong character in the course of her lifetime. Both
Augusta Millinder in *The House of Five Talents* and Ida
Hartley in *Portrait in Brownstone* are survivors, but they
are also characters who have accepted a particular role
and grown in it. By the time they reach their sixties, both
women are self-confident individuals and powerful
forces in their families. Most of their growth occurs in

middle age — that is to say, in a phase of life not covered in the earlier novels, which end when their heroines are still young. Auchincloss's portraits of his female protagonists are, as always, sympathetic, but by extending the period of time in which the women are seen in the later novels he has eliminated the uncertainty and fuzziness that trouble the endings of the earlier works.

The two novels are also given added depth by finely developed historical perspective. In each novel Auchincloss traces the life of a particular family over several generations and shows how customs and attitudes change over periods of time. His brilliant depictions of fashionable life in New York and Newport in the 1890s and the first decade of the twentieth century are reminiscent of Edith Wharton's backward glances at the New York of her childhood in *The Age of Innocence* and *Old New York*, but, unlike Wharton, Auchincloss is creating a world that existed before he was born. In this respect his achievement is remarkable.

To write the novel of manners in America at all has always been a difficult enterprise. Writers from James Fenimore Cooper to Henry James to Lionel Trilling have even argued that it is an impossible task. Whether this is true or not, American society with its fluidity, its lack of fixed social forms, and its absence of a clearly defined class structure has always presented special problems for the novelist of manners.[1] As Hugh Holman has observed, "the impact which democracy makes on manners converts the novelist from being a tester of character by established standards to a portrayer of character under the persistent impact of change. The social novelist's subject becomes mutability rather than order, and his testing cruxes occur when change rather than stasis puts stress on the moral values of his characters."[2] Although Holman was writing about John P. Marquand, another American novelist of manners, his remarks help to define the challenge Auchincloss faced in *The House of Five*

Talents and *Portrait in Brownstone*. Auchincloss meets the challenge in his own way, however. In both novels his central character, even though she becomes a stronger and more confident person, serves as a kind of fixed point against which we can measure the changes from previous to later generations.

In *The House of Five Talents* and to a somewhat lesser extent in *Portrait in Brownstone*, Auchincloss confronts another persistent challenge to the American novelist. Despite their egalitarian pretensions, Americans have always been fascinated by the rich. Indeed, Auchincloss maintains that the impetus for writing *The House of Five Talents* came from his irritation at people who had automatically assumed that his earlier novels were primarily about the rich. "Irked by the insistence of critics and friends that the most important thing in the shaping of my characters had to be their money, I decided that it might be interesting to write the novel that everyone thought I had been writing." Most American novelists have been ambivalent about the rich, and insiders' views of the rich have been rare in American fiction. Here again Auchincloss is unique. Drawing upon lore from previous generations of his wife's family as well as his own, he writes with special authority. Yet, as Robie Macaulay has commented, Auchincloss also brings a cool objectivity to his task. "He is untouched by Fitzgerald's resentments, by Edith Wharton's rather romantic despair, or by [any of] the deceptive aphorisms" about the rich that one usually encounters in the tradition.[3]

Though Auchincloss himself has wondered whether *The House of Five Talents* "does not belong more to history than to literature," neither it nor *Portrait in Brownstone* is a sociological tract. Of all the paired novels among Auchincloss's works, these two are the most clearly related. Indeed, *Portrait in Brownstone* was initially conceived as a sequel to the earlier novel.[4] Yet the two novels diverge thematically. *The House of Five Talents* is more directly concerned with the effects of a large fortune on a family somewhat like the Vanderbilts, whereas *Portrait in Brownstone* examines the question whether a large but tightly knit family can survive in the twentieth century in a city such as New York. In both novels, however, Auchincloss shows us the costs to the human spirit of growing up in an upper-class American family at the turn of the century, and he charts the always difficult process of finding personal identity in such a family or any family. In telling the stories of Gussie Millinder and Ida Hartley, Auchincloss evaluates the costs and defines the benefits of the lifelong experiment by which one comes to know oneself. *The House of Five Talents* and *Portrait in Brownstone* develop the themes latent in Auchincloss's earliest novels and mark his emergence as a contemporary novelist of first rank.

The House of Five Talents

Published in 1960, *The House of Five Talents* is a first-person narrative told by Augusta Millinder, the granddaughter of Julius Millinder, the German immigrant who established the family fortune. Augusta's account spans five generations of the family from the 1870s to 1948. As Augusta points out, the novel is not "the story of a family," but "the story of a fortune," a tale of what people do with their money and what their money does to them. It is a novel filled with the objects that various members of the family have bought with the Biblical talents alluded to in the title. Indeed, at many points in the novel, things — houses, paintings, works of sculpture — seem to stand in for the people who own them. Although Gussie Millinder's perspective is sometimes limited and her actions flawed, she is sympathetically portrayed. In their mixture of tart commentary, pathos, and comedy, her reminiscences constitute Auchincloss's most effective first-person narrative.

The novel, however, is also the story of Gussie's interventions in the lives of other members of her family. While acknowledging the failure of many of her attempts to control others, Auchincloss at the same time makes us aware of the poignant losses Gussie suffers both because of her family position and because of her own character. Despite her losses, Gussie triumphs by accepting and learning how to play, honestly and vigorously, the role she has been handed. As life changes around her, she remains the same. But, paradoxically, even while she becomes an anachronism — a sort of glorious old fossil — as the Victorian respectabilities of her childhood yield to more modern customs, she also becomes a stronger and happier person.

Gussie writes her narrative in 1948, when she is seventy-five. She has no intention of showing it to anyone in her lifetime, because she wants her past to remain her own. "Everyone wants to do something to the poor old past," she observes. "It is difficult enough to catch and isolate even the faintest aroma of past events without being confused by the advice and the pasts of others." In her account of the Millinders, Gussie is determined "to be impartial and give the money its due but no more than that." Significantly, however, money receives its due almost immediately. The first episode of the novel involves a bitter argument between Gussie's father and mother over her grandfather's will. Although the family inherits more than they could ever spend, Mrs. Millinder is upset because her husband has received only half the fortune his younger brother has. Mr. Millinder is unhappy because he hadn't wanted even that much money.

With the inheritance, Gussie's mother builds a large house in Newport, where she attempts to make her mark in society by marrying her older daughter Cora to Lancey Bell, the son of the social arbiter of the resort. As-

sisted by Gussie, who is herself in love with the young
man, Mrs. Millinder gets Lancey Bell to propose to Cora,
but Cora refuses to break her previous, hasty engagement to a French count, whom she marries in Paris.
Even after this fiasco, Gussie is befriended by Mrs. Bell.
At his mother's urging, Lancey eventually proposes to
Gussie and she accepts. Out of fears about her own inadequacy and doubt whether Lancey loves her or is marrying her for her money, Gussie breaks off the engagement shortly before the wedding date. Her mother is
furious and gives up trying to find her a husband. At age
twenty-five, Gussie takes courses in history and art at
Columbia. Though she teaches briefly in a girls' school,
for the rest of the novel she largely plays the role of cousin
or aunt, encouraging and advising other members of the
family in a series of crises. In the next decade she sup-
ports her cousin Lucius Hoyt's rebellion against his father, and she wins back the loyalty of her mother by taking her side in her parents' divorce. After the divorce,
she leaves teaching to help her mother in building her
art collection.

Her mother's death in 1916 marks the midpoint in
both the novel and Gussie's life. Realizing that her years
as her mother's advisor have been a way of postponing
any decision about her own life, Gussie lapses into severe
depression. She is rescued from her gloom by Ione Locke,
the impoverished widow of one of her brother Bertie's
friends who comes to live with her and persuades her
that her role as an "old maid" could be satisfying. With
the advantages of her inheritance and the increased respect accorded her age, she intervenes even more actively
in the lives of those around her. She is responsible for her
brother's marriage to her friend Ione and later breaks up
Ione's affair with a young cousin, Sandy Herron. She
covers up the embezzlements of another cousin's husband, Collier Haven, and sees to it that he retires from
the brokerage business. As Aunt Gussie, she also takes

over the lives of her two nephews. Her interventions
achieve mixed results at best. Her older nephew, Lydig,
whom she loves as a son, marries unhappily and dies in
a mountain-climbing expedition in the Himalayas. His
younger brother, Oswald, lives as a Bohemian in Greenwich Village and becomes a Communist fellow-traveler
in the 1930s. At Gussie's urging he marries his pregnant
mistress. When Oswald divorces her, Gussie helps her
keep custody of their child, Julius. The former mistress
proves an unfit mother, however; and at the end of the
novel, when Oswald has fled to Guatemala after giving
evasive testimony to a congressional committee, Gussie
is left to raise his child.

As well as being the central character, Augusta Millinder is an admirable narrator because she possesses just
the right amount of insight to evaluate the actions of the
rest of her family without ever going beyond the believable range of attitudes and ideas of a woman of her time
and class. She always remains a "character" — a crusty
old maid with strongly held opinions who displays a
good deal of gusto in expressing them. Much of the comedy in the novel comes from Gussie's acerbic remarks
about other members of her family. Because of her train-
ing as an art historian, she is also a credible voice for the
sort of historical analysis in which Auchincloss delights.
In her narrative, literary allusions and comments on
works of art do not sound out of place as they sometimes
do in the mouths of businessmen or socialites in other
novels by Auchincloss. The use of a first-person narrator
in *The House of Five Talents* allows sympathy and distance at the same time and eliminates the jarring conflict
between a predominantly sympathetic view and occasional ironic distance that one encounters in the portrayals of the protagonists in the earlier novels.

In considering Gussie Millinder's development from
childhood to old age, Auchincloss displays the keen sense
of family politics that he had developed in his writing

during the 1950s. The single most important influence
on Gussie's personality is her mother, a powerful, domineering woman who wants to use her daughters as ve-
hicles for her own social advancement. Like several other
mothers in Auchincloss's fiction, the strong-willed Mrs.
Millinder regards her daughters as extensions of herself.
As Gussie's governess tells her, "Your mother is not like
other people" because she does not yield to emotional
appeals. By adolescence Gussie had "learned once and
for all that there was no point in playing rough games
with Mamma. She never knew when to stop." Throughout the novel, Gussie identifies herself with the statue of
the White Captive that was in her grandfather's gallery
when she was a girl. She thinks of herself as standing
before the "bleak, denigrating stare" of her assembled
family like the naked girl of Erastus Dow Palmer's statue, "her hands tied to a post, her eyes raised to her
enemies in a proud defiance that could not wholly conceal her bewilderment and fear."[5]

Growing up in the shadow of her beautiful older
sister is also difficult for Gussie. As the ugly duckling in
the family, Gussie resents the attention paid to Cora. As
Auchincloss carefully shows, her motives in serving as in-
termediary between Cora and Lancey Bell and in helping her mother promote their engagement are a complex
mixture of girlish romanticism and envy. Yet even Cora,
whose beauty attracts several highly eligible suitors in
addition to Lancey, is frightened by Mrs. Millinder's intense desire for a socially successful marriage. Her decision to marry Prince Antoine de Conti is in part an attempt to escape her mother's machinations. At the same
time, however, the failure of her match with Lancey also
illustrates the pervasive power of the Millinder family's
money and its tendency to distort human relationships.
Lancey Bell first rejects marriage to Cora because Mrs.
Millinder throws the family fortune in his face in a humiliating way, but when he proposes again, Cora can

no longer be certain about his reasons and prefers to marry Conti because he has been much more honest about his need for money to maintain his family's estates. Ironically, Cora and Antoine's children turn out to be grandfather Millinder's "happiest and most successful descendants." European society offers them a definite position and predetermined roles, and as a result they have none of their American cousins' ambivalence about riches or social position.

Gussie breaks off her engagement to Lancey for more complicated reasons, but even in her case the family fortune has an unhappy distorting effect. Gussie was very much in love with Lancey and would have made a far more congenial wife for him than Cora, who had none of his wit or intellectual sophistication. Even fifty years later, Gussie recalls Lancey's proposal as the most important event of her life. At a dinner party many years after Lancey's marriage to someone else, Gussie asks him if his proposal had been serious. Before he can answer, she stops him — not, as he thinks, because she is afraid that he will say he had not loved her, but rather, as she puts it, because she "could not bear to contemplate the idea that Mamma had been right and that I had wrecked my own life." In this instance Auchincloss gives the money "its due" but definitely "no more than that," as Gussie might say.

Though Gussie may well have thrown away her best opportunity for conventional happiness when she rejected Lancey Bell, the role she constructs for herself with the assistance of Ione Locke represents a sort of comic triumph. Auchincloss underlines the authenticity of the role by connecting it with the old family brownstone in which Gussie chooses to remain after her mother's death. Ione encourages her to redecorate the mansion to "suggest, albeit pleasantly instead of vulgarly, some of the pushing spirit of the decade of its construction," and she persuades her that the role of "a rich, respectable, intelligent old maid" could be far more significant than she had imagined. An old maid could be a sort of mediator between the generations, able to reach both young and old.

An old maid, at least a rich one, could wear big jewelry and ride around in an antique town car and wear fussy clothes out of fashion and weep at the opera and threaten naughty street urchins with her stick; she could join the boards of clubs and charities and be as officious and bossy as she liked; she could insist on giving the family party on Christmas Eve; she could even, in her new, shrewd, noisy way, become the head of the remnants of the Millinders. She could become, in short, to two generations of relatives and friends, the redoubtable, the in-domitable "Aunt Gussie" and earn for herself . . . the ultimate compliment of an easily hoodwinked world: she could be "wonderful." (*House of Five Talents*, p. 217)

Gussie's acceptance of a role such as this may seem an odd sort of salvation, and as Auchincloss's description implies there is a decidedly humorous dimension to her character. But her triumph is nonetheless quite real. Unlike many earlier Auchincloss protagonists, Gussie is emphatically *not* cast in the one role she cannot play in life. It helps perhaps that she is a woman and therefore not subjected to the demands for conventional success that overwhelm such men as Michael Farish, the trust officer who commits suicide in *Venus in Sparta*, but Gussie's self-acceptance is courageous and unique in a world where far better equipped people ruin themselves trying to play roles for which they are totally unsuited. Even the seemingly self-assured Cora is a person who "looked to perfection a part that she had no wish or capacity to play." Whereas Cora must in effect run away from her family to keep from destroying herself, Gussie remains in the setting that produced her and manages to adjust happily; Auchincloss convinces the reader that this is no mean achievment.

If Gussie and Cora's experiences show the effects of

the Millinder fortune on members of the family, Ione Locke presents an example of its effect on people outside the family. Ione and her husband had been a popular couple about town before he died, leaving her with very little money. Gussie saves her from an uncomfortable existence as a dependent on Gussie's insensitive Aunt Daisy. Other members of the family think that Ione dupes Gussie when she moves in with her and redecorates the Millinder brownstone, and their opinion of her as a social adventuress is only confirmed when she ends up marrying Gussie's bachelor brother Bertie. Yet Gussie, who loves Ione and for a time is possessively attached to her, realizes that all of Ione's relationships with her family are reciprocal: "Ione always gave more than she got, and nobody ever got very much from the Millinders." Here, as in Auchincloss's later novel *The Embezzler*, who uses whom is not an easy question to answer. When she realizes that Bertie is interested in Ione, Gussie thinks of her as a "white captive" much like herself, but she later encourages Bertie to marry her "for our team" when a rival appears from outside the family. Not to break up the relatively harmless affair with Sandy Herron is the one favor Ione ever asks of Gussie in all their years of friendship, and Gussie refuses her. As Gussie later realizes, "I had tried to possess her by purchase," just as the other members of the family had. When Ione marries the rich but boorish Harold Faye after Bertie's death and becomes richer than all the Millinders, Gussie perceives the final irony in the symbiotic relationship: "We had made her in the end a true Millinder."

The tale of Ione Locke, like other episodes in the novel, reveals what Robie Macaulay has called the "expenses of spirit" resulting from great wealth.[6] Yet it also shows how Gussie is characteristically a flawed agent in the world of the novel. When Gussie attempts to influence events, she seldom achieves the results she intends. When she reports her father's affair with a

former actress, she expects to endear herself to her
mother and become a central figure in reconciling her
parents. Her mother is grateful, but she rather than
Gussie dominates the divorce proceedings, and the handsome settlement Mr. Millinder's attorney offers her finally permits her to withdraw even further from human
relationships and to spend most of her fortune on the
things she collects. Gussie's cousin Lucius Hoyt, who initially seems a sensitive aesthete, becomes with Gussie's
assistance the harshest businessman in the family — even
more calculating than the father against whom she had
encouraged him to rebel. When Gussie releases Collier
Haven from the promise he had made to retire from the
brokerage business, she gets blamed by the rest of the
family for his subsequent embezzlements, even though
it was she who had loaned him the money to cover up
his first misappropriations. Though all these vignettes involve the distorting effect of money, Auchincloss seems
also to be suggesting in each one of them the radically
unpredictable effects of human actions.

Of all Gussie's emotional involvements in the second
portion of her life, her relationship with her nephew
Lydig is the most intense and poignant. Gussie's position
as an old maid aunt in her fifties allows her to get close
to Lydig in a way that his ambitious and rather cold
mother cannot. She encourages him in school and college and provides him with a second home. By far the
most intelligent and appealing figure in his generation,
Lydig is another character who strives to excel in the very
role for which he is unsuited. A born businessman, he
tries to be a philanthropist and art collector. When his
brittle wife becomes bored with him and displays an interest in his hunting, fishing, and polo-playing friend
Townie Fales, a man with none of his intellectual substance or warmth, he tries to become an even greater
athlete and sportsman. After Lydig dies in a climbing
accident in Nepal, Gussie feels that by encouraging his

conventional achievements and denying him the company of her small group of elderly friends — the only setting in which he had felt relaxed — she has failed him, much as she had failed Ione Locke. In Lydig's death she has lost almost a son, almost a lover, and the years following his loss are the gloomiest in her life.

Gussie's involvement in the life of Oswald, Lydig's unappealing younger brother, is far less intense, but it gives rise to the numerous ironies that shape the conclusion of the novel. Almost inevitably, a family as large as the Millinders that was living in the 1930s and 1940s would have contained at least one Communist or fellow-traveler. Auchincloss neatly explores the possibilities of such a character and context. By a sort of perverse poetic justice, Oswald's comments on his family are among the most trenchant analyses in the novel. It is Oswald, for example, who sees most clearly that Lydig's aspirations are out of keeping with his true character. When Gussie makes Oswald marry his mistress, Millie, he warns her that she is "opening up a Pandora's box of respectabilities." Because Millie cannot adjust, she becomes a liability in the new, more respectable life that Oswald enters as a minor novelist (the author of a trashy novel on the Collier Haven episode) and host for leftwing artists and intellectuals, and she is duly divorced. Oswald becomes a leading liberal and works as the public relations officer for his Uncle George Millinder's foundation. When it is discovered that Oswald was a fellow-traveler who had used his uncle's name to support a number of Communist front organizations, George, the very model of a respectable modern millionaire and therefore anathema to Gussie, must mount a new public-relations campaign to dissociate himself from his former public relations officer.

Though Gussie reacts with mild glee at George's discomfiture, her own espousal of Millie's cause meets with equally ironic results. She assists Millie in her battle to keep her son in the face of attempts by Oswald's mother, Julia, to get legal custody of the child by offering a large cash settlement. A few years later, however, when Millie turns out to be an unfit mother as Julia had predicted, Gussie ends up offering her the same sort of financial settlement that Julia had. Gussie is honest enough to see the ironies and Julia discreet enough not to mention them.

Oswald names his and Millie's son for his great-grandfather Julius Millinder — an act that "was widely considered a hopeful sign of reform" at the time. Yet in the aspirations of this fifth-generation Millinder and his contemporaries Auchincloss gives us a final index of how greatly the attitudes of the family have changed. Rather than emulating his namesake who built the conspicuous family houses, who tried to buy the Republican Party, and who was not quite respectable in his own time even after he had made a hundred million dollars, little Julius gives himself an allowance no larger than that of the average boy in his form at Chelton School and hopes to enter Yale to become a doctor. He emulates his cousin Lydig Millinder, Jr., who has become a typical suburbanite with "a job in a law firm downtown where he works at least three nights a week." This scion of a robber baron "is married, has two children, two cars, a house in New Canaan and lives like his neighbors. The fact that he spends less than a third of his income after taxes is generally known in his community and generally approved." Lydig Jr.'s mode of living and the respectable, socially responsible philanthropy of George Millinder's son Alfred embody the story of the Millinder fortune in the post–World War II era. "What more painless and dignified death could I ask for the family name," Gussie says, "than it should descend into the dust of uniformity from which it arose?"

Yet Auchincloss shrewdly reminds one that appearances can be deceptive. Despite its new, less obvious manifestations, the Millinder fortune has not disappeared. As Oswald observes, "nothing could be falser" than the old adage, "Three generations from shirt sleeves to shirt sleeves." "Take the twelve living grandchildren of Julius Millinder," he says. "Every last blessed one of them is rich. . . . Why, they're spread all over the globe! I figure that it takes no less than a thousand human souls to wait on the old pirate's progeny!" There is no evidence that the fortunes of the fourth and fifth generations have radically declined; all that has changed is their manners.

As Gussie states at the outset, her memoir is the story of a fortune. But it is also very much the story of the artifacts acquired by the various generations of Millinders. Though Auchincloss often follows a tradition in American fiction — both realistic and romantic — that regards houses and possessions as symbols of their owners, objets d'art of various sorts are more prominent in *The House of Five Talents* than in any other of his novels. Consider, for example, Gussie's remarks early in the novel about one of her nephews:

Young Alfred has what I call a "mansion" on Ninetieth Street, but he insists that he bought it only to house his collection of modern art. It seems to me that a cellar would have done as well for that. But then Alfred loves to be described in picture magazines as a "daring collector" and to be photographed in his shirt sleeves, pipe in hand, squinting at some practical joke by Picasso that he has just bought for a higher price than my mother paid for her great Holbein. It's all part and parcel of his silly campaign to identify the family name with something he calls "public responsibility." I'm afraid I was a bit snappish when he explained this to me. I think he actually wanted me to move out of my conspicuous old brownstone shell to help his campaign. (*House of Five Talents*, p. 5)

Alfred's desire to "dry-clean" family history is one of the reasons Gussie decides to write her memoir, and this passage is a good example of the way Auchincloss establishes just the right tone for his narrator. At the same time, it also reveals how moral and aesthetic judgments are subtly interconnected throughout Gussie's narrative.

In a story of money in which objects often seem to stand for people, Gussie's recollections may themselves be regarded as a sort of family museum. The story begins in Grandpa Millinder's gallery, whose large, dark academic paintings on historical subjects and American landscapes of the Great Plains and the sea suggest both the size and the newness of the family's fortune. The great Gérôme painting of the assassination of the Medici that dominated the grandfather's gallery is relegated by Gussie's mother to the dark summer place she builds in Bar Harbor. In a similar fashion, Gussie's family house in Newport built in indigenous American shingle style by Stanford White exemplifies her mother's good taste versus the ostentation of Aunt Daisy's "late Gothic French chateau of dull, featureless limestone" built by Richard Morris Hunt. In the third generation, Gussie's cousin Lucius Hoyt collects French Impressionist paintings, and in the next generation Alfred, of course, buys Picassos.

The most striking instances of the linkage between works of art and character in the novel are associated with Gussie's mother, an obsessive collector whose tastes develop and change over several decades. Toward the end of her life, Mrs. Millinder stops acquiring landscapes and paintings of human subjects altogether, turning instead to French and Oriental porcelains — a change that reflects her almost total withdrawal from human relationships. The only two paintings that she retains in her collection tell much about her character. The great Holbein portrait of an unknown English lady is really an image of herself, and the tiny Vermeer of a household maid holding a blue and white cup is, as Gussie realizes, "more of a still life than a portrait," its focal point being the china cup rather than the maid. Mrs. Millinder dies of a stroke while traveling in the Orient in search of porcelains and jades for her collection. Unable to speak, she spends her last days with Gussie at her side in the English hospital in Hong Kong. At the very end, in a chilling scene, she ignores Gussie and gazes steadily at the finest of her acquisitions, "a small yellow glaze jar, of a simplicity and depth of color that made it a perfection among man-made things."

As her comments on her nephew Alfred's collection indicate, Gussie is herself associated with the family's brownstone mansion, in which she remains an indomitable resident even as the neighborhood around her becomes completely commercial. She identifies herself with the late nineteenth-century world that produced her. As she wryly observes late in the novel, she plans to will most of her fortune to the Mayan Institute for archeological work since "after all, I am a bit of a fossil myself." The final image of Gussie, however, is one of art rather than paleontology. Having told the tale of her family as explicitly and honestly as she can, she allows herself "to toss and turn for a while in the downy bed of more romantic concepts." In the last paragraph of the novel, she returns again to the solace of her grandfather's gallery during her girlhood. She imagines all the paintings and their subjects. "Standing beneath them all, on the top of the ottoman," she says, "is still, of course, the white captive, her hands tied to the post, her eyes fixed upon her captors with defiance and bewilderment. She has simply grown old, that is all." This final symbolic artifact in the novel not only suggests Gussie's essential vulnerability but also establishes an almost Proustian continuity between past and present. Yet, in the broadest perspective, it also reminds one of the fundamental artfulness of all recollections. Like any attempt to reconstruct one's own past, Gussie's history is as much a product of her own imagination as an objective account, and it is fitting that, at the very end, Gussie herself should join the family collection as the unfashionable but poignant statue of the white captive.

Though Gussie retreats into the romantic world of

her own imagination, her narrative as a whole raises the question implied in Scott Fitzgerald's famous remarks about the rich — a question considered in many of the novels in the tradition of which *The House of Five Talents* is a part. "Let me tell you about the very rich," Fitzgerald wrote in an early story. "They are different from you and me." Gussie denies this. "I sometimes think," she writes in the concluding chapter of her narrative, "that my family were at all times simple, ordinary people, pursuing simple, ordinary tasks, who stood out from the crowd only in the imagination of those observers who fancied from reading the evening papers that tiaras and opera boxes made an organic difference. Perhaps that is my ultimate discovery of what the money meant, that it meant nothing at all, or, at any rate, very little." Gussie's opinion, of course, reflects Auchincloss's own assumption that human nature and human problems are fundamentally the same despite differences in class or milieu. Yet Gussie herself shies away from her opinion. She wants to see the Millinders as special in some sense, and the whole burden of her narrative is to suggest how money changes members of the family, by heightening their insecurity about other people's motives or exaggerating traits already present in their own personalities. Though Auchincloss affirms the fundamental similarity between rich and poor on some basic level, in Gussie's narrative he has also produced a subtle and carefully balanced definition of the complex transformations wrought by money in the lives of a particular family.

The House of Five Talents is the first fully satisfying novel of Auchincloss's maturity. In Gussie Millinder, he succeeds in creating not only an authentic voice for the themes of the novel but also a unique and distinctly memorable character. Though some of the minor characters are less fully realized, the unpredictable ironies of their fates give life and interest to the complex plot

much of a "moper" for the breezy, cheerful Denisons, whose family code condemns any sort of emotional excess as "sloppy." Throughout the novel, the shy, somewhat intellectual Ida is contrasted with her flamboyant cousin Geraldine, "the golden-haired darling of the block," who is both mischievous and willful. Geraldine enjoys the intrigue connected with a secret romance between her brother Scotty and their Italian-born cousin Livia, but Ida feels compelled to reveal the secret and then feels guilty about doing so. The first portion of the novel ends with Ida's trip to Paris as a chaperone to her grandmother Trask and an elderly widower — an experience Geraldine would have found amusing, but Ida finds painful and embarrassing.

In the second part of the novel, Ida is courted by Derrick Hartley, an ambitious Bostonian who makes his way into Linn Tremain's firm and soon becomes a partner. She falls in love with him, and they exchange a chaste kiss in the Egyptian Room of the Metropolitan Museum, but, as soon as he sees Geraldine, Derrick is infatuated. When Geraldine, acting under intense pressure from the family, rejects him for a wealthier suitor, Derrick returns to Ida, who accepts him in spite of her wounded pride. After a decade of marriage, Ida realizes that she cannot change Derrick and decides to accept his dominance. Fifteen years later, when Geraldine returns from Europe after the death of her second husband, the rivalry between the cousins is renewed. Derrick sets Geraldine up in an apartment he owns, and she becomes his lover. Ida knows this, but accepts the affair as the price of Geraldine's forced rejection of Derrick's proposal. At the end of the novel, however, after her cousin has committed suicide and many years after the end of the affair, Derrick tells Ida that it was Geraldine rather than he who broke off the relationship when she found that he was never going to divorce his wife.

The remaining portions of the novel involve Ida and

Derrick's children. Dorcas, the older child, who had
identified closely with her father when she was a girl,
marries Robin Granberry, an editor and would-be novelist. A weak, self-pitying figure, Robin is precisely the
sort of man her father does not wish her to marry. The
birth of a son reconciles Derrick to his daughter, but
Robin is destroyed, partly through his own weakness and
partly through Derrick's overbearing financial assistance. Dorcas divorces him and later marries her lawyer,
Mark Jesmond. In Mark she has found a powerful man
very much like her father — indeed, Mark joins Derrick's
firm and eventually supplants him as senior partner.
Derrick and Ida's son, Hugo, on the other hand, refuses
to go into his father's business, preferring to work in the
Denison family auction gallery and live at home. Always
his mother's favorite, he seems unwilling to settle down
and is quite content to remain a bachelor and extra man.

In the last section of the novel, entitled "The Emergence of Ida," Ida finally asserts herself. Her emergence
begins immediately after Geraldine's suicide and is most
prominently displayed in her efforts to arrange Hugo's
life. In a show of social dexterity worthy of her mother
and an exercise of power worthy of Derrick, she breaks
up Hugo's engagement to an older divorcée and makes
sure that he will marry his cousin Alfreda Denison. At
the same time, Derrick realizes that Dorcas has shifted
her loyalty to Mark and is actively assisting him in his
plan to take control of the family brokerage firm. After
a terrible argument which lays bare Mark and Dorcas's
true feelings about him, Derrick suffers a heart attack.
In the closing scene of the novel, which takes place at
Hugo's wedding, Ida has become the central force in
the family. Derrick, now confined to a wheelchair, acknowledges that "no woman could have lived with me
but you," and other members of the family pay their
court to her. Ida has asserted herself in the name of
preserving the family, but now that she has succeeded

she wonders if the Denisons as she conceived them ever existed, and she suspects at the end of the novel that they no longer exist, in the sense of being a cohesive, effective institution, outside of her own mind.

Always an acute social historian, Auchincloss is perhaps at his best as an observer of changing manners in *Portrait in Brownstone*. In his depiction of mothers and daughters in four generations of the family, for example, he provides a miniature history of attitudes toward sex and marriage among upper-class New Yorkers from the Civil War to World War II. For Ida's mother, marriage is a desirable social institution frequently, but not necessarily, accompanied by intense romantic feeling. For the Denison family in 1911 — and for Ida as well — Derrick and Ida's kiss in the Egyptian Room of the Metropolitan Museum is a virtual seal of their engagement. Twenty-five years later, however, Ida herself recommends that her daughter Dorcas sleep with Mark Jesmond before deciding to marry him. As James Tuttleton has pointed out, the very setting of Ida's first kiss suggests how "the manners and mores of [her] youth have become archeological curiosities."[8]

Under the layer of conventions associated with the Egyptian Room, there is another, even earlier set of conventions connected with Ida's grandmother, Mrs. Trask. On their voyage to France Ida and Mrs. Trask meet Miss Polhemus, an old friend from Mrs. Trask's childhood whom she regards as a definitive social arbiter because her fortune is older and considerably larger than her own. Miss Polhemus is shocked because Mrs. Trask is traveling to Europe on the same ship as Mr. Robbins, a widower who, along with his own wife when she was alive, used to travel with Mrs. Trask and her late husband. Because of Miss Polhemus's objections, Ida's grandmother completely changes her itinerary to avoid staying in the same hotels with Mr. Robbins. When Mr. Robbins proposes to her in Paris, Mrs. Trask rejects him because she is worried that she will have to meet her first husband in heaven and confess that she has married again. For Ida's mother, who had joined her daughter in Paris, Mrs. Trask's scruples about remarriage seem quaint. In her brisk, modern view, nothing should stand in the way of two people's search for happiness, and she efficiently persuades her mother-in-law to marry Mr. Robbins. In the final analysis, however, Mrs. Trask's forced conversion to the modern idea of marriage produces unhappy results. Though her old-fashioned ideas may have been silly, she is not really content in her second marriage. She has been sacrificed on the altar of modernity as a victim of the Denison family's penchant for neat domestic arrangements. The episode reflects Auchincloss's underlying view of social change. Though he does not advocate a return to the past, he recognizes both loss and gain as the past gives way to the future. The result is a blend of pathos and very mild comedy.

If Auchincloss is alert to changes in ideas of courtship and marriage, he is also aware that some forms of behavior do not change. In the downtown world represented by the family brokerage firm, individual behavior repeats itself in recurring cycles. In each generation the tough managing partner is replaced by a younger man very much like him who has married into the Denison family. Linn Tremain, who had married into the family after buying out their banking business, is succeeded by Derrick Hartley, who in turn is followed by his son-in-law Mark Jesmond. Neither of the two older men yields gracefully. Both of the usurpers are outsiders — New Englanders from middle-class backgrounds — who conquer the New York financial world by aggression and intelligence. Derrick and Mark Jesmond both anticipate such successful outsiders in Auchincloss's later novels as Rex Geer in *The Embezzler*. All three men who marry into the Denison family gain a place in respectable society, but in each generation the Denisons also get full value from their acquisitions. Without the new blood, neither the family nor the family business would have survived.

Derrick Hartley is Auchincloss's first full portrait of a totally self-absorbed, hard-driving businessman. Though there are hints of him in the character of George Dilworth in *A Law for the Lion*, Derrick's single-minded devotion to success and his unlimited energy set him apart. He has none of the sexual insecurity of George Dilworth and other successful men in the earlier novels. Like a Balzac hero, as one critic observed, Derrick declares war on the very society he seeks to enter.[9] His sheer power makes him appealing to Geraldine, even after she returns from Europe. He is "a man interested only in ultimate favors." But this strong will also ensures that, having decided precisely what he wants, Derrick will not leave Ida to marry Geraldine, no matter how strong his sexual attraction.

Rather unexpectedly, Ida turns out to be the perfect wife for Derrick. Auchincloss shows how she manages not only to endure but also to prevail, as first Geraldine and then Derrick burn themselves out in the course of the novel. This process of development over a whole lifetime is missing in the novels dealing with similar women that Auchincloss wrote at the beginning of his career. Always a bit in awe of her brisk and self-assured mother, Ida feels closer to her father, Gerald Trask, a gentle figure who seems to have been taken over by the more energetic Denisons around him. During his final illness he tells his daughter: "In life you can be a leader or you can be led. It doesn't make much difference which you choose, as long as you *do* choose." This advice applies well to Ida's development in the novel. Though her own passion, combined with the pressure exerted by the rest of the family, causes her to accept Derrick's proposal of marriage, she finally decides consciously to be led at the time Derrick takes control of the family firm and fires

her favorite cousin, Scotty Denison. Her sense of having
made a choice allows her to weather Derrick's affair with
Geraldine and her own difficult relationship with Dorcas during the 1930s. When Geraldine commits suicide
in 1950, Ida is somehow prepared to exert the strong
leadership her mother displayed in her childhood — to
become in her own view, at long last, a true Denison.
She manages to rout Kitty Tyson, Hugo's self-assured
mistress, and prevents her from marrying him by a
shrewd threat that is really a bluff. She conducts a successful campaign to acquire control of the family gallery
so that Hugo will have a suitable position to persuade
Alfreda to marry him. After Derrick's heart attack, she
even controls his brokerage firm, and Mark Jesmond
must consult her before making major decisions.

Yet paradoxically Ida becomes the commanding
figure in the Denison family only after she has been
forced seriously to question her ideal image of the family. Geraldine's death not only frees her from comparison
with a lifelong rival but also removes her "ancient sense
of guilt at having come between the archetypes of male
and female" in preventing the "innately fitting" union
of Derrick and Geraldine by claiming Derrick for herself. As she goes through Geraldine's papers after her
death, she discovers that her cousin not only carried on
an affair with Derrick but also had tried to get him to
divorce her. Ida's anger at Geraldine's dishonesty and at
the tawdriness of the affair is a liberating force that permits a new beginning, that gives her psychological per-
mission to change.

Though Derrick is himself biased, his analysis of
Ida's situation in the final pages of the novel is acute.
"The Denisons themselves were your invention," he tells
her. "And you were very careful, being a guilt-ridden
child, to invent an ideal that you could emulate but
never approach. The Denisons, in your definition, were
a crazy patchwork of inconsistencies. They had to be gay

and lighthearted, even when they were being pure and
dutiful. They had to be fearless, even when they were
cautious. They had to be gallant and wear rubber boots
in the house. They had to be endowed with all your terrors and yet never suffer from them. You made up the
Denisons to prove to yourself that you were alone in the
world!" Derrick then offers his tribute to Ida, telling her
that, "your reality, my dear, is much finer than your
myth ever was. If your mother and aunt could see you
now, they would see that you had made something very
beautiful out of the pieces and patches that they left you
with" (*Portrait in Brownstone*, pp. 369–70). This too is
true, but the fact remains that, even though Ida's vision
of the family may no longer exist, Ida herself has become
a worthy successor in the family tradition she has in part
created. She has become a figure not unlike her vision
of Aunt Dagmar or her mother. What has changed,
however, is that there is no longer any cohesive family
structure around her solitary figure. This is perhaps the
final irony in the novel and Auchincloss's main point
about American social history in the seventy-five-year
period he describes. Like Auchincloss's own relatives the
Dixons, the Denisons — as a tightly knit family with
shared values based upon duty and loyalty — represent
New York society before World War I. By the time the
action of the novel closes in 1950, the sense of family as
institution embodied in the Denisons had long since van-
ished.

Like *The House of Five Talents*, *Portrait in Brownstone* is a highly allusive novel. Rather than being an art
museum, however, it is a library. It abounds in literary
allusions — almost all of them appropriate to the brownstone past Auchincloss seeks to convey. Where Gussie
Millinder values the art of the nineteenth century and
is in part defined by the objects she values, Ida lives
through its literature. In one of the earliest episodes in
the novel, for example, Auchincloss establishes the con-

trast between Ida and Geraldine by associating Ida with
the poetry of Tennyson. At a birthday party for Aunt
Dagmar, Ida wants to recite the dedication to Queen
Victoria from *Idylls of the King*, whereas her cousin
decides to do a takeoff on the popular actress Maude
Adams, then appearing in *As You Like It*. The choice
of Tennyson perfectly conveys Ida's girlish, but painfully
earnest character and foreshadows her subsequent concern for the family. Crucial moments later in the novel
are expressed as repetitions of, or references to, Austen,
Browning, Scott, and other nineteenth-century authors.
Moments involving other characters recall such twentieth-century writers as Proust and Wharton, but these incidents significantly do not involve Ida.

If *Portrait in Brownstone* is slightly less successful
than its predecessor, it is so for two reasons. First, the
later episodes in the novel, especially the sections on
Hugo's love affairs, do not attain the luminous quality
of the earlier portions set in Ida's childhood. Hugo's marriage to Alfreda Denison seems rushed, and Derrick's
newly found admiration for his wife is not entirely convincing. Secondly, Auchincloss's complex narrative technique, which switches back and forth between past and
present and between first-person and third-person point
of view, is distracting. The great strength of the novel
remains its portrait of the Denison family. It is this aspect
of the novel that engages Auchincloss most fully. Here,
as perhaps nowhere else in his fiction, he explores his
own attraction to his mother's family. And Ida in her
final triumph is a convincing embodiment of that mysterious and enviable power Auchincloss himself sensed as
a child in the feminine world represented by his mother.
Even as *Portrait in Brownstone* reminds us that the era
evoked in its title is gone, it successfully memorializes
that era, bringing turn-of-the-century New York to life
again.

After the publication of *The House of Five Talents*,

Auchincloss's prominence as a novelist was established. His growing reputation as a writer capable of astute commentary on human character and intelligent re-creation of the past was signaled by the appearance of a front-page review of *Portrait in Brownstone* in the *New York Times Book Review*. Together, *The House of Five Talents* and *Portrait in Brownstone* set readers' expectations about Auchincloss and prepared the way for his next — and best known novel — *The Rector of Justin*, which appeared two years later. *The Rector of Justin* is not primarily a novel of manners, but the abilities displayed in the two preceding novels enrich Auchincloss's consideration of the character of his protagonist Francis Prescott.

5

~~~~~~

Novels of the Great World

Auchincloss's experiences as a lawyer have always nourished his fiction. Nowhere is this more true than in the novels directly concerned with men who work downtown in the "great world" of law and finance — attorneys in major Wall Street firms, bankers and trust officers, stockbrokers. In five novels, ranging from *The Great World and Timothy Colt* in 1956 to *I Come As a Thief* in 1972, Auchincloss has depicted the lives and behavior of men in this world with unique authority and insight. In another, related novel, *The Embezzler* (1966), he looks back upon the life of a central figure in a major Wall Street scandal of the 1930s. As his fellow-novelist Gore Vidal has observed, "almost alone among our writers he is able to show in a convincing fashion men at work — men at work discreetly managing the nation's money, selecting its governors, creating the American empire."[1]

Yet the insider's view of men on Wall Street presented in these novels and in numerous short stories is hardly cheerful. In *A Writer's Capital*, Auchincloss recalls a boyhood visit to lower Manhattan and his father's law firm. His father proudly pointed out the sights: J. P. Morgan & Co., the Stock Exchange, Wall Street. But young Auchincloss was terrified: "Never shall I forget the horror inspired in me by those dark narrow streets and those tall sooty towers and by Trinity Church block-

ing the horizon with its black spire — a grim phallic symbol." This disquiet is reflected in almost all of the protagonists of the novels. Though they are successful or
plainly bound for success, all are troubled by hidden feelings of inadequacy or grimly debilitating memories from
their childhoods that lead them to court professional or
personal disaster. The protagonist in one novel and a
central figure in another commit suicide. Several other
protagonists destroy their marriages; all except one are
indicted or sentenced to jail. In most of these novels, the
world of Wall Street, as Wayne Westbrook has pointed
out, is a fallen world.[2] Yet at the same time it is a world
where men are corrupted not so much by the temptations
of material success as by flaws that are deeply rooted in
their own psyches. As Auchincloss himself learned (in
part through psychoanalysis), "a man's background is
largely of his own creating." In these novels, as elsewhere in his fiction, the principal characters come increasingly "to create their own worlds," in the sense that
reality as they see it is largely the subjective product of
their inner mental states and psychological needs.

Like the more conventional novels of manners such
as *Sybil* or *The House of Five Talents*, the novels of the
great world are filled with sharply observed detail. Auchincloss carefully establishes the social backgrounds of
his characters, but more importantly he extends the
range of the novel of manners by precisely placing his
lawyers and trust officers in the elaborate but often tac-
itly defined hierarchies of the firms in which they work.
Even in twentieth-century America, a society in which
class distinctions have allegedly disappeared, Auchincloss
achieves some of the same impressions of a fully articulated class structure that Anthony Trollope managed
in his description of the various levels of the British clergy
in ninteenth-century England.[3]

Auchincloss's novels about men in the great world
fall into two distinct groups. The three novels published

in the late 1950s — *The Great World and Timothy Colt*, *Venus in Sparta*, and *Pursuit of the Prodigal* — involve characters who cannot adjust to the world in which they live. Often driven by anger or despair, they brush up against evil by committing minor technical crimes or by allying themselves with other characters who lack their moral perception but who are not flamboyantly dishonest. In the second group, a pair of novels published in 1968 and 1972, Auchincloss's vision of evil darkens. The protagonists of *A World of Profit* and *I Come as a Thief* both commit serious offenses, and the world in which they move is more overtly corrupt. Martin Shallcross in *A World of Profit* is motivated wholly by greed, and Tony Lowder and his partner become entangled with the Mafia in *I Come as a Thief*. In these two novels of the Vietnam era, Auchincloss is most strongly preoccupied with evil and most inclined to emphasize the disintegration — and even rottenness — of the world of law and finance as it is threatened by historical change.

The Embezzler, published in the years between the two groups of novels about men in contemporary law or finance, is, as I have suggested, a novel about Wall Street. As such, it shares many of the themes and motifs found in the other five novels. Yet, in its concern for a vanishing past and its evocation of New York and Newport society in the early years of the century, it is very close to Auchincloss's major novels of manners, *The House of Five Talents* and *Portrait in Brownstone*. Because it is an interesting hybrid of several strains in Auchincloss's fiction and because it deals explicitly with the past, *The Embezzler* will be discussed in a separate chapter.

Though Auchincloss employs a variety of narrative techniques in the novels of the great world, certain plot patterns, character types, and motifs recur frequently. Not only are most of the protagonists troubled by a guilty secret of some sort, but almost all of them strike bargains with sinister, sometimes devil-like business or legal partners. Often their psychological problems are manifested — or their moral guilt or innocence evaluated — in a dramatic courtroom scene that hinges upon a nice legal distinction or interesting technical question. For most of the main characters, courtroom testimony is not only an opportunity to purge one's guilt but also a way of defying or striking out at the world around one. Sometimes these recurring motifs seem formulaic, but their shifting combinations and the interesting variations Auchincloss makes on them allow them to embody a series of complex moral and psychological themes. Though not all of the novels are of equal quality, Auchincloss's combined achievement in the complete series including *The Embezzler* is impressive: a sustained consideration of the world of Wall Street matched by no other American novelist.

The Great World and Timothy Colt

Based on a short story of the same title published in 1954, *The Great World and Timothy Colt* is Auchincloss's first full-scale consideration of men in professional life. Although a few of the minor characters are slighted, Timothy Colt is a convincing character placed in a situation that enhances the significance of his actions. Although the conclusion of the novel remains ambiguous, Auchincloss does not divert the reader's attention to a subsidiary character as he does in the final chapter of his previous novel, *A Law for the Lion*. The novel reflects Auchincloss's years as an associate in the law firm of Sullivan & Cromwell and admirably captures the experiences of a young lawyer starting out in a large firm in the years after World War II. Above all, however, *The Great World and Timothy Colt* is the story of a particular young man driven by his own nature to destroy himself. In Auchincloss's narrative, the ethical and legal perplexities raised by the events of the plot invariably lead us inward and backward to the psychological uncertainties of the main character.

The novel is divided into two parts. In the first, Timothy Colt works happily as an associate in the corporate department of Sheffield, Knox, Stevens & Dale, directly under the managing partner Henry Knox, who has brought him into the firm and become a second father to him. A brilliant corporation lawyer, he is, even without Knox's backing, on the verge of becoming a partner. At the request of Sheridan Dale, the partner in charge of estates and trusts, Knox puts Timmy in charge of a complicated corporate acquisition deal being worked out by George Emlen, the obnoxious nephew of Dale's wife. Working with Emlen brings Timmy close to a breakdown, and at the party held to celebrate the successful completion of the deal, he publicly insults him. When Knox suggests that he apologize to Emlen and Dale, Timmy at first refuses. Under the urging of his wife Ann, he finally apologizes, but is so angry with Knox that he tells him he will leave the corporate department and join the managing partner's hated rival Dale in estates and trusts. Knox, who suffers from a heart condition, dies suddenly on the same evening. Timmy is left desolate and guilty.

At the beginning of the second section, Timmy is made a partner in the firm and becomes right-hand man to Sheridan Dale. He enters "the great world" as he sees it — the world of savage competition and expediency — with a vengeance. He alienates his former friends by carrying out Dale's reorganization plan for the firm, makes money from insiders' tips given him by Dale, and ironically even serves as trustee for one of the Emlen family estates. Unable to stomach the new Timmy, Ann leaves him, and he has an affair with Dale's step-daughter, Eileen Shallcross. When George Emlen wants to take unfair advantage of his sisters in the division of their father's trust, Timmy knowingly conceals information from the beneficiaries and the other trustees.

This last angry concession to "the great world" brings about the denouement of the novel. When Eileen Shallcross hints that George has taken unfair advantage of them, the two Emlen daughters bring charges against Timmy in surrogate's court. The charges are complicated, and there is no hard evidence against Timmy; but just as it appears that his friend Larry Duane has won the case for him, Timmy confesses his breach of trust and refuses to exonerate himself in any way. After the trial he returns to Ann, still unsure about his motives in confessing but prepared to begin some sort of new life.

The central act in the novel is not Timmy's breach of trust, but his switch of allegiance from Henry Knox to Sheridan Dale, the significance of which Auchincloss underscores by the essential but fortuitous death of Knox. In *A Writer's Capital* Auchincloss suggests that Timmy "lives in a Miltonic universe of good and evil with a compulsion to join the latter." Indeed, Satan's words in *Paradise Lost* as he first beholds Eden might well serve as an epigraph for the second portion of the novel:

So farewell hope, and, with hope, farewell fear,
Farewell remorse! All good to me is lost;
Evil be thou my good. . . .

At the death of Henry Knox, Timmy casts away hope, and, in his anger and guilt, elevates evil to be his good. His view of the world — and of the law firm — is fundamentally Manichaean. There is no middle ground: if he must compromise with the Dales and Emlens of the world, then he will join their side entirely. Yet the actions that cut him off from his former happy state are the result of his basic insecurity and deeply buried anger rather than of any willful disobedience. Though George

Emlen is an infuriating client, Timmy's obsession with
him is, as Knox points out, childish. Emlen is unjust in
accusing him of "doping off" because he omits a small
sliver of land from a real estate description, but Timmy
believes that there is truth in the charge. As Ann puts it,
Timmy sees George Emlen as a fiend "because he sees
Timmy as Timmy sees himself" — as lazy, shiftless, in-
competent. And earlier in the novel, at the end of their
first meeting, George observes with sinister irony, "By
the time you're through with this deal, Timothy, you're
going to feel that you and I are twins."

When, on the other hand, Timmy is able to imagine
himself on the side of good, he cannot compromise. The
business of apologizing to Emlen and Dale is simply not
the matter of conscience Timmy makes it out to be. As
George's lawyer and as a guest in his home, he was
doubly impolite, and Knox is correct in seeing his self-
righteous account of his behavior as "more appropriate
to a boy's boarding school than to a law firm." For their
attempts to bring him to reason Henry Knox and his
wife get only resentment: Timmy abruptly shifts from
self-righteousness to opportunism in accepting Sheridan
Dale's materialistic offer to leave Knox and work in his
department. Timmy's final argument with Knox is revealing, for it suggests not only the naive rigidity of Timmy's views of his profession but also something of what
he loses in going over to Dale. "All during the war I never
wavered in my desire to come back and work for you,"
he tells Knox. "It didn't matter to me that society was
disintegrating so long as I was not on the side of the
disintegrators. So long as I was constructive. For several
years you gave me that sense. Of having my own little
smithy in a crazy world. It was all I needed." But now,
according to Timmy, Knox has plunged him into "the
lower regions" — all in the name of giving him experience
in the real world: "You wanted me to make my peace
with the devil. Well I've made it! You won't catch me

making an ass of myself again. Now I'm with Dale, I'm staying with him."

The sad thing, as Knox realizes, is that there is some truth in Timmy's remarks. He really had been the ideal lawyer Knox had envisioned, and Knox is honest enough to accept his rebuke without reply. In joining Dale, however, Timmy loses his old sense of the law as noble work. Several characters refer to him as an artist, and Auchincloss nicely conveys the intense pleasure a legal craftsman like Timmy can feel as he works on a complicated corporate transfer:

He loved the abstractness of the practice of law; he found it actually exciting that on the signing of the final paper, the passing of the final check, after the hurly-burly of the conference table and all the talk, there would have been no change in anything physical, no alteration in the appearance of a mill smoking by a sleepy river, no shift in the vast, ordered weight of bales in a soot-stained warehouse. If this was sterility to a vulgar mind, it was beauty to him, the approach to the essence of things without disarrangement. (*Great World*, pp. 58–59)

Timmy's idealistic enthusiasm is part of his strength as a lawyer, but it is also related to the self-destructive side of his personality.

In abandoning Henry Knox, Timmy also rejects a father figure and hero. Timmy, who had been six when his father died, first met Knox when employed as a tutor to his daughters during a summer vacation from Columbia Law School. Knox was so impressed with Timmy's legal acumen that he hired another tutor and put Timmy to work on an important memorandum to the SEC. As Knox's closest associate in the firm and almost a part of his family, Timmy responds to his death like a hurt child. At the funeral that closes part one of the novel, he finds himself "trembling," in the midst of his tears, "with a passionate anger that his guide and mentor should have so betrayed him, even by dying, so deserted him in his hour of need."

After Knox's death, Sheffield, Knox, Stevens & Dale becomes Sheffield, Dale & Stevens, and Sheridan Dale takes control. Dale's transformation of the firm, carried out largely by Timmy himself, represents another fall into "a lower realm" in the novel. Knox, the idealistic son of a New England headmaster, had conceived of the firm as "a group of gentlemen loosely associated by a common enthusiasm for the practice of law" and subscribed to the old-fashioned notion that lawyers should not become overspecialized. Dale, a parvenu from Brooklyn whose "manners seemed to verge on the greasy" and who had increased his income by marrying a wealthy client, sees the firm as a big business and believes it should be run like one. With his usual precision, Auchincloss contrasts the styles of the two partners. Even their offices and apartments reflect their differences. Knox's gentlemanly ideals are plainly superior to Dale's harsh doctrine of expediency and shady practices, but Auchincloss shows how they are based in part on illusions. Knox has constructed a myth of the firm centered on the senior partner, Mr. Sheffield, who may not have been the hero he made him out to be — it was Sheffield, for example, who promoted Sheridan Dale. Knox knows this, and although he continues to profess the ideal of the lawyer as generalist, he has in fact represented nothing but large corporate clients for years. As in his portrayals of New York society at the turn of the century, Auchincloss combines a mild nostalgia for the passing of a golden age with a clear recognition that such an age may be in part an imaginary construction.

Auchincloss's depiction of life in Sheffield, Knox is rounded out by deft portraits of minor characters: Mr. Sheffield, the semiretired senior partner; Timmy's fellow associate Austin Cochran, who works as hard as Timmy, but whose idealism is focused on community service rather than the abstractions of corporate law or advancement within the firm; and Larry Duane, Timmy's friend and the son-in-law of Henry Knox, who seems at first to be an easygoing young socialite, but who turns out to be coldly ambitious. The result is a convincing anatomy of a unique twentieth-century American institution, the large Manhattan law firm.

Timmy's defection from Knox to Dale is closely followed by his affair with Eileen Shallcross. Although she does not share her stepfather's duplicity or unctuous manners, Eileen embodies another facet of Timmy's image of the great world in her glamour and sophistication. Like the alliance with Dale, the affair is partly motivated by anger at Ann for urging him to apologize. Timmy had met Ann when he was a student at Columbia Law School and she was at Barnard. Almost the perfect wife for Timmy and a finely drawn character in the tradition of Eloise Dilworth in *A Law for the Lion*, Ann is warm, somewhat awkward in her sincerity, a casual housekeeper, a bit of an intellectual who is content to stay at home reading while Timmy works late at the office. She shares Timmy's idealism but also recognizes the necessity of his apologizing to Dale and Emlen and sees that some adjustments in their lives will be necessary as Timmy moves up in the firm. But she cannot understand the extreme change in his personality or accept his new indifference to her. Her feelings about their new life are vividly expressed at a party given by the Dales, where she quite uncharacteristically gets drunk and throws up on Mrs. Dale's bed. The next morning she suggests a temporary separation to Timmy. Still angry at her, he accepts the idea, though part of him rebels against his decision. When Larry Duane criticizes Ann as a bad lawyer's wife, Timmy wants to defend her, but his grim commitment to the values of the great world is still too strong. He remains silent, "wondering if he was really man enough to stick to his chosen path." The original, short-story version of *The Great World* ends with the incident in which Ann gets sick. After Timmy leaves the party with Ann, the first-person narrator of the story comments: "There would be nothing easy for them, as for Mr. Hayard [Knox's equivalent in the story], in compromise, nothing of grace." This is equally true in the novel.

Eileen Shallcross is a character less satisfactorily developed than Ann. Auchincloss sees her as a woman whose nature demands that she bestow unconditional love on one man, but whose very perfection ensures that he will reject her great gift. Closely associated with David Fairchild, a cynical interior decorator who comes uncomfortably close to the stereotype of the bitchy, artistic homosexual, Eileen is a sympathetic figure but ultimately remains an image of the high fashion and social grace that both Timmy and Ann lack.

Eileen plays an important role in the conclusion of the novel. It is she who tells George Emlen's sister Anita that something is wrong about the distribution of the Emlen trust, and her testimony spurs Timmy to confess his breach of trust. But from the very beginning Timmy's decision to go along with the unfair division of the trust is the product of the self-destructive forces that make him leave Ann. He immediately suspects a plot between Dale and Emlen when he receives Dale's memo suggesting that all the shares of Emlen Fibre, a family-owned company in the trust, go to George. He knows that George will benefit far beyond the book-value of the shares because the family company holds valuable patents desired by a large textile company in which George and Dale have an interest. And he even confronts Dale with this knowledge. But as he considers what to do, a voice keeps repeating in his head, "This is the world. *Your* world!" Dale's promise that he will give him a lucrative client if he goes along is a lurking challenge, "the dark hirsute thing behind the green leaves of his new prosperity." Though he needs the money and recognizes his own ambition, he realizes that these are mere pre-

texts for something he is going to do anyway. Auchincloss
describes him as pecularly passive — not even a character
in a play, but a character in a movie:

Wasn't it rather that he was sitting alone in a darkened pro-
jection room, watching the unreeling of his own life, inextricably bound up in its logic? For it was because of this logic,
because of this only consistency, that he oddly enough felt
himself bound to sacrifice everything. He had made decisions,
had he not, crossed Rubicons? Was it seemly now, even feasi-
ble, to turn his steed and go galloping back pell-mell before
atonished spectators on the road he had so defiantly taken the
day before? (*Great World*, p. 217)

When Timmy discovers that George's scheme has
been revealed, he feels "a sensation of curious relief."
Auchincloss again employs an image from the cinema.
Since the final distribution of the trusts, Timmy "had
lived in a state of suspended animation," unable "to
identify sympathetically with the central character of his
own drama. Those two weeks had been like a film when
the sound track was broken; now, with the sudden jar
of the resumed noise, it was not altogether misery to
know that his story was again moving forward." After
a scene with the Emlens and Sheridan Dale in which he
refuses to explain his conduct and dares George's sisters
to hire their own attorney, he goes to Eileen and angrily
rebukes her for being just like her stepfather Dale. Even
then, he sees himself as a misplaced actor uttering heroic
bombast in the midst of a comic scene. But "at least he
was performing again," and whatever the costs "there
would be an end to it."

Though he has not cleanly broken with Eileen, he
returns to Ann almost immediately — something he had
always suspected might happen. He seems to accept her
suggestion that he betrayed his trust to punish himself
for the death of Mr. Knox, and he assists Larry Duane
in preparing his defense. With Larry's encouragement,
he even entertains the possibility that, after the trial, he

can return to corporate work and his former life. "Was there a moral obligation always to expect the worst from the universe? To insist on punishment or penance?" he asks himself. "Wasn't it better to be reborn and reborn joyfully, to go back to the family he loved and support them doing the work he loved?"

At the end of the novel, the answers to these questions are not simple. They hinge on the reasons for Timmy's confession in court. Timmy could have put all the pieces of his old life together by going along with Larry's defense that he merely suspected rather than knew that the Emlen Fibre stock was more valuable than it appeared, and he is ready to do so until Eileen perjures herself in a minor way to help save him. His confession, because it brings out the complete truth, would seem to represent a final escape from the dishonesty of the Dale world, but does it? Or is it another melodramatic, self-destructive episode in the drama of Timmy's life? When Timmy finally talks to Ann, whom he has avoided for several days after the trial, he has almost convinced himself that his confession was an act of reparation to Eileen in return for her sacrifice of her basic honesty in trying to save him. But he cannot be sure. Auchincloss, however, tentatively endorses Ann's reassuring assertion that "there are moments above the damned subconscious. Like the moment when you told that judge the truth." Though what Timmy said on the stand remains "a kind of truth, a *willed* truth," it is a truth that he and Ann can build on. And when, in the final paragraph of the novel, Timmy's two sons come in waving a copy of the newspaper with his picture under a headline that reads "Trust Revelations," the reader may perhaps trust the pun. However guarded, however ambiguous the truth, Ann and Timmy have reached a human revelation they can trust.

The Great World and Timothy Colt is not a perfect novel, but it is the first work in which Auchincloss gives

a clear indication of his full powers. Some characters
are scanted, some, like David Fairchild, verge on ster-
eotypes, and the ending of the novel is rushed. But in the
character of Timmy Colt, Auchincloss offers an acute
psychological portrait that is alive to the ambiguities of
human motives, to the narrow escapes we often make,
or fail to make, from the traps set by our own minds.
And in his depiction of the Sheffield, Knox law firm
Auchincloss presents an outstanding view of the time and
place in which Timmy Colt and others like him existed.
In its comic ending, *The Great World and Timothy Colt*
mirrors the comic complexity of life itself.

Venus in Sparta

Venus in Sparta is perhaps Auchincloss's most emotionally powerful work. Published in 1958, the novel traces the
inexorable process by which its hero destroys himself in
a series of futile attempts to live up to a false image of
masculinity. Michael Farish's impulses to destruction are
even more deeply rooted than the self-loathing that com-
pels Timmy Colt's angry attempts to wreck his marriage
and career in *The Great World and Timothy Colt*. Unable to break free of the unresolved contradictions of
his childhood emotional life, Michael lives, as Auchincloss has written, in "a grim world of phallic symbols,"
plagued by fears of sexual inadequacy and by guilt over
the early death of his father. In each of his marriages,
he unconsciously re-creates his childhood relationship
with his mother, and he deliberately subverts his professional career out of fear that he cannot live up to the expectations of his dead father. Though at times burdened
with obvious sexual symbolism, *Venus in Sparta* is Auchincloss's most compelling account of an apparently
successful man's desire to escape the trap of his own
success.

Unlike Timothy Colt, Michael Farish is very much an insider. He is heir apparent to the presidency of the Hudson River Trust Company, the venerable Wall Street institution of which his grandfather had been president and his father senior trust officer. In the course of the novel he marries the daughter of the current president, who is also a former daughter-in-law of Ambrose Parr, the chairman and largest stockholder in the company. Michael is himself highly talented. Described as a man who looked like the perfect modern trust officer, he moves easily among the wealthy clients of the firm. He is also a man of considerable intellectual ability. Ambrose Parr values him as much as a hunting companion and confidant as the greatest managerial asset of Hudson River Trust. As expected, Michael rises to the top of the firm, but his apparent success and seemingly secure place in the world mask disaster: *Venus in Sparta* ends with his suicide.

In the plot of the novel, as in *The Great World and Timothy Colt*, Auchincloss intertwines the personal and professional crises of the main character. Michael Farish owes much of his success to having brought in, when he was just beginning his career, one of Hudson River Trust's largest clients, the Winters Estate. But most of the income the bank receives from the estate is based upon a dubious interpretation of a letter from Michael to Mr. Winters that Michael has concealed but never destroyed in the sixteen years since Mr. Winters' death. Danny Jones, the surly young assistant trust officer who discovers the letter in the bank's files early in the novel and calls into question Michael's integrity, turns out also to be carrying on an affair with Michael's wife Flora. At the same time that he begins to suspect the affair between Flora and Danny, Michael is summoned to Averhill Academy because his son has been disciplined for his role in an ugly racist incident. Michael's competence is thus simultaneously shaken on three fronts — as a businessman, a husband, and a parent.

After a strange, humiliating scene in which he watches Danny make love to Flora in his own bedroom, Michael leaves Flora and files for divorce. He resigns the vice presidency of Hudson River Trust when Mrs. Winters, acting on information from Danny Jones, brings the matter of the concealed letter to Surrogate's Court, and he travels to Mexico while waiting for his divorce and that of his old friend Alida Parr, whom he intends to marry, to become final. Even in Mexico, however, he realizes that marriage to Alida, like his success at Hudson River, is just another trap; but by then he has gone too far to back out. When word comes that he has been exonerated in Surrogate's Court and he is asked to return to his post as vice president, he feels no elation whatsoever. A year later, restored to his position at Hudson Trust and once again a member of the same Long Island summer community as his ex-wife and his mother, Michael lives a kind of posthumous existence, drinking heavily and only going through the motions in his job. He is violently attracted to his former stepdaughter, Ginny Dexter, and pursues her throughout the summer. In the same night that he consummates the affair, he swims out into the ocean and drowns himself.

Auchincloss's narrative technique in *Venus in Sparta* is an important achievement. It is not only aptly suited to tracing the disintegration of Michael's life, but it also reinforces one of the central themes of the novel: the power of the past in determining an individual's actions. The ongoing account of events in the narrative present of the novel is interrupted by five carefully placed retrospective chapters, each of which illuminates the episodes that immediately precede it. As the events in the present time of the narrative move forward toward Michael's suicide, the reader looks back on crucial episodes that have made his destruction almost inevitable.

In the first flashback Auchincloss returns to the beginning of Michael's career and shows how he came to write the letter to Mr. Winters that later causes his resignation. The next retrospective chapters — one dealing with Michael's friendship with his schoolmate Peter Teriot, another covering his courtship and marriage to his first wife Flora, and a third describing his wartime affair with Alida Parr — take the reader from Michael's adolescence to a point five years after the episode with Mr. Winters. They fill in the major events of Michael's private life and provide an illusion of development and forward motion. This illusion is shattered, however, by the final flashback, which takes us back farthest into the past, to Michael's boyhood and the death of his father. The second, third, and fourth retrospective chapters reveal troubling patterns in Michael's relationships with other people, but only after the fifth flashback does one realize how deeply Michael is haunted by the past. As Michael moves toward destruction, the reader moves toward discovery, in a process not unlike psychoanalysis that peels away successive layers of actions to reveal underlying patterns of character.

From the very beginning of the novel, Auchincloss establishes a sense of foreboding. Even the description of the Hudson River Trust Company that opens the first chapter suggests an unsettling disparity between appearance and reality. The Richard Morris Hunt building, Auchincloss tells us, "tried to express the maximum of solidity in the minimum of space. Happily, its bluff, if bluff it was, had never been called." If it had fallen into disrepair, "it would have lacked the dignity of a Roman ruin. Its arches might have seemed only pompous and its beetling cornice an empty boast." The application of this descriptive passage to Michael's situation is obvious. One is not surprised to find that, though he "looked to perfection the part of the modern trust officer," he feels some sort of disquiet, "a sense of damp anticipation un-

comfortably different from the mild, hollow, familiar
depression that he was apt to feel an hour after lunch and
for which he had a compensatory pill." More than an
anxious businessman under stress, Farish is a man who
regards himself as radically out of place in the world in
which he finds himself.

Michael's anxiety seems at first to stem from his success in acquiring the Winters Estate for the bank. When
Mr. Winters had selected Hudson River Trust as executor
and trustee of his estate, he had made Michael agree to
write a letter limiting the *total* commissions on his estate
to one and a half percent. Winters had died before Michael could have the letter typed, and on the basis of the
wording of the equivalent clause in Winters' will, which
had not included the word "total," Hudson River Trust's
counsel had advised that the limitation applied only to
regular commissions and not to the commissions on the
family's real estate holdings, which comprised more than
half the estate. Having neglected to mention the letter,
Michael could simply have destroyed it. Instead, he held
onto it and then put it into the Winters file, where it
could easily be found. Part of him tells him "to get on
with the ascending process that seemed to be the business
of life," but another part of his personality fears the
responsibility that comes with success and dares him to
take the self-destructive gamble with the letter, to "be
a sportsman with the shade of Mr. Winters," as he puts
it. Over the years, Auchincloss tells us, the knowledge
that someone might discover the letter "had changed
gradually from a fearsome thing to one that had a strange
element of comfort. There was actually a queer little
relief in the idea that whatever happened to him in
Hudson, *here* was always a way out, like the poison
capsule that spies wore around their necks in case of capture in enemy lands." Michael's image of himself as a spy
in enemy territory is revealing. He finds the idea that
Danny Jones should discover the secret ironic and a little sickening, but he nevertheless feels relief.

The second major crisis in the novel reveals a good deal more about the sources of Michael's anxiety. In dealing with his son Seymour's misconduct at Averhill Academy, Michael must return to the scene of his own first encounters with the harsh expectations of the masculine world. The high ideals of his old school, embodied in its legendary former headmaster Mr. Minturn (a figure obviously modeled on Endicott Peabody),[4] have impelled Michael's progress toward worldly success, but at the same time the expectations that accompany such ideals have been a source of unrelenting and rather frightening pressure. As Michael drives up to the school, the Gothic tower of the chapel looms up threateningly over the Georgian buildings around it, "a giant phallic symbol to remind one that duty is never done."

Thinking of Mr. Minturn, "the small, brisk, simple silver-haired man who had oscillated between the extremes of a chuckling benevolence and a terrifying wrath and who represented God to two generations of Averhill graduates," Michael is relieved that he is no longer alive to hear about his failure with Seymour, who along with his roommate Rex Webb, has burned a cross on campus and left a ball of tar and feathers in the room of the school's only black student. Minturn's stern morality and warnings against "sentimentality" among the boys, though Michael regards them as part of "the truer male world" that holds Averhill Academy and adult life in its "heavy muffled grasp," represent only one of two divergent ideals. Seymour's friendship with Rex Webb reminds Michael of his own friendship with Peter Teriot, who had held out "the dazzling vision" of a different sort of manhood when they were together at Averhill. Unlike Michael, who wanted to do the "right" things to be popular and get his name into the school yearbook, Peter was an individualist who saw through Mr. Minturn and scorned the conventions of the school but who succeeded through charm and talent anyway. Michael's intense friendship with Peter shows him the other, warmer side to Averhill. When Mr. Minturn summons Peter back from Harvard to rebuke him for letting several Averhill students drink at a party and banishes him from the school, Michael knows that he is committed to Peter's side. Significantly, however, the commitment is never tested. Rather than having to confront Mr. Minturn, Michael goes on to be one of his senior prefects, and Peter dies in the summer after his first year at Harvard. Peter's death becomes "an interesting if depressing revelation of how the conflict of values between any friend of his and Mr. Minturn might be resolved," and the whole episode simply underlines Michael's sense of inadequacy. After Peter's death, he still feels he ought to be like both the headmaster and his friend but senses that he will not succeed in emulating either of them. "One's leaders, of course, were always potentially reconcilable, if over nothing else than their joint discouragement with one's own ineptitude at following them." This desire to satisfy two contrary impulses in his personality remains with Michael throughout his life. The contradiction between the ideals represented by Minturn and Peter Teriot can only be resolved self-destructively, either by failure or by evasion.

The reminders of Michael's inadequacy during the visit to Averhill Academy precede almost immediately the full revelation of his wife's affair with Danny Jones. Indeed, Michael's discovery is anticipated when he walks out in the evening to visit the memorial erected to Peter Teriot on the campus. There he hears an imaginary voice — seemingly that of Peter, but really his own, more realistic alter ego — reminding him of his "big bosomy wife with an eye for the boys" and suggesting that his trip to the school has been an evasion. "If I were Peter, do you think I'd be in Averhill? Wouldn't I be in New York, perched on a window sill, to watch old Flora and her muscle-bound boyfriend make love?" The voice of the alter ego convinces Michael of what he had been

avoiding all along—that there is something going on between Flora and Danny. Michael rushes back to New
York only to have the words of the mocking voice come
almost literally true.

The scene in which Michael actually catches his
wife and Danny is peculiarly humiliating. Not only does
Michael look helplessly on from his perch on a bureau
placed next to the transom window above the door between his dressing room and the bedroom, but he is
reminded of another equally humiliating scene from his
childhood when he had spied on his mother taking a bath.
Before he could see anything, his mother had caught
him, summoned him back, and insisted that he look at
her as she took off her bathrobe. Utterly ashamed, Michael had looked down at the floor and fled in abject
terror. On the later occasion, as is the case with several other Auchincloss characters, Michael feels discon-
nected from his experience: "He had ceased to be himself in reserving a front seat for the tragi-comedy of
Michael Farish." Michael's strange sense of standing outside himself suggests how little he is able to deal with
the reality around him, and the recollections of the scene
with his mother show that, even at forty-five, he still has
not conquered his childhood fears about sexuality. Indeed, the basic action of the scene—Michael's observing
his wife and Danny through the door transom—recalls
a scene in Proust's *Remembrance of Things Past* in which
the narrator-hero spies on the lovemaking of Baron de
Charlus and the tailor Jupien. This allusion not only suggests the deeply literary nature of Auchincloss's imagination, but also raises the possibility of repressed homosex-
uality in Michael.[5]

Michael's courtship of Flora Dexter—which we learn
about in the flashback chapter that follows Michael's
discovery of the affair with Danny—is his first large-
scale attempt to quell his fears of sexual inadequacy.
Bitter that at twenty-three, "after taking all those hur-

dles of his adolescence," he should fail in the last and
most important test, Michael admires Flora from afar
at the summer colony where both their families have
vacationed for years. She is twenty-nine, already a mother, and unhappily married to Bobbie Dexter, who has
carried on a series of flagrant affairs since their honey-
moon. After taking Flora out for most of the summer,
Michael finally sleeps with her and ends up later that
evening knocking down her husband in a flamboyant
display of masculinity in a fight that occurs when Bobbie returns home with his current mistress. After Flora's divorce, in which he is named as corespondent, Michael marries her, against the wishes of his mother and
Mr. Minturn. When Minturn displays the ultimate sign
of disapproval by asking him not to visit the school, it
seems to Michael "that he held his Averhill diploma at
long last in his hand."

But Michael's relationship with Flora is a romantic evasion. Before his fight with Bobbie Dexter, Flora
treats Michael as a kind of pet, using him to entertain herself while Bobbie is occupied with his mistress. Even
Michael recognizes at points that Flora is not strongly attracted to him. He is nonetheless willing to save her from
Bobbie Dexter without really asking for anything in return. This pattern continues in the marriage, up to the
point at which Michael discovers the affair with Danny
Jones, and at least one character suggests that there were
others before Danny Jones. Clearly Michael is capable
of self-deception, but his essential passivity and subservi-
ence to Flora emerge most plainly in the details of the
scene in which they first make love. Michael stares at the
floor as Flora undresses, just as he had done when his
mother had taken off her bathrobe when he was nine.

Michael's fear of and embarrassment with the naked
female form are picked up by Auchincloss's ironic title,
based on a quotation from Plutarch that serves as the
novel's epigraph. According to Plutarch, the Spartans

honored their gods by adorning them wilth military weapons and armor. Even "Venus herself, who in other nations was generally represented naked, had her armor too." In his fearful attitude toward the sexual power of his mother and Flora, Michael has created armed goddesses in his own mind. And in his ambivalence about his career, he displays much the same attitude toward the bitch-goddess success.

Michael's second wife, Alida Parr, initially seems quite different from Flora and Michael's mother, but in the end she too becomes another threatening Venus. Unlike Flora, Alida is younger than Michael and sexually atttacted to him when they are thrown together at the naval base in England to which they are both assigned. Unlike the other important events in his life, the affair with Alida had not been planned. Yet in retrospect Michael sees that he had carried on the affair with much the same anxious sense of masculine duty that had made him woo Flora — "the same almost obligatory sense that a wartime affair was expected of sailors in wartime." When Michael turns to Alida after he has discovered Flora's infidelity, he again acts reflexively: having lost one wife, he will prove himself with the one other woman he has ever been involved with. Michael spends the night after he has discovered Flora and Danny in the spare bedroom of Alida's apartment. Even then, Alida is firmly in control. She puts him to bed in a motherly fashion, giving him an aspirin and a goodnight kiss on the forehead. Michael envisions her as a sort of Amazon leading him through a dense forest: "Alida, happily, would know her way. He seemed to sense her firm stride ahead in a darkness that had no terrors for her." As she blazed the trail, "he would not lose sight of her a second time."

Since Alida is caught in a wretched marriage with Jimmy Parr, the son of the chairman of Hudson River Trust, she is quite eager to marry Michael. She manages their two divorces with daunting efficiency. Michael soon learns to defer to her opinion in all matters of importance. Yet, before he is completely under her control, he makes one more self-destructive break for freedom. The day after Michael has seen him with Flora, Danny again raises the question of the commissions on the Winters Trust. Michael virtually defies him to report the matter and drives him to resign from the bank. When Mrs. Winters gets the information from Danny and brings her attorney to the bank, Michael feels "something like exhilaration." He urges her to take her complaint to the Surrogate's Court and promptly resigns from the bank—much to the surprise of the worried Charlie Meredith. Here, as in *The Great World and Timothy Colt*, the central character's guilt or innonence turns upon a rather nice legal distinction. As Michael points out, if the bank's commissions on real estate had been limited to one and a half percent, the real estate business would have been given to a collection agent who would have charged the Winters estate the same amount of money it had paid over the years anyway. But, although Auchincloss is interested in the gray area in which ethical problems are most likely to arise in professional life, his primary concern is Michael's psychological motivation.

Even after Michael resigns from the bank, he does not feel free, for his bondage has been largely self-created. On the flight to Mexico where he joins Alida and her aunt to wait for his and Alida's divorces to become final, he enjoys "what he was quite aware would be only the fleeting satisfaction of turning his back on ancient obligations. When he saw Alida and her aunt in the waiting room to greet him, . . . he was quickly reminded of new ones." As he tours Mexico City with the two women, he has "a curious feeling" that his true self had been left behind in New York, not unlike the sense of disconnection he felt as he watched Flora and Danny. And when word comes that he has been cleared by the Surrogate's Court and that Charlie Meredith and Ambrose Parr have approved of his marriage to Alida and want him back at the bank, he is discouraged rather than elated. Again his mind returns to an unhappy episode in his childhood: the dismal experience of being sent back to Averhill one winter when he had expected to recuperate from a respiratory infection in Arizona.

More than another revelation of Michael's entrapment in recurring patterns of obligation, the Mexican episodes are crucial in the novel. In three striking scenes that follow closely upon each other in a single chapter, Auchincloss signals Michael's approaching destruction. In the first, Michael climbs alone to the top of the pyramid of the sun at Teotihuacan. There, as he thinks about the Aztec sacrificial victims who had been in his place centuries before, he arrives at a dark vision. He realizes that "there was always the answer of death. It was the only answer to Mexico, the only relief from the glare of colors. That was her message: violence and death, the same for the Aztecs, the same for Spain." But Michael wonders, "If Mexico seemed a reproach to himself, even a sneer, was it not because violence was what he had been avoiding all his life, violence that was man's estate, violence that was the shunned heritage of his father? And without violence was it possible to achieve the release of death?" These questions loom increasingly large in Michael's despair. Death seems the only answer to violence, but "one had to live before one could die."

This vision of universal violence is reinforced only two days later when Michael wanders into a movie theater and sees a wildlife film. To him all the animals seem "wholly absorbed in the task of eating each other," but he realizes that the passive victim is as much a part of the process as the predator: "One did not *have* to do such things; that was the beautiful simplicity of being weak. One could always die." In a third scene, Auchin-

closs most explicitly prefigures Michael's eventual situation. Michael attends a very bad bullfight in which he
finds himself identifying with the bulls while the inept
matadors toy with them in the ring. As the warning is
sounded for the last bull, the matador moves in for the
kill, but his blade merely glances off the back of the
stunned animal. Crowds of scornful spectators rush into the arena, and Michael prays that the bull will charge
again. The bull does so and knocks down several boys
before he follows the oxen docilely out the gates. Michael
is ecstatic, but he soon finds that the bull has survived
only to be killed when he reaches his pen. When he hears
this he faints, apparently from the altitude and a fever
he had caught. Significantly enough, however, the first
news he hears when he comes to is that Jimmie Parr has
agreed to a divorce and Alida is free to marry him.

Like the bull, Michael has survived in vain. The
long aftermath of the trip to Mexico sees Michael return
indifferently to the bank. Though everything has turned
out perfectly for him, his success has become "a soiled
stiff shirt after a long and tiring evening." In his last affair with his stepdaughter Ginny Dexter, Michael seeks
to prove that he has lived, so that he may die. Auchincloss describes Michael's attraction to Ginny as "a mad-
ness of the blood," something quite different from his
idealized interest in Flora and Alida. Uncharacteristically, Michael pursues her directly, even whispering ob-
scenities in her ear as he dances with her at the beach
club parties where they meet. But the self-destructive
side to his newfound ardor is depressingly familiar. Alida
is partly right in seeing this relationship as another way
out of the trap of success. At the same time, however,
it is another even more flamboyant attempt to live out
the false masculine ideal he has been emulating all along.
"This was simply the way *other* men behaved," Michael
concludes after a particularly suggestive exchange with
Ginny. Yet finally there is something adolescent about

Michael's conduct, almost as if he were turning back the clock more than twenty years and approaching Ginny as he thinks he should have approached Flora. Ginny seems the realization of one of his most extravagant boyhood fantasies. Her figure resembles "the Ingres odalisques that he had looked at as a boy, who returned to envelop him in bold alabaster arms, the wide-hipped Bouguereau nudes who dragged him, naked, up to an azure sky where winged cherubs puffed at horns."

Michael's obsession with Ginny is foolish and somewhat pathetic, but there is a certain integrity in it. Though he is ultimately a victim rather than a tragic figure, Michael does confront the violence he sees at the heart of things and in his confused way does escape from the world of duty that has constrained him. Though he has none of the grandeur of a Lear raging against the elements on the heath, the events that lead to his suicide are a dramatic stripping-down process in which Michael sheds all the paraphernalia of his conventional life. First he gets into a fight with a young man who wants to take Ginny home from the club dance; then he argues with Alida and walks out of their house, with the expectation that he will never return. As he makes his way down the beach to Ginny's house, he takes off his tie and steps out of his shoes. After making love to Ginny, who, it turns out, has been eagerly awaiting him, he walks out onto the beach again, strips, and swims out to his death in the sea. On the verge of his suicide, Michael realizes what he has finally done: "To become a man, as other men, to become an animal, as other animals, he had, quite simply, destroyed himself. He had equated manliness with hardness and lust; he had wanted to be a beast, and he had become a beast." In this moment he realizes the irony of his situation, but he has gone too far to turn back — even if he wants to. In his own confused terms, he has lived. His vision on the pyramid of the sun "had now a striking validity.

If he had at last achieved the vitality of the living, he had surely earned the right to cease to live."

Though it comes dangerously close to melodrama, the suicide scene is moving, and the five chapters that lead up to it give *Venus in Sparta* much of its power. In the face of this power, the psychological explanation offered by Michael's analyst Dr. Jennison and elaborated in the last of the flashbacks seems a bit too neat: "his father's death, coming when it did, had paralyzed him with a sense of overwhelming responsibility" resulting in "an acute sense of inadequacy." This theory is plausible but inadequate — almost as if Auchincloss had not quite grasped the full horror at the heart of things that Michael discovers in the final year of his life. In light of the conclusion to the novel, Dr. Jennison's optimistic predictions that, if Michael "could learn to concentrate on his accomplishments and not his failures," he would feel better about himself and "his fear of the opposite sex might be expected to decline" become almost ludicrous. Yet the fact is that Michael stops seeing Dr. Jennison after only six sessions and never does resolve his feelings about his father. Even as he contemplates his affair with Ginny, Michael thinks of his father and "the hopelessness of ever ceasing to disappoint this loving and all-forgiving parent." In the last flashback, we learn that Michael's father dies before Michael can redeem himself in his eyes. His death merely fixes Michael's inadequacy permanently. Like several other Auchincloss protagonists, Michael never escapes the past he has created for himself. His father remains "the vast, too encouraging figure" of his childhood, "constantly throwing balls that had somehow to be caught." And in spite of his success Michael remains the vulnerable little boy, painfully out of place in a man's world, in the menacing Sparta he sees all around him.

Venus in Sparta skirts several dangers — a tendency toward the melodramatic, the seeming contradiction between the pat psychological explanations for Michael's behavior and the intense anguish he actually experiences. The symbolic scenes in Mexico, while absolutely essential to the novel, underline Michael's approaching fate perhaps a bit too obviously, and all but the most hard-boiled Freudians could do with fewer direct references to the phallic tower of the chapel at Averhill Academy, but *Venus in Sparta* is a remarkably well-crafted work. Auchincloss manages the succession of revealing flashbacks expertly, and his customary control of detail enhances the larger thematic patterns of the novel.

Above all, *Venus in Sparta* is a compelling portrait of an insider in business and society who simply does not fit. As James Tuttleton has observed, "society offers only one role — complete with props" to Michael, "a role he cannot play."[6] As a Farish, Michael is brought up with a set of inherited expectations that become increasingly burdensome: he must be president of Hudson River Trust; he must demonstrate conventional masculinity. In succeeding in meeting most of the demands of family and class, he destroys himself. In his self-destruction, he is not a tragic figure; but Auchincloss convinces us that his pathos is significant. Even as he follows the rules for a well-regulated ascent in the world, Michael longs for something beyond the quotidian. That his conception of the world beyond is confused and his attempts to escape futile finally does not matter.

Although *Venus in Sparta* was written within a year of his marriage, during what was apparently a very happy time in Auchincloss's life, it offers the bleakest view in all his fiction of the dangers posed by the masculine activities associated with the downtown world of his father. In Michael Farish we see the most extreme version of the horror inspired by "those dark narrow streets and all those sooty towers" that Auchincloss saw as a boy when his father took him to Wall Street and that he later associated with his father's nervous breakdown. From

these grim sources, perhaps, *Venus in Sparta* ultimately draws its peculiar intensity and power.

Pursuit of the Prodigal

Published only one year after *Venus in Sparta*, in 1959,
Pursuit of the Prodigal is the final work in the first
group of novels about men in the great world. It portrays
a lawyer from a background very much like that of Michael Farish. After the usual seasoning at St. Lawrence
Academy, Harvard College and Harvard Law School,
followed by service in World War II, Reese Parmelee
goes to work in the law firm founded by his grandfather
and moves into the former gatehouse on his family's
estate on the North Shore of Long Island at Parmelee
Cove. His problems are the obverse of Michael Farish's.
Both men wish to escape the conventional world to
which they have been destined from birth, but Reese
has always been a rebel rather than a conformist. An intensely physical man with no doubts about his masculinity, Reese prides himself on his integrity and blunt-
ness and disdains the compromises that "nice" people
inevitably end up making. He feels hemmed in by his
work at the family law firm and by living among three
generations of Parmelees in the family compound. As
Benjamin DeMott observed when the book first appeared,
Auchincloss in his early descriptions of Reese almost
brings off "an extraordinary stunt, that of setting a
brute — not a comedian, or a mere British Decent, but
a thoroughly nasty man — down in the dull unsuspecting
world" of the novel.[7] Twice in the course of the novel,
Reese attempts to break free from the structures that
confine him. First, he has an affair, divorces his wife,
and leaves the family firm to work with a less respectable
uptown firm. Yet he returns to Parmelee Cove with his
second wife, and, after a second attempt to flee, settles
down there to stay as the sole male member of his generation in the family colony.

In its concern for changes in several generations of the same family and in its juxtaposition of the contrasting milieux of Parmelee Cove and the world of minor artists and writers connected with the fashion magazine for which Reese's second wife works, *Pursuit of the Prodigal* points forward to Auchincloss's next two novels, *The House of Five Talents* and *Portrait in Brownstone*. But much of the novel is concerned with Reese's legal career, and, as in the previous novels, Auchincloss draws significant connections between the personal and the professional. By working for an uptown practitioner like Amos Levine, Reese not only escapes the confinement of the family firm but also sees himself as striking a blow against the hypocrisy of elite corporate law. He regards both his second marriage and the partnership he is eventually offered by Levine as entanglements that threaten his integrity and independence. Reese defends Levine against charges of misconduct in a dramatic courtroom trial, but he never knows whether his partner's behavior has been entirely ethical. At one point Rosina, his second wife — acting, ironically, at the suggestion of his *first* wife — conspires with Levine to conceal information Reese needs to make up his mind about his partner's conduct. As in the previous novels, the partner's conduct, while not technically illegal, falls into a gray area. Reese's emotional response to Levine's less fastidious style of doing business becomes progressively more important in the novel, and the real issue for Auchincloss becomes psychological rather than ethical: whether Reese's ideas of integrity represent sound morality or self-destructive egotism.

Auchincloss never quite answers the questions posed by Reese's doubts about Levine because, in the rapid conclusion to the novel, one never fully sees why Reese returns to his marriage with Rosina and his partnership with Levine. Nonetheless, the central irony posed by Auchincloss's title *Pursuit of the Prodigal* remains and gives the novel much of its interest. In a family like the

Parmelees in the twentieth century, Auchincloss suggests, it is almost impossible to be a prodigal son. As Reese finds as he watches a family party in progress, "People no longer waited for the prodigal to return; they chased him, shaking sticks and rattling pans" to drive him back into the pen. Time and again, Reese is drawn back into the orbit of his family. Yet perhaps it is finally those who remain in the tottering "old stockade" of the family who are the true prodigals, "spending their tiny capital of integrity in the endless task of adapting themselves cheerfully to the new, anything new." Despite the pursuit, Reese returns in the end, but it is hard to tell whether he does so because of his love for Rosina or because he now recognizes the futility — or the immaturity — of even attempting to flee. Though Reese returns to Parmelee Cove, presumably he does so in order to regain the values of the past rather than to embrace "the new" as those who have never left continually strive to do.

Although *Pursuit of the Prodigal* adds several aspects to Auchincloss's picture of the great world, it is the least successful of the three earlier novels. Auchincloss convincingly describes the world of uptown legal practice, and in the character of Amose Levine he offers a detailed and finely drawn portrait of the shady partner figure who is found in most of the novels in the series. In portraying Reese Parmelee, he approaches the problems of men at work from an interesting and fresh perspective, but his development of Reese's character in the later portions of the novel is flawed, as Benjamin De-Mott has suggested. The sections of the novel that describe the various branches of the Parmelee family are quite fine, but unfortunately the relationships within the extended family do not remain at the center of the novel, as they do in *The House of Five Talents* or *Portrait in Brownstone*. One must ultimately conclude that Auchincloss handles the same sort of material better in novels that are more explicitly concerned with manners. In its critique of "the new," however, *Pursuit of the Prodigal* anticipates the examination of moral values that one finds in the last two novels in the series.

A World of Profit and *I Come as a Thief*

In the final pair of novels, *A World of Profit* and *I Come as a Thief*, Auchincloss's vision of the past fades, and his view of the present darkens. Neither novel is among his best works, though *I Come as a Thief* is especially interesting because it deals so explicitly with religious issues. In both novels, Auchincloss abandons his earlier partial faith in the decency of the older, established community connected with the downtown law firms and large financial institutions. Characters such as Henry Knox, the senior partner in *The Great World and Timothy Colt*, or even Rex Geer, the investment banker in *The Embezzler*, though they are by no means perfect human beings, are redeemed by a fundamental honesty and humanity. Analogous characters in the two later novels are not. In the later novels, too, Auchincloss extends his consideration of men in the great world by choosing protagonists who do not come from Old New York or the ranks of middle-class New England males who work their way up in the world of law or finance.

The central character in *A World of Profit* is Jay Livingston — a seemingly unlikely protagonist for Auchincloss, since he not only is Jewish but also has made his fortune in real estate in Queens and the Bronx. A young man somewhat reminiscent of Fitzgerald's Gatsby and based in part on the financier, Edward M. Gilbert,[8] Jay tries to marry into the old New York family of the Shallcrosses. Auchincloss sets him down in the midst of a group of people motivated almost entirely by greed, and he emerges as the only even mildly appealing male figure in the novel. He does not really need to tempt the lawyers and brokers from the older families and respectable downtown firms into his shady real estate investments and subsequent dealings in the stock of a corporate conglomerate, for they are, if anything, more corrupt than he is. Early in the novel, Jay joins the Shallcross family in a scheme to raze their old family estate in Queens and build a veterans' housing project on the site. Significantly, however, the idea of selling the family property had come not from Jay but from Martin Shallcross, the son in the family, for whom the lure of quick profits from borrowed federal housing funds far outweighs any attachment to a symbol of family tradition. Though Jay is ruined at the end of the novel by his illegal efforts to acquire control of the Atlantic Corporation, he retains an energy and innocence that the more respectable characters lack. His erstwhile partner Martin, unable to bounce back from failure, commits suicide by jumping off the commuter train to Greenwich. Though there is something mildly sociopathic in Jay's opportunism and indifference to legal niceties, Martin's younger sister Sophie is probably right when she says that he "was the only one of us who had the guts to live. We all sensed that and fed off him."

In the final chapter, Judge Eben Shallcross, Martin's father and the philosopher figure in the novel, accuses Jay and his son's friends of being part of a bankrupt generation. But then he admits that his own generation made "the mess of messes" between the two World Wars and calls his philosophizing "a lot of crap." Though the judge's point is that one cannot make valid generalizations about human behavior, the past in *A World of Profit* is invested with none of the luminosity of Guy Prime's recollections in *The Embezzler* or similar accounts in Auchincloss's novels of manners, and neither the newcomers nor the old families in the novel have much probity or integrity. Judge Shallcross takes unseemly glee in bringing Jay's misdeeds to the attention of the former district attorney and in the process violates professional ethics since Jay is at the time a client of his law firm. With his heavily leveraged real estate deals and his attempts in the Atlantic Corporation to build a financial conglomerate, Jay is the very type of the modern corporate raider, but old-fashioned values as they are exemplified by the Shallcrosses and others seem moribund at best in *A World of Profit*. Indeed, if one takes into account the fact that many aspects of the work are modeled upon Edmond and Jules Goncourt's 1864 novel, *Renée Mauperin*, it may be seen as an attack on bourgeois values in general.[9]

In *I Come as a Thief*, published in 1972, Auchincloss again reaches beyond the world of established New York families on the Upper East Side for his protagonist. Tony Lowder is a third-generation Irish lawyer and a liberal Democrat with political aspirations. Like other Auchincloss heroes including Jay Livingston (who was guilty of plagiarizing a story he published in his prep school literary magazine), he is troubled by an episode in his past. When Tony was ten, he stole his grandfather's gold knife and was branded a thief by his father. And like earlier protagonists going back to Timmy Colt, he is associated with a shady law partner, whom he dubs "Max Satanicus" at one point in the novel. When some of his and Max's investments go bad, they are forced to go to the Mafia for a loan. Yet the corruption in the novel is located not just in the underworld but reaches to the highest level of one of the most important brokerage houses on Wall Street. In return for forgiveness of the loan, Tony is asked, in his capacity as special assistant to the regional director of the SEC, to delay a crucial investigation in order to give the firm time to cover up financial irregularities. He does so and thus enters into a silent partnership with the corrupt but urbane head of the firm.

Up to this point in the novel, events have proceeded in a manner in keeping with the action in Auchincloss's earlier novels about lawyers or brokers. But about midway in the narrative, something strange happens. Tony undergoes what can only be described as a religious experience akin to the dark night of the soul defined in Christian mystical tradition. At a birthday party for his mistress, Joan Conway, he senses "the sky darkening outside as if the sun had been clouded over." Even at lunch in a crowded room he cannot rid himself of an ineffable "impression of darkness . . . permeating the harsh light, so that black and white seemed to coexist in a queer blend of blindness and vision." He feels that "he had hurled himself out" of Paradise and "fallen into a strange limbo where he existed alone." The people around him "were the ghosts of the people he had known in Paradise, and, like all ghosts, they existed without pleasure or taste. Without companionship. And there was no seeming end to it."

This strange experience leads Tony to confess and accept his guilt, but in the corrupt world of the novel his virtuous actions estrange him from everyone around him, even for a time his wife. His father-in-law, Mr. Bogardus, a tax attorney and partner in a large downtown firm who represents the sterility of the established world, hates him all the more because of his mystical experience. When Tony tells him over lunch at the Down Town Association that he plans to confess, Mr. Bogardus asks him if he has thought of his wife and children. Tony explains that he now realizes that above all he must become a person his family can respect: "Jesus Christ told his disciples there should be nobody between him and them: no wife or child or parent. That always used to shock me, but now I think I see what he meant. There shouldn't be anyone between a man and his conscience. If there is, it's really because he's using them as an excuse." Mr. Bogardus is scandalized, not so much by

Tony's crime as by his religious sentiments. "To talk about Christ in the Down Town Association was grossly improper," he thinks. "People who talk about Christ in that way were always very odd people indeed." As the voice of narrow practicality, Mr. Bogardus urges Tony to keep quiet and go back to work. As Auchincloss observes, after Tony is convicted of his crime, "he was alone because he had taken himself out of his world."

Though Tony's confession and testimony against his associates at his trial retain some of the questionable absolutism of Timmy Colt's or Reese Parmelee's actions, the validity of his religious experience is affirmed by the novel. Against the cold hatred of Mr. Bogardus, who sees to it that Tony will be convicted and urges his daughter to divorce him, and compared to his own ineffectual parents, Tony is a vivid and significant character. His spiritual experience remains mysterious — "all I know is that I took a bribe and went to hell," he says toward the end of the novel — but it is genuine and powerful. As Tony goes off to prison, however, it becomes clear that he has been granted some sort of salvation, no matter how murky, and that he will be able to rebuild his life.

The conclusion of *I Come as a Thief*, in which Tony is reconciled with his wife Lee, is reminiscent of the comic ending of the first novel in the series, *The Great World and Timothy Colt*. But the novel as a whole is the shortest and the least elaborately detailed of any in the series. Though *I Come as a Thief* therefore seems somewhat schematic, Auchincloss's religious perspective provides a solid underpinning for Tony's change in character. Tony sins. Then, in something like the first step in the process of conversion in Evangelical theology, he is gripped by the conviction of his utter sinfulness and estrangement from God. He confesses his sin, is vouchsafed an experience — however vague — of grace, and finally receives forgiveness. This underlying religious pattern makes *I Come as a Thief* much more successful

structurally than *The Great World and Timothy Colt*.
It also makes the work the most hopeful of Auchincloss's
novels of the great world. Though Tony's fall is greater
than that of any other protagonist and he knows that it
will be very difficult to put his life together again when
he returns from prison, he clearly has something to build
on. What he has gone through "has to be enough to build
a life on," as he tells Lee at the end of the novel.

Because of his mystical experience, Tony, more
than any other character in the novels discussed in this
chapter, escapes not only the ordinary world around him
but also the world of his past. In taking the bribe, he
recapitulates the guilty episode in his boyhood when he
had stolen his grandfather's knife. But unlike the protagonists of the earlier novels, he does not seem doomed
to go on forever repeating the pattern of his past. The
"presence in himself" he experiences at the luncheon
party—"Was it grace? Was it God?" he later asks himself—enables him to break out of the pattern. Like the
divine voice at the Last Day in the book of Revelation
to which Auchincloss alludes in the novel's title, the experience comes "as a thief," suddenly, unexpectedly. And
like divine grace, it comes *to* a thief, to someone who is
essentially underserving. Tony refuses to make too much
of the voice he has heard, but he does believe in it, and
it offers solid hope for a new beginning, if not for the
Biblical "new heaven and new earth." Auchincloss's decidedly religious perspective in the novel, in turn, underlines his fundamental conservatism. Major changes
in people's lives, he implies, will not come from moral
improvement schemes or through some sort of rational
education. They must come from outside ordinary experience, from something, that is, like grace. In *I Come
as a Thief* Auchincloss offers his own sardonic commentary on the basic incongruity of genuine religious experience in the everyday world, while for the first time

showing us fully how characters in that world can escape from the burdens of their own pasts.

Seen in the light of the four related novels that precede it, *I Come as a Thief* is testimony to Auchincloss's continuing versatility as a novelist. Novels that deal sympathetically and intelligently with businessmen and professionals are rare in recent American fiction, so these novels of the great world stand out. Within their recurring patterns and motifs and within their shared symbolic universe, the attentive reader can see growth as well as variety.

6

ᛏᛏᛏᛏᛏᛏᛏᛏᛏᛏᛏᛏᛏᛏᛏᛏᛏᛏᛏᛏᛏᛏᛏᛏᛏᛏᛏᛏᛏᛏᛏᛏ

The Great World
Revisited:
The Embezzler

Like the novels about businessmen and lawyers discussed
in chapter 5, *The Embezzler* may be said to be a novel
of Wall Street—but it is considerably more than that.
The five novels in the series extending from *The Great
World and Timothy Colt* to *I Come as a Thief* all portray contemporary life in the world of Manhattan finance. *The Embezzler*, on the other hand, looks back
on an earlier era in that world and evokes the elegance
of New York society before World War I. Though its
protagonist Guy Prime is a stockbroker, *The Embezzler*
is closely related to the novels of manners that Auchincloss wrote in the early 1960s. Indeed, its essential action recalls an episode in *The House of Five Talents* in
which Gussie Millinder makes a loan to her relative Collier Haven so that he can replace funds that he has em-
bezzled from customers' accounts at his brokerage firm.
Haven is forced to retire from business for awhile but
returns to Wall Street and resumes his illegal activities,
finally disappearing from sight after he has stolen money
from a family trust. Another member of the Millinder
family writes "a trashy but sensational novel" based on
the episode. Though *The Embezzler* is not that novel,
it reminds us of Auchincloss's tendency to quarry his own
previous works for material for his fiction.

In addition to mediating between the novels of manners and the novels of contemporary Wall Street, *The Embezzler* also reflects — and extends — the experiments with multiple narrative perspectives in Auchincloss's previous novel, *The Rector of Justin* (1964). As in his portrayal of Francis Prescott in *The Rector*, Auchincloss explores the complexities of human character and how we perceive it by showing us Guy Prime's life from several distinct and conflicting viewpoints. As in his preceding novel, too, he takes the career of a well-known person as his starting point.

In spite of the various ways in which it recalls previous novels, however, *The Embezzler* remains unique. To turn from the earlier novels about lawyers and trust officers to *The Embezzler* is to see, once again, the variety Auchincloss is capable of achieving in depicting the world of Manhattan finance. The protagonists of the three novels written in the 1950s remain, in many respects, little boys who cannot work out their childhood anger or resolve their guilt. Guy Prime, on the other hand, is an egotistical overreacher who brings about his own ruin with little remorse and few of the signs of debilitating insecurity that plague many earlier Auchincloss characters. Yet at the same time his illegal actions are more than coincidentally related to his discovery that his wife is unfaithful, and, like Timothy Colt or Michael Farish in *Venus in Sparta*, he is very much the creator of the psychological world in which he lives.

Like many of the novels that follow it, *The Embezzler* is a historical novel in at least two senses. First, it attempts to capture the spirit of a particular period of Wall Street history — the golden age of the 1920s and 1930s before the establishment of the Securities and Exchange Commission, an era when the stock exchange operated more like a gentleman's club than a public institution. As in his novels about old New York, Auchincloss is keenly interested in changes in society and man-

ners over periods of time. In *The Embezzler* he looks
back upon the world in which Guy Prime lives with a
double vision — aware of its flaws, but at the same time
sensitive to what was lost as the New Deal tamed Wall
Street. Second, the novel is also historical in a more
literal sense. Many of the events and details come from
a particular episode in Wall Street history — the Richard
Whitney scandal. A former president of the New York
Stock Exchange and a leading broker with close ties to
the investment banking firm of J. P. Morgan, Whitney
was convicted of embezzlement in a highly publicized
trial in 1938.[1] Because Whitney was still alive when the
novel appeared, *The Embezzler* occasioned much of the
same consternation among friends of Auchincloss's parents that his previous novel, *The Rector of Justin*, had
aroused among some graduates of Groton School. (Whitney himself was a Groton graduate.) Auchincloss was ac-
cused of opening an old wound, and, indeed, the parallels between surface details in the novel and the facts of
the Whitney case are numerous. Richard Whitney misappropriated bonds belonging to the New York Yacht
Club, of which he was treasurer. Guy Prime uses bonds
from the country club of which he was president to cover
personal loans. Where Whitney's fortunes had foundered
in wild investments in a firm called Distilled Liquors,
Guy ruins himself trying to prop up the value of his holdings in Georgia Phosphates (a name not only suggested
by Whitney's investments in fertilizer firms but also borrowed from Auchincloss's own past, since his grandfather was owner and agent for phosphate mines in
Florida).[2] A minor character like the timid cashier of
Guy's club probably has his origin in the clerk of the
Stock Exchange Gratuity Fund, from which Whitney
also misappropriated funds. Guy's best friend, Rex Geer,
possesses a combination of attributes drawn from two
major participants in the Whitney scandal. Rex's background and professional career resemble those of

Thomas Lamont, managing partner and house intellectual at J. P. Morgan and Company, and Guy's dealings
with Rex are reminiscent of those between Richard
Whitney and his brother George, who was also a Morgan partner and bailed him out several times in his
career.[3]

Despite these and other external similarities to the
Whitney case, Guy is not, finally, a literal portrait of
Richard Whitney. Rather, the puzzling questions raised
by Whitney's conduct and never quite answered in his
trial or subsequent life serve as the germ for Auchincloss's
novel.[4] By borrowing details from the historical record
and altering many of them when he sees fit, Auchincloss
creates a character of his own. He explores Guy's psychology and motives and presents several theories to explain his behavior, but he does not offer any final solu-
tion to the mystery. Though some of the theories about
Guy's behavior seem considerably more plausible than
others, the reader must ultimately, as in *The Rector of
Justin*, make up his own mind about the central character.

What one is to make of Guy Prime remains at least
partly ambiguous because of Auchincloss's narrative
technique in the novel. Auchincloss tells Guy's story
through three interlocking first-person narratives. The
novel begins with Guy's own account of his life, which
is followed by memoirs written by Rex Geer and Guy's
wife Angelica, who by the time she writes has divorced
Guy and married Rex. Rex reacts to Guy's memoir, and
Angelica in turn comments on both Guy and Rex's narratives. Angelica's narrative has more authority than the
others, but it is not definitive. The result is reminiscent
of Robert Browning's successive dramatic monologues in
The Ring and the Book, except that, unlike his Victorian
predecessor, Auchincloss leaves a number of the questions about Guy unanswered.

The Embezzler is, above all, a retrospective work.

Guy Prime writes in 1960 from exile in Panama, where he has gone after his release from prison to live out his days in obscurity, and where he has become a local character, presiding over a "round table" of cronies every afternoon in the men's bar at the Rivoli Hotel. He writes for posterity, in hopes that his grandchildren will know him as something more than a figure in old newspaper clippings. Because both Rex and Angelica's accounts are written after Guy's death, they look back not only on the first memoir but also on Guy's life as a whole. In this novel, the climactic courtroom scene one finds in almost all of Auchincloss's novels of the great world becomes a congressional hearing rather than an actual trial and occurs at the beginning of Guy's memoir rather than the end, enhancing the effect of retrospection. After mentioning the trial, Guy's narrative turns back to the first hints of trouble and works its way forward to Guy's final ruin. Along the way, Guy tells about his life from childhood to his twenty-second wedding anniversary in a series of flashbacks.

Guy begins life as a Prime—a member of a large old family that includes an early settler in New York and a former bishop and rector of Trinity Church. During his junior year at Harvard he befriends Rex Geer, the son of a poor country parson and the most brilliant student in his class. He saves Rex from having to drop out of school and introduces him to Marcellus de Grasse, the great investment banker, who offers them both jobs in his firm. Rex stays with de Grasse, rising to partner, but Guy soon leaves to travel in Europe and to start his own brokerage firm. Before the two young men go their separate ways, Rex falls in love with Guy's cousin Alix, but the romance is broken up by the girl's family, and Rex marries his childhood friend Lucy Ames.

During his travels in Europe, Guy meets Angelica Hyde, the high-strung daughter of an artistic Catholic family. He marries her in Paris in spite of his father's reservations. Though Guy and Angelica's interests are incompatible, the marriage works for a time. But after Guy returns from World War I, their marriage turns into a convenient arrangement in which Angelica ignores Guy's numerous affairs in return for unlimited money to build and maintain her country estate with its stables and kennels. Only after ten years or so does Angelica fall in love with Rex Geer. Guy recognizes what is going on when he asks Rex for a loan of one hundred thousand dollars and Rex agrees without any questions.

The knowledge that Angelica is desired by his friend makes Guy want her again. On their twenty-second wedding anniversary, he pushes matters to a crisis and tries to get Angelica back. His crude efforts only drive her away, and on the same evening she runs off to Rex's house. Her mother persuades her to return, the affair is temporarily broken off by Rex, and she becomes pregnant with Guy's child. When she suffers a miscarriage — brought on deliberately, Guy thinks — Guy's embezzlements begin.

As Guy sees it, Angelica and Rex have destroyed his faith in himself. There is now no point in his living except as a rich man and as "king" of his self-created realm at the Glenville Country Club. When the club's bonds are called in, he turns again to Rex for assistance. This time Rex demands (just as George Whitney had of his brother Richard) that he liquidate his brokerage firm. This is the final blow to Guy's pride — spiritual cuckolding, as he calls it. He accedes to Rex's conditions but continues his speculations and embezzlement on an even grander scale. When his bluff is called again, Rex does not bail him out. Guy accepts his fate and goes to prison, cutting all ties with his former life, refusing to see Angelica, and telling her to get a divorce. After leaving prison, Guy goes to Panama, where he marries again. Angelica moves to a house on Rex's estate, and when Rex's wife dies after a long illness, she marries him.

More perhaps than any other character in Auchincloss's fiction, Guy Prime demonstrates the truth of
Auchincloss's remark that "a man's background is largely
of his own creating." Many of Guy's problems in the
novel stem from his tendency to construct myths — of his
family, of himself, and of those he admires. He views his
father, for example, as a "paragon of the age of elegance"
who married a living embodiment of the age of innocence for love rather than money. Yet this view of the
past, like many of the statements in Guy's memoir, is
shown to be largely illusory by the other two memoirs.
Rex, in his exaggerated and self-serving fashion, sees Mr.
Prime as "a boundless snob who could not be bothered
to conceal his small opinion of his son's unprofitable new
friend" and Mrs. Prime as a saint. Angelica, however,
comes much closer to the truth: "The Primes were a
shabby lot, and were so regarded, when I was a girl, by
most of the people whom they sought to impress." Rather
than marrying for love, Guy's father simply had miscal-
culated the amount of his future wife's fortune. Rather
than a saint and martyr, Guy's mother was a hypochon-
driac who made life miserable for her children.

Guy grows up with the dream of elegance and
financial success that his father desires for him. It is his
father, who never worked a day in his life, who sets him
up with his own seat on the stock exchange. He does this,
as Guy proudly points out, "by using all the money, in
a single magnificent gesture, that he had *not* borrowed
from his rich brothers in all the long hard years of his
married life." This grandness of gesture is what Guy
seeks as he sets up his club and as he maintains the Mead-
owview estate for his wife. With some of this same gran-
diosity, Guy faces "the bleak void" of his impending
conviction and imprisonment: "I was happy that I had
engaged with life, that I had married a beautiful woman
and made and spent fortunes and founded a great club.
New York would not soon forget Guy Prime. And if all

ended hideously, New York would forget him even less."

At one point in his memoir, Guy denies the commonly held theory about his behavior — that he "suffered from megalomania" and saw himself as a sort of king of Wall Street. Yet there is some truth in this idea. When he asks Rex for the first loan, he thinks of himself as "an institution on which a small multitude of people depended."[5] After Rex has made him agree to liquidate his business, he wonders if Rex and Angelica "were not bound in some kind of unholy conspiracy to fetter me and reduce me to helplessness." Rex despises him, he thinks, because "Guy Prime, the symbol of well-born affluence, of the grandeur of old New York," represents too vividly "the very world he had spent a lifetime trying to conquer."

In moments of crisis, Guy behaves with grand obliviousness. At a family dinner after he has already told Rex about his misappropriation of the Glenville Club bonds, Guy coolly discusses the failure and suicide of Count Landi, an international manipulator with a record similar to his own. He even asks everyone at the table for his or her opinion. When his own failure finally comes, he delivers a speech to a house full of friends announcing his pending indictment. Angelica is convinced that Guy's "little oration" was fully rehearsed: "Guy was delivering a long-planned valediction." With his sense of style, inherited from "that sporty old fraud" his father, Guy did not, of course, worry that his conduct was illegal or dishonest when he misappropriated the bonds, but when he is caught he does not deny his crime.[6]

The great contrast to Guy in the novel is Rex Geer. Their friendship is the central relationship in Guy's life, and probably in Rex's as well, but, like Guy's marriage, it fails. In Auchincloss's historical scheme, Rex represents the new forces entering the older world of the Primes. Rex, the poor, earnest outsider from a country parsonage, rises in the old world of finance by his industry and

asms," this becomes a special failing. While this
ency has unfortunate consequences for Guy, it is also
oral virtue—a point that Rex fails to see. Guy's con-
tions of those around him are invariably generous:
infused his imagined world, not only with glory and
gance but with love and good will." As Angelica looks
ck on Guy's life, it gives her "a nostalgic pleasure to
member that Guy's vision of his world, although not
particularly fine one, was a good deal finer than its
ality. And perhaps it is important for me to remember
, too, for I seem to be the only person living (except
erhaps for a little widow down in Panama) who has still
kindly feeling for Guy. The others think he blackened
ur world. Perhaps so. But only after years of trying to
give it a spot of color" (*Embezzler*, p. 234).

Unlike Rex, Angelica refuses to believe that Guy
deliberately involved the people around him in his own
disgrace.

I am sure that he had no conception of how great the scandal
of his trial would be. He intended to bow quietly out of society as simply another of the numberless embezzlers of financial
history and start a new life for himself. He intended to leave
all of us better off by his departure, even Rex, who, if he lost
the money that he had put up, was to be compensated with
me. Guy was a testator who planned to survive the probate
of his own will and to watch from afar his legatees enjoying
their bequests. But what he was going to enjoy most of all was
his own liberation into a new life: a life that would be just like
the old with one all-important exception. He would not disappoint anybody in it, including himself, because nobody in it
would have expected anything else of him, including himself.
This life he was to find in Panama. (*Embezzler*, p. 273)

This view of Guy is intriguing, for it finally relates him
to the other less flamboyant protagonists in Auchincloss's
great world. Like Michael Farish in *Venus in Sparta* or
Reese Parmelee in *Pursuit of the Prodigal*, Guy is a person of whom too much is expected. At the end, he, too,

intellectual brilliance. With his stern morality, Rex also
reflects the contrast between Guy's elegant, aesthetic
father and his religious mother. There is, as Guy admits,
"a grasshopper and cricket aspect" to their relationship,
but Guy also invests their friendship with some of the intensity of a love affair. "To fill the great gap in my young
and surging heart, I needed a friend, a particular friend,
a Pythias, a Jonathan, who would direct me as well as
understand me, who would help me prove to myself that
I was a man as well as a Prime." And there is more of
the cricket in Guy than might first appear, for he sees
a partnership with Rex as a vehicle for achieving his
dream of greatness. With Rex's ability and Guy's connections in New York, their partnership would make
Guy as successful as his father had hoped.

Like Guy's image of his father, the friendship with
Rex is built upon Guy's fatal tendency to idealize those
whom he admires or loves. When Rex's infatuation with
Guy's cousin Alix Prime is brutally checked by her family, Guy's relationship with Rex deteriorates. But even
after the episode with Alix Prime, Guy continues to help
Rex. One of the ironies of the relationship is that Guy
is responsible in part for Rex's success. He introduces him
to Marcellus de Grasse and even encourages his courtship of Alix Prime. Yet, while admiring Rex, Guy also
envies him and sees him as a rival. This accounts—
though only partially—for Guy's oddly ambivalent feelings when he discovers the affair between Rex and
Angelica and for his later refusal to live up to his promise to liquidate his business.

Rex's memoir is the least appealing of the narratives
that comprise the novel. Though Auchincloss does not
do enough to distinguish the prose styles of the three narratives, Rex tends to be more factual and less expansive
than Guy, and more abstract and less vivid than Angelica. Sometimes his memoir descends to the level of
a fussy point-by-point rebuttal of Guy. Yet Rex is rela-

tively honest in his own fashion, freely admitting, for example, that he has hurt Guy by brusquely rejecting his offer of a partnership. Through his own moralistic spectacles, Rex views Guy as a wicked figure when he discovers his embezzlement. But in the end, he regards him as the destroyer of the world of business in which they both operated: "Either he would become the richest man in Wall Street or he would destroy Wall Street," turning it over in ruins "to the jackals of the New Deal." When it became clear he would fail, "Guy moved to enmesh me in his fall. It was essential to his plan that I should become his creditor, with full knowledge of his embezzlement."

This Machiavellian view of Guy is obviously incorrect, and, indeed, in the light of Auchincloss's other novels about the great world, it is Rex rather than Guy who plays the role of the sinister partner-figure. Yet the story of Guy's fall is not a simple morality play. Though Rex triumphs in the end, he is not a wholly Satanic figure, and Guy's fall is not so much from any actual Eden as from his own world of illusions — from a vision of the past that never existed and a dream of the future that was largely wishful thinking. Rex's success finally reminds one of Guy's own lack of the cold intellectual brilliance that makes such success possible. Guy may well not be capable of the great things to which he aspires, and his failure is another sign that efficient intellectual technicians like Rex hold the key to the future in the world of business, as they do elsewhere in Auchincloss's fiction in the legal world.

Though Guy and Rex are opposites in many respects and their narratives present sharply contrasting views of the facts, both share a special sort of egotism and a penchant for exaggeration that Auchincloss often associates with male characters in his novels. When Guy wonders whether Rex is involved in a conspiracy against him because he symbolizes the affluence and grandeur of old

New York, he is engaging in mu...
thinking that Rex displays when ...
deliberate destroyer of Wall Stree...
more truth in Guy's view than in ...
engage in self-aggrandisement and te...
as titanic figures at the center of the w...
move.

Angelica's memoir is the shortes...
corrective to the two men's memoirs. ...
women in Auchincloss's novels, she is ...
idealistic illusions or intellectual abstra...
males around her. She not only deflates ...
exaggerated sense of the elegance of the Pr...
also straightens out the puzzling question ...
ly happened in Bar Harbor between Rex a...
was a nymphomaniac attracted to both R...
and her family had to take her away from ...
not so much to prevent a match with Rex as ...
out of trouble. Angelica's account also revea...
uine pain that Guy caused her, both by his ...
the time of the affair and by his refusal to le...
him at the time of his failure. Though she and ...
poorly matched, Angelica was initially a happy ...
did not become disillusioned with Guy until she s...
indiscriminate he could be in his hero-worship. ...
illusionment coincides with Guy's return from Par...
the war — his own last chance at greatness. It is ...
significant that in his narrative Guy glosses over the ...
years of his marriage and the period of Angelica's a...
with Rex in two very short chapters.

Though it does not solve all the mysteries of ...
character, Angelica's final view of Guy is validated ...
the novel as a whole. Early in their marriage she realiz...
that "his estimates of people were always wrong." Sh...
calls him "a hero-worshipper who lived in a gallery of ...
plaster-cast figures that he took for marble." In some-...
one "so intensely gregarious and of such multiple en-

intellectual brilliance. With his stern morality, Rex also reflects the contrast between Guy's elegant, aesthetic father and his religious mother. There is, as Guy admits, "a grasshopper and cricket aspect" to their relationship, but Guy also invests their friendship with some of the intensity of a love affair. "To fill the great gap in my young and surging heart, I needed a friend, a particular friend, a Pythias, a Jonathan, who would direct me as well as understand me, who would help me prove to myself that I was a man as well as a Prime." And there is more of the cricket in Guy than might first appear, for he sees a partnership with Rex as a vehicle for achieving his dream of greatness. With Rex's ability and Guy's connections in New York, their partnership would make Guy as successful as his father had hoped.

Like Guy's image of his father, the friendship with Rex is built upon Guy's fatal tendency to idealize those whom he admires or loves. When Rex's infatuation with Guy's cousin Alix Prime is brutally checked by her family, Guy's relationship with Rex deteriorates. But even after the episode with Alix Prime, Guy continues to help Rex. One of the ironies of the relationship is that Guy is responsible in part for Rex's success. He introduces him to Marcellus de Grasse and even encourages his courtship of Alix Prime. Yet, while admiring Rex, Guy also envies him and sees him as a rival. This accounts — though only partially — for Guy's oddly ambivalent feelings when he discovers the affair between Rex and Angelica and for his later refusal to live up to his promise to liquidate his business.

Rex's memoir is the least appealing of the narratives that comprise the novel. Though Auchincloss does not do enough to distinguish the prose styles of the three narratives, Rex tends to be more factual and less expansive than Guy, and more abstract and less vivid than Angelica. Sometimes his memoir descends to the level of a fussy point-by-point rebuttal of Guy. Yet Rex is relatively honest in his own fashion, freely admitting, for example, that he has hurt Guy by brusquely rejecting his offer of a partnership. Through his own moralistic spectacles, Rex views Guy as a wicked figure when he discovers his embezzlement. But in the end, he regards him as the destroyer of the world of business in which they both operated: "Either he would become the richest man in Wall Street or he would destroy Wall Street," turning it over in ruins "to the jackals of the New Deal." When it became clear he would fail, "Guy moved to enmesh me in his fall. It was essential to his plan that I should become his creditor, with full knowledge of his embezzlement."

This Machiavellian view of Guy is obviously incorrect, and, indeed, in the light of Auchincloss's other novels about the great world, it is Rex rather than Guy who plays the role of the sinister partner-figure. Yet the story of Guy's fall is not a simple morality play. Though Rex triumphs in the end, he is not a wholly Satanic figure, and Guy's fall is not so much from any actual Eden as from his own world of illusions — from a vision of the past that never existed and a dream of the future that was largely wishful thinking. Rex's success finally reminds one of Guy's own lack of the cold intellectual brilliance that makes such success possible. Guy may well not be capable of the great things to which he aspires, and his failure is another sign that efficient intellectual technicians like Rex hold the key to the future in the world of business, as they do elsewhere in Auchincloss's fiction in the legal world.

Though Guy and Rex are opposites in many respects and their narratives present sharply contrasting views of the facts, both share a special sort of egotism and a penchant for exaggeration that Auchincloss often associates with male characters in his novels. When Guy wonders whether Rex is involved in a conspiracy against him because he symbolizes the affluence and grandeur of old

New York, he is engaging in much the same grandiose thinking that Rex displays when he regards Guy as the deliberate destroyer of Wall Street. There is probably more truth in Guy's view than in Rex's, but both men engage in self-aggrandisement and tend to see themselves as titanic figures at the center of the worlds in which they move.

Angelica's memoir is the shortest and serves as a corrective to the two men's memoirs. Like most other women in Auchincloss's novels, she is far less given to idealistic illusions or intellectual abstractions than the males around her. She not only deflates Guy and Rex's exaggerated sense of the elegance of the Prime family but also straightens out the puzzling question of what really happened in Bar Harbor between Rex and Alix: Alix was a nymphomaniac attracted to both Rex and Guy, and her family had to take her away from Bar Harbor, not so much to prevent a match with Rex as to keep her out of trouble. Angelica's account also reveals the genuine pain that Guy caused her, both by his conduct at the time of the affair and by his refusal to let her help him at the time of his failure. Though she and Guy were poorly matched, Angelica was initially a happy wife. She did not become disillusioned with Guy until she saw how indiscriminate he could be in his hero-worship. Her disillusionment coincides with Guy's return from Paris after the war — his own last chance at greatness. It is highly significant that in his narrative Guy glosses over the early years of his marriage and the period of Angelica's affair with Rex in two very short chapters.

Though it does not solve all the mysteries of his character, Angelica's final view of Guy is validated by the novel as a whole. Early in their marriage she realizes that "his estimates of people were always wrong." She calls him "a hero-worshipper who lived in a gallery of plaster-cast figures that he took for marble." In someone "so intensely gregarious and of such multiple enthusiasms," this becomes a special failing. While this tendency has unfortunate consequences for Guy, it is also a moral virtue — a point that Rex fails to see. Guy's conceptions of those around him are invariably generous: "He infused his imagined world, not only with glory and elegance but with love and good will." As Angelica looks back on Guy's life, it gives her "a nostalgic pleasure to remember that Guy's vision of his world, although not a particularly fine one, was a good deal finer than its reality. And perhaps it is important for me to remember it, too, for I seem to be the only person living (except perhaps for a little widow down in Panama) who has still a kindly feeling for Guy. The others think he blackened our world. Perhaps so. But only after years of trying to give it a spot of color" (*Embezzler*, p. 234).

Unlike Rex, Angelica refuses to believe that Guy deliberately involved the people around him in his own disgrace.

I am sure that he had no conception of how great the scandal of his trial would be. He intended to bow quietly out of society as simply another of the numberless embezzlers of financial history and start a new life for himself. He intended to leave all of us better off by his departure, even Rex, who, if he lost the money that he had put up, was to be compensated with me. Guy was a testator who planned to survive the probate of his own will and to watch from afar his legatees enjoying their bequests. But what he was going to enjoy most of all was his own liberation into a new life: a life that would be just like the old with one all-important exception. He would not disappoint anybody in it, including himself, because nobody in it would have expected anything else of him, including himself. This life he was to find in Panama. (*Embezzler*, p. 273)

This view of Guy is intriguing, for it finally relates him to the other less flamboyant protagonists in Auchincloss's great world. Like Michael Farish in *Venus in Sparta* or Reese Parmelee in *Pursuit of the Prodigal*, Guy is a person of whom too much is expected. At the end, he, too, feels the need to escape the expectations of his parents, class, and era.

When *The Embezzler* first appeared, R. W. B. Lewis called it "technically speaking . . . Auchincloss's most satisfying work," "a better-wrought if slenderer work" than *The Rector of Justin*.[7] *The Embezzler* is indeed an appealing work, and its narrative technique is successful. The multiple points of view function more smoothly than they did in the earlier novel. Yet, in the final analysis, Guy Prime, though an attractive and puzzling figure, is not so substantial as Francis Prescott in *The Rector of Justin*, and an attempt to unravel the mysteries of his character does not lead to the larger ethical and moral issues raised by Prescott's life.

The great strength of *The Embezzler* lies in its evocation of the world of the Primes — the world of New York, Bar Harbor, Europe before World War I, of an elegant past that was disappearing even as Guy was building it in his own mind. In telling Guy's tale from three perspectives, Auchincloss captures a character in the particular moment when the old gives way to the new. When he realizes that he has finally ruined himself, Guy thinks that "the long Manhattan career of the Primes had ended in a hell as bright as any in the Bishop's sermons." Yet, by providing the other two memoirs, Auchincloss leads us to ask whether a past of the sort Guy envisions is ever anything more than one individual's personal impressions. Guy and Rex are both caught up in the same historical moment, but for each man that moment is different. And in looking at Guy Prime as a man seeking success in the great world, Auchincloss again reminds us that much of the drama in that world too — the friendships and betrayals, the hopes and disappointments, even Guy's catastrophe itself — is played out on a personal, and ultimately private, stage.

The Embezzler is a work of great charm. In telling the story of Guy Prime, Auchincloss succeeds in combining the sort of novel of manners represented by *The House of Five Talents* with the novel of Wall Street. Though Guy Prime is not so substantial a figure as Francis Prescott, the three narratives enact the central theme of the novel admirably. Though some aspects of Guy Prime's character remain in doubt, *The Embezzler*, in its varied perspectives and occasional contradictions, reminds one of the almost universal human tendency to create highly personal versions of reality. Beyond even the quest for Guy's true motives, this tendency is Auchincloss's central concern in the novel.

7

The Stories

Auchincloss's productivity as a writer of short stories rivals his output as a novelist. In the past three decades he has published over ninety stories and sketches, which he has gathered in eight collections. Although his literary reputation will no doubt ultimately rest on his novels, he is an able practitioner of short fiction. Gore Vidal has called him "a superb short-story writer,"[1] and he has been praised for his "thoroughly disciplined technical skill and artistry" in William Peden's standard study of modern American short fiction.[2] Occasionally Auchincloss's stories are overly contrived, and several of the longer ones seem outlines for novels, but at their best they are very good indeed. They display their author's psychological acuity and quick grasp of the ironies interwoven in complex human relationships. They achieve their effects — often pathetic as well as ironical — with admirable ease and economy of means, and in several of the stories that depict contemporary manners, an almost uncanny prescience accompanies Auchincloss's usual verisimilitude of detail.

When they have been published separately, Auchincloss's stories have appeared almost exclusively in general-circulation magazines. None have appeared in the "little" magazines, and, though Auchincloss has published three stories in *The New Yorker* and several in *Harper's* and *The Atlantic*, most of his work has made its way into magazines that cater to an even broader popular audience, magazines ranging from the old *Sat-*

urday Evening Post to *McCall's, Cosmopolitan,* and *Playboy.* In an age of shrinking markets for short fiction, Auchincloss has been fairly successful as a short-story writer, though he has achieved nothing on the scale of the commercial success of such earlier writers as John Marquand or even Edith Wharton.[3] Despite this modest success, however, it seems unlikely that he will participate in the revival of the short story apparently taking place in the 1980s. He is a member of an earlier generation than the currently popular writers, most of whom are in their thirties or forties.

Anyone who considers Auchincloss's short stories, however, encounters much the same paradox that is raised by the novels. Because the stories are not self-consciously difficult on the surface, they appeal to a popular audience. Yet, at the same time, they are marked by a profound literariness. While they meet the expectations of the average reader much more completely and easily than many stories published in, say, *The New Yorker,* they are frequently allusive and sometimes depend for their full effect upon knowledge of particular literary antecedents. Plot is also much more important in a typical Auchincloss story than in the stories of such writers as John Cheever and John Updike, both of whom share Auchincloss's interest in contemporary manners, but whose stories are often vignettes or brief impressionistic sketches. Auchincloss's stories, in contrast, often deal with events that develop over many years, and they may rely upon unexpected twists in plot or ironic conclusions. Almost always, they fulfill our conventional expectations for narrative, for a "good story."

Though the publications in which his stories have been published tell us much about Auchincloss's fiction, their wide appeal should not be overemphasized. Auchincloss has never aimed for a particular magazine audience. He has never been influenced by contracts with a magazine publisher, like Wharton and Marquand,

nor has he been exclusively associated with a single journal, like Updike or Cheever. Indeed, almost half of Auchincloss's stories were first published as parts of collections rather than in periodicals.

Within the obvious limits imposed by their author's
choice of social milieu and geographic location, Auchincloss's stories display a good deal of variety, and his interests as a story writer have changed as his career has
developed over the years. As in his early novels, Auchincloss is often interested in the weak — failures or misfits
who nonetheless possess peculiar strength despite their
awkwardness or oddity. Though the settings of the earlier stories are always richly realized and authentically
portrayed, Auchincloss's primary focus is upon the psychology of his characters. Throughout his career, he
has been interested in the figure of the artist; like Henry James he frequently depicts writers, artists, or people who spend their lives acquiring works of art. Even
though several collections are set in law firms, that has
not limited him from pursuing extralegal interests in
many of the stories involving lawyers. The more recent
stories, especially those written since the late 1960s,
have often tended to deal with social change in the worlds
they portray. With his sardonic wit and elegant eye,
Auchincloss has always been a fine chronicler of his
times. Some of his keenest commentaries on contemporary life are contained in his stories.

The Collections

More than most other short-story writers, Auchincloss
has attempted to construct unified collections of stories.
All his collections have coherent rationales — either a
unifying theme or a set of recurring characters. In some
cases Auchincloss's quest for unity has led to a literary
form that mediates between the usual collection of unrelated stories and the novel. Indeed, several reviewers

have mistakenly referred to two of his collections, *The Partners* and *The Winthrop Covenant*, as novels, and one of his recent novels, *The Book Class* (1984), comes close to being a collection of short stories. Since all the collections are so carefully planned, it is useful to describe each one briefly.

The first volume of stories, *The Injustice Collectors*, published in 1950, takes its title from a term coined by the psychoanalyst Edmund Bergler. Injustice collectors, as Auchincloss explains the term, are "people who are looking for injustice, even in a friendly world, because they suffer from a hidden need to feel that this world has wronged them." Each story focuses upon one such collector — the girl who destroys her chances of marriage to the most eligible young man in the Maine summer resort by unleashing her impossible parents in a nasty dispute with the boy's father, for example, or the LST commander who ruins his career by his inability to accept assistance from his executive officer in his first attempt to bring his ship alongside a larger supply ship. The characters and settings are typical of Auchincloss's early work: shy girls and matrons in New York society, expatriate Americans in Paris, eccentrics in Maine resort towns. Each story is related with precision and dry humor, often by a first-person narrator who is himself the subject of Auchincloss's ironic scrutiny. Because of its craftsmanship, *The Injustice Collectors* remains in many respects Auchincloss's finest collection.

The Romantic Egoists (1954) depicts a similar group of outsiders, many of whom also display the same self-destructive tendencies. Though the outsiders in *The Romantic Egoists* share a self-preoccupation that is romantic in its intensity, the collection is unified not so much by a common theme as by the use of a single first-person narrator, Peter Westcott, whose responses to the cruder, but more vital characters he observes often shape the individual stories. F. Scott Fitzgerald adopted an almost identical title, "The Romantic Egotists," for the original version of his first novel, *This Side of Paradise*, and Peter Westcott is Fitzgeraldian in his sympathy and urbanity. The characters and situations depicted in the collection are more varied than those in *The Injustice Collectors*. In addition to "The Great World and Timothy Colt," which Auchincloss reworked and expanded into the novel of the same title, there is another law-firm story, as well as a fine story about prep-school life, "Billy and the Gargoyles," two stories about life in the U.S. Navy, a Fitzgeraldian study of a rich schoolmate, a sketch of an elegant divorcée transformed by her boorish second husband, and a powerful story about a middle-aged American in Venice, "The Gemlike Flame." Even in *The Romantic Egoists* there are hints of the unifying techniques that characterize the more tightly integrated collections that follow. Auchincloss repeats characters and settings. Lorna Treadway, the elegant divorcee in one story, appears again as a minor character in "The Great World and Timothy Colt." The first two stories in the collection deal with overlapping events from Peter Westcott's prep-school days.

Auchincloss's next collection, *Powers of Attorney*, published in 1963, makes full use of interlocking characters and situations. All the stories involve the partners and employees of the Wall Street law firm of Tower, Tilney & Webb. Rather than producing boring homogeneity, this unifying device yields a broad panorama of characters from secretaries to senior partners. Several of the stories portray weak or pathetic characters — the old partner who is so irrelevant to the firm that no one even blames him for a costly mistake in a will that he has officially approved, or the nostalgic executive secretary at a farewell reception who delivers a tipsy speech punctuated by her own hiccups — while others portray the hard-driving litigators and managing partners in the firm.

At the center of the collection is Clitus Tilney, the head of the firm, and the man who has transformed Tower, Tilney into a modern, highly efficient corporate organization. Tilney is not above forcing a rival representing the older, less organized style of legal practice out of the firm by giving secret advice to the other side in a lawsuit brought by the rival. Although Tilney's conduct is unethical, Auchincloss does not sit in judgment. He does not see the senior partner as radically evil, and in the final story in the collection, "The Crowning Offer," he celebrates Tilney's innate pleasure in practicing law. As in *A Law for the Lion* and *The Great World and Timothy Colt*, Auchincloss stresses the bureaucratization of legal practice and the ways in which modern Wall Street firms have become subservient to their largest corporate clients.[4] Although every story involves a member or employee of the firm, several stories diverge from law-firm life per se to describe the personal dilemmas of wives or clients.

In *Tales of Manhattan* (1967), Auchincloss again uses the device of interconnected stories. In this volume, however, the tales are grouped in three separate sets. The first section, "Memories of an Auctioneer," includes five stories told in the first person by Roger Jordan, the vice-president of a leading auction gallery. The final story in the section, "The Money Juggler," which Auchincloss later expanded into the novel *A World of Profit*, recounts four friends' memories of their college classmate, a shady businessman whose tactics they deplore, but from whose activities they have all profited. In each of the preceding stories, items offered for sale by Roger's gallery lead him into interesting quests that reveal the personalities or lives of their owners. As in *The House of Five Talents*, material possessions take on a life of their own, embodying essential traits of their owners.

The second group of stories in the volume, "Arnold & Degener," is another law-firm series. Each story is cast as a chapter in the firm's history written by a specific partner. Here the very act of telling becomes an act of appropriation as each writer attempts to impose his own image on the firm, to assert his dominance over his subject, or to express long-concealed anger or jealousy. As in *The Rector of Justin*, which immediately preceded this collection, and in *The House of the Prophet*, published twelve years later, writing biography becomes an attempt to assert personal power as well as a search for the true pattern of events.

The final section, entitled "The Matrons," contains three stories and a one-act play. At the center of each work is the sort of upper-class woman well beyond middle age for whom Auchincloss seems to have special sympathy and affection. Two of the stories depict figures from the turn-of-the-century New York described in *The House of Five Talents*. One is an aged "extra man," somewhat like the protagonist in Edith Wharton's "After Holbein," who is taken under the powerful wing of his wealthy hostess. The other is a gentle alcoholic who becomes for a brief time manager of the Metropolitan Opera House, whose experiences are recalled by his elderly niece who knew him in her girlhood. Another story is a study of the relations between a "perfect," noninterfering mother and her daughters on the occasion of her seventieth birthday.

The relation between a mother and her grown daughter generates the action of Auchincloss's slightly Ibsenesque play, *The Club Bedroom*, which was performed at the A.P.A. Theatre in December 1967 and televised on the New York educational channel. Influenced by the popular monologues of Ruth Draper, the play is Auchincloss's only stage production. It does not seem out of place in *Tales of Manhattan*, for the events of the plot build to an ironic climax reminiscent of the endings of several of the stories. In the final scene, Mrs. Ruggles, the genteel but impecunious protagonist whose

dwindling resources help support her daughter's affair
with a married man, is denied her one small hope for
the remaining years of her life — a permanent room in
the fashionable ladies club to which she belongs. The only person who might conceivably have a grudge against
her, the wife of the man with whom her daughter is involved, happens ironically to be chairwoman of the committee that must approve requests for rooms in the club.

Auchincloss's fifth collection, *Second Chance: Tales
of Two Generations*, was published in 1970. Although
not all the stories are equally successful, *Second Chance*
is arguably Auchincloss's best collection of stories of
manners. As the subtitle suggests, many of the stories
deal in some way with the so-called generation gap, a
source of much painful discussion in the late 1960s. Auchincloss is concerned not only with the relationships
between parents and children but also with the connections between grandparents and grandchildren, old people and young, contemporary figures and their historical antecedents; and he is interested as well in different
"generations" of behavior within the lives of individuals. In the fine title story of the volume, for example, a
middle-aged business man abandons the assumptions of
his own generation and lives out the "new morality" of
the young. *Second Chance* is decidedly Auchincloss's
most topical collection. "The Cathedral Builder" was
obviously suggested by the decision of the Episcopal Di-
ocese of New York during the late 1960s to abandon
plans to finish the construction of the Cathedral of St.
John the Divine, and other stories in the collection involve a black English teacher at a private school and
the takeover of a publishing house by a large conglomerate.

In *The Partners* (1974), perhaps his most popular
collection, Auchincloss returns to the technique of interlocking stories involving members of a large Wall Street
law firm. *The Partners* is also his most highly unified

collection. The central character, Beekman ("Beeky")
Ehninger, a senior partner in the firm of Shepard, Putney & Cox, appears in all but two of the fourteen stories and is thus far more fully developed than Auchincloss's usual protagonists. In contrast to Clitus Tilney,
the aggressive, self-confident senior partner in *Powers
of Attorney*, Beeky is a conciliator and negotiator who
often doubts himself. Married, like Michael Farish in
Venus in Sparta, to an older woman who has been divorced, he is troubled by a milder and nondebilitating
version of Michael's sexual insecurity. As in the previous
law-firm collections, Auchincloss provides a number of
incisive views of human relationships in large corporate
firms. Though several stories are satiric or critical, the
collection as a whole comes around—in the final story
especially—to a wry but genial endorsement of the special desire of some men to practice law in firms. Having
negotiated the merger of Shepard, Putney & Cox with
a larger firm headed by an old prep-school rival of his,
Beeky decides to retire. He makes the decision at a party, in a kind of comic epiphany: he will retire from the
firm only to set up "a crazy new law firm" composed entirely of "duplicates," the redundant lawyers who must
be dropped from the two firms because of the merger.
At the end of the story, Beeky goes to bed happily, clutch-
ing this new "fierce little resolution." In all the stories
in which he appears, Beeky's great gifts are his gregar-
iousness, loyalty, and fellow-feeling; he is, above all, a
man who shares the love Auchincloss's own father felt
for his law firm as a human institution.

   The Winthrop Covenant, Auchincloss's seventh collection, grew out of the American Bicentennial in 1976.
It is an attempt to explore one strand in the American
character—"the rise and fall of the Puritan ethic in New
England and New York"—as displayed in the lives of
members of a single family, the Winthrops. Written especially for this volume, the nine stories cover the years

from 1630 to 1975. Though Auchincloss does not fully achieve his ambitious historical aim, the collection contains several fine stories, such as "The Arbiter" and "In the Beauty of the Lilies," set in those particular periods of American history in which Auchincloss is most at home. The volume as a whole reflects Auchincloss's growing historical consciousness, which will be considered more closely in the discussion of the eight novels he has written since the appearance of *The Winthrop Covenant*.

In his most recent collection, *Narcissa and Other Fables* (1983), Auchincloss returns to the looser organization found in his earliest collections. Though none of the stories are fables in the conventional sense of the term, each deals in some way with a favorite Auchincloss theme: the moral confusion that arises when older values lose their legitimacy and are not replaced by anything even remotely satisfactory. As a sort of coda, there are twelve "Sketches of the Seventies" — a new genre for Auchincloss but one well suited to his sensibility. None of the sketches is longer than a page or so, but each captures a moment in which the ironies or shortcomings of fashionable life in the 1970s are revealed. The range of settings, situations, and types of stories in the volume — from sketches to long stories, from a tale about an elegant expatriate in Florence in the 1920s to a wry first-person narrative by the victim of a corporate takeover in the 1970s — reminds one of the variety that Auchincloss is capable of and attests to his continuing vitality as a short-story writer.

Because of their sheer numbers, it is impossible to analyze all, or even a significant fraction, of Auchincloss's stories in detail here. The rest of this chapter, however, will suggest the variety and range of the stories as well as some of Auchincloss's artistry by considering a sampling of his work: two strong early stories; a series of stories on a single theme, writers and writing;

and several recent tales in which Auchincloss offers keen commentary on the changing manners of the last two decades.

"Greg's Peg"

Most of the early stories tend to be more obviously polished performances than the more relaxed stories in some of the later volumes, and two of them, "Greg's Peg" and "The Gemlike Flame," are especially powerful and carefully crafted. The former story, published in *The Injustice Collectors*, depicts the improbable rise to social prominence of a thirty-five-year-old innocent, Gregory Bakewell, who is taken up by the members of the fast set at a Maine summer resort. The tale is told by the middle-aged headmaster of a boarding school who befriends Greg and urges him to make something of himself. In a carefully controlled narrative, Auchincloss sketches the strange rise and fall of Greg, while at the same time revealing the enigmatic character of the narrator.

Greg is an unprepossessing, even grotesque character, "an oddly shaped and odd-looking person, wide in the hips and narrow in the shoulders," whose "face, very white and round and smooth, had, somewhat inconsistently, the uncertain dignity of a thin aquiline nose and large, owl-like eyes." Dressed in white flannels and a red blazer — garb seldom seen outside a schoolboy's sixth-form graduation ceremony — Greg is "a guileless child" who still lives with his widowed mother. Having been educated by private tutors, he has never left home or really done anything with his life. Thus he presents a challenge to the headmaster, who takes him mountain-climbing and advises him to spend the winter away from his mother so that he can "learn to think." Though Greg seems deaf to the narrator's appeals, he does respond in his own way. Over the next three summers, he carries out an elaborate campaign to make himself a social leader in the resort community. Beginning at the bridge table with his mother's elderly friends, Greg gradually comes to meet their children and grandchildren and is finally adopted by the hard-drinking, sophisticated set in the resort. In showing Greg's social progress, Auchincloss provides a succinct anatomy of the various generations and groups in an old-line summer resort.

Greg becomes a "character" in Anchor Harbor, and thus immune to criticism, but his new role as "one of the respected citizens of the summer colony" does not really represent an advance for him. Though "his spotless white panama was to be seen bobbing on the bench of judges at the children's swimming meet," and he has become a sponsor for the summer theater and outdoor concerts, his winning costume at the annual fancy dress ball reveals his true nature: twice in a row, he goes dressed as a baby. Greg starts to drink too much, and, as his mother realizes, his frenetic new life is killing him. The climax of the story occurs when, for the last time, Greg does the little drunken dance that gives the story its title. The narrator, who has carefully avoided seeing "Greg's peg" before, observes his actions at the tennis club dance with fascination and horror:

His eyes were closed, and his long hair, disarrayed, was streaked down over his sweating face. His mouth, half open, emitted little snorts as his feet capered about in a preposterous jig that could only be described as an abortive effort at tap dancing. His arms moved back and forth as if he were striding along; his head was thrown back; his body shimmied from side to side. It was not really a dance at all; it was a contortion, a writhing. It looked more as if he were moving in a doped sleep or twitching at the end of a gallows. The lump of pallid softness that was his body seemed to be responding for the first time to his consciousness; it was only thus, after all, that the creature could use it. (*Injustice Collectors*, p. 244)

Greg's macabre dance is cut short by some rowdy visitors who hoist him on their shoulders in mock triumph
and throw him into the swimming pool. The young
visitors are put to rout by Greg's indignant friends, who
fish him out of the pool, but he is never the same again.
He seems to realize that even the admirers who applauded
him and called for his dance that summer were really
on the side of the young men. Rather than become a
social leader, he has turned into a pet or mascot. The
Bakewells do not return to Anchor Harbor the next summer, and two years later the narrator learns that Greg
has died in Cape Cod, where he is remembered dimly,
if at all, as "a strange, pallid individual" carrying a
marketbasket for his mother.

Like the characters in the other stories of *The Injustice Collectors*, Greg is impelled to seek out his own
humiliation. Part of the effect of the story comes from
the pathos and oddity of his situation. Yet Auchincloss
carefully avoids the predictable psychologizing that a
character like Greg might evoke. Rather than the conventional domineering mother one might expect, Mrs.
Bakewell turns out to be a brisk, efficient woman who
does not pressure her son to stay at home and who recognizes far more clearly than the narrator the evil and
destructiveness of the frivolous society Greg has entered.
Indeed, she is both a comic figure, as she announces to
the headmaster that she has read his books and disapproves of them, and a moral voice in the story, when
she questions his belief in heightened awareness as the
ultimate goal in life.

It is Auchincloss's expert handling of the narrator,
however, that gives "Greg's Peg" its distinctive interest.
Though honest and perceptive, the headmaster also has
a gloomy, misanthropic side. When he first meets Greg,
he is still recovering from the death of his wife. He takes
pleasure in coming to Anchor Harbor, a place not unlike
Bar Harbor, Maine, in the early fall after most of the

summer people have gone. His headmasterly desire to
improve Greg's character leads, ironically, to Greg's
downfall, and his partial complicity in the downfall
gives the story its bleak edge. After he finds that Greg
has never heard of him or his wife, the headmaster finds
himself "oddly determined to imprint my ego on the
empty face of all he took for granted." For him Greg is
"a perfect *tabula rasa*," and he eagerly seizes the "responsibility of writing the first line." His grand miscal-
culation is to presume that the blank surface that Greg
presents is capable of being inscribed with any sort of
definite message. Greg remains, throughout, the "lump
of pallid softness" that is revealed in his little dance, incapable of being shaped by the headmaster's version of
muscular Christianity.

When the headmaster finds out what his advice has
wrought, he angrily abandons his protégé. A couple of
times thereafter, and especially as he watches the grotesque little dance, he thinks he glimpses an appeal for
rescue in Greg's eyes, but he is uncertain and takes no
action. When Mrs. Bakewell suggests that he save Greg,
he points out that "people don't *save* people at Anchor
Harbor." The headmaster is of course not directly responsible for Greg's downfall — he could not, after all,
have predicted Greg's elaborate campaign for social self-
advancement. But the vehemence with which he rejects
Greg's overtures for continued friendship and the im-
passive tone in which he relates the story suggest puzzling depths in his character. One shares the narrator's
uneasy interest in Greg's fate, while Auchincloss skillfully leads one to ask uncomfortable questions about the
narrator's own role. Though it might initially seem merely a story about an eccentric in the fashionable setting
of an old summer resort, "Greg's Peg" is an elegantly
unsettling examination of a perceptive but flawed individual who intervenes in someone else's life without fully
knowing his own motives.

"The Gemlike Flame"

"The Gemlike Flame," first published in *New World Writing* for 1953, and reprinted in *The Romantic Egoists*, is a brilliantly developed portrait of another lonely figure. The story depicts Clarence McClintock, an American expatriate in Venice, at a crucial and revealing moment in his life. Like "Greg's Peg," the story, in its sympathy and focused intensity, is a good example of Auchincloss's early style at its best.

Clarence McClintock is seen through the eyes of his cousin Peter Westcott, the young novelist who appears in all the stories in *The Romantic Egoists*. Peter is an ideal narrator, a sympathetic observer who knows Clarence's past but is objective and honest about his own responses. He encounters Clarence — a sort of legend in his family, "personally distinguished and prematurely bizarre" — on a visit to Venice. Emotionally scarred by a domineering mother who waged a bitter custody battle for him when he was a child, Clarence had come to Italy many years before "to admire it and be left alone." Since he had never bothered to make any friends in Venice during all this time, Clarence clings to Peter as an embodiment of a past that remains very real to him. When Peter is beginning to feel trapped, he introduces his cousin to Neddy Bane, a charming but feckless college classmate who has left his wife and now dabbles in painting. Inevitably, their relationship is broken up by Clarence's mother, who arrives in Venice for an elaborate masked ball that represents everything the serious and almost ascetic Clarence abhors. "Quite remorseless in her pursuit of pleasure," his mother in effect steals Neddy away. At the end of the story, having desperately tried to keep his friend away from the ball, Clarence catches sight of Neddy in a silly costume kneeling at the feet of his mother, and he stalks off alone into the night.

Early in the story Clarence warns Peter that he "burns with a hard gemlike flame." The phrase, from the Conclusion to Walter Pater's *Studies in the History of the Renaissance*, points to the heart of the story: Clarence's unexpected intensity as revealed in perhaps his only serious relationship with another human being. Practically everyone except Peter — and especially Clarence's mother — is eager to see his friendship with Neddy as a tawdry homosexual affair, but Clarence regards it, ironically, as an ideal love and his own highest contribution to Art, insofar as he supplies the order and discipline Neddy needs to paint. That Neddy is a totally unworthy object of devotion ultimately means very little, for Clarence has found "a love that I've looked for all my life." Even Peter has difficulty understanding that there is something ineffable in his love, "a quality in his feelings that was over and above what is called sublimation, a quality that made of it something higher than — ." Peter's sentence breaks off as he realizes how hopeless the task of explaining that "something higher" would be, and the story proceeds to the final scene, in which Clarence turns away to guard the gemlike flame alone: "Should not true flame-tenders, the people like himself, enjoy in solitude the special compensations of their devotion?" he seems to ask. Clarence continues to walk resolutely away from the scene of the ball, as described in the strong final image of the story, "away from the lighted palace and the gondolas that swarmed about it like carp."

"The Gemlike Flame" is a fine story not because of the exotic, Jamesian situation of wealthy Americans abroad, but because Auchincloss refuses to cheat the reader of the complexity of Clarence's feelings, even though he offers no alternative to the psychological explanation that comes to Peter's mind. Despite the abundance of specific detail, the power of the story comes from the absolute economy of its essentials. In *A Writer's*

Capital, Auchincloss recalls his extreme pleasure when Norman Mailer told him at a party that he would not mind having written the story himself. Though Mailer's sensibility and interests are radically different from Auchincloss's, he was right to admire this story.

Stories on Writers and Writing

Peter Westcott's presence in all the stories of *The Romantic Egoists* is only a suggestion of the prominence of writers and the act of writing in Auchincloss's stories. No fewer than ten stories are directly concerned with writing fiction, biography, or autobiography, and the essential situations and characters in another half dozen stories are drawn from previous works of literature. Several of the latter stories are explicit homages to James or Wharton. Given Auchincloss's admiration for James, this persistent interest in art and the artist as a theme for short fiction is hardly surprising. What is distinctive, however, is Auchincloss's repeated attention to the effects of all sorts of writing on not only authors but other people as well. The stories about writers and writing, which come from all periods of his career, are among his most characteristic and effective.

In Auchincloss's fiction, the activity of writing is invariably more than a simple recording of events or a form of creative expression. Writing may well be a mode of communication or self-revelation, but at the same time it may also be an act of aggression, a defense mechanism, or a means of appropriating, and thereby controlling, someone else's life. This sense of writing-as-appropriation, as has been suggested, is particularly prevalent in some of the law-firm stories (as well as in the biography-novels, *The Rector of Justin* and *The House of the Prophet*). One of the "Arnold & Degener" stories in *Tales of Manhattan* raises the issue in a striking, though comic fashion.

In "The Senior Partner's Ghosts," Sylvaner Price decides to write the biography of Guthrie Arnold, founder of Arnold & Degener and his mentor. Though he appears to others as "a man of no accessories, no appendages, no stray bits or loose ends," Price fancies himself a romantic a la Victor Hugo. Unlike the usual law-firm history, his biography will be a work of art, a vivid evocation of Arnold's true personality. As Price sits down to dictate portions of his book, horrible revelations of cutthroat buccaneering practices on Arnold's part tumble out of his mouth. Shortly thereafter, as if possessed by "the evil genius of Guthrie Arnold," Price makes a speech at a meeting of the firm urging his partners to take business away from a rival firm whose senior corporate expert is dying of cancer, and a few days later he finds himself involuntarily tearing up a page from the will of a deceased client. After the latter episode, Price suffers a stroke and is hospitalized. His partners make him consult a psychiatrist, who assures him that his visions are merely the result of long-suppressed guilt. After one more disquieting excursion into sensational biography, Price gives up private composition and free association and dictates an ordinary, boring firm history in the presence of his censorious secretary. Though the new biography kills off any humanity in its subject, "what did it matter, so long as there was peace?"

On one level, "The Senior Partner's Ghosts" offers a humorous explanation for the dullness of many official histories of law firms. At the same time it also points up the disparity between the respectable front of the large corporate law firm and the aggressive activities of some of its partners. Even if Sylvaner Price's memories of Guthrie Arnold are the product of an overheated imagination as the psychiatrist suggests, they describe plausible instances of dubious professional conduct — behavior no doubt occasionally encountered by the lawyers who first read the story in *The Virginia Law Review*.

More generally, the story is a study of an ordinary, seemingly bloodless professional man who cherishes a secret romantic streak in his nature. Price is silently pleased, for example, to learn that a young partner's wife has compared him to King Philip II at the Escorial. The comic denouement of the story suggests how difficult it is for a man like Price to escape the bounds of the professional persona he has assiduously cultivated for forty years. Perhaps the psychiatrist is right: in Price's mind, only his godlike mentor Guthrie Arnold is permitted to get away with expressing the romantic side of his nature. Yet, like several other psychiatric opinions in Auchincloss's fiction, this diagnosis, though correct in its way, seems reductive. Sylvaner Price creates his own hero and a myth of the firm, which he can control, but the hidden power of the subconscious mind is more difficult to contain. Though its tone is fanciful rather than portentous, "The Senior Partner's Ghosts" reminds us of the dangerous power of the writer's imagination. It is not a major story, but it illustrates Auchincloss's masterful skill in balancing a number of disparate elements in a single story without capsizing what is admittedly a light vessel.

In two other law-firm stories, both from *Powers of Attorney*, Auchincloss further explores the uneasy connection between writing and human relationships. For Morris Madison, the tax attorney in "The Single Reader," writing fulfills some of the same secret desires that it reflected in the mind of Sylvaner Price. Madison, however, is not troubled by "ghosts" as Price was. Over a period of thirty years he fills more than fifty morocco-bound volumes of his diary with carefully polished and often bitingly satiric entries. As the years go by, the diary takes over his life. He rearranges all the engagements outside the office in order to provide the best possible raw material for the diary and even leaves money in his will for its posthumous publication. When he shows a few representative volumes to the woman he wishes to marry — the "single reader" of the title — she recoils in horror, not because the diary is bad (it is brilliant), but because she fears becoming a human sacrifice to its insatiable appetite.

In "The 'True Story' of Lavinia Todd," writing is not only self-expression but also a rueful emblem for failed communication and the inconspicuous self of the writer. Mrs. Todd, a middle-aged woman who is deserted by her husband, pours out the story of her betrayal in a long account that is accepted for publication in a woman's magazine. Rather than offend her husband, the candid story of their marriage and his callous behavior seems to bring him back to her side. He invites her out for dinner, praises the story, and asks for a reconciliation. She discovers, however, that he has never read the story and has only praised her work because his colleagues and several powerful clients have expressed their admiration. The "true" Lavinia Todd remains unread, and the art of the story, which has merely mirrored life, is once again mirrored in her own life.

The stories in which Auchincloss borrows situations or characters from previous authors may strike contemporary readers as overly derivative. This is not the case at all. Somewhat like the early films of François Truffaut, the best of these stories are *hommages*, or tributes, to Auchincloss's masters, James and Wharton. A good example of this type of tribute in its simplest form is "The Evolution of Lorna Treadway." This slickly written tale from *The Romantic Egoists* involves a sophisticated divorcée who marries a boorish Texas oilman and adopts all his values, becoming vulgar and trivial herself as she throws large parties to advance her husband's business career. While the narrator of the story talks with the husband, he momentarily plays with a Jamesian conclusion for his tale. "How neat it would have been," he thinks, if the oilman "had become with marriage the suave, accomplished man of the world, if

he and Lorna, in other words, had changed places," so
that people would pity him for being tied down to the
giddy, unsophisticated "bride of his earlier and poorer
days." But, of course, "that would have been strictly fiction." Though the pliant heroine might have come out
of an Edith Wharton story such as "The Other Two,"
Auchincloss's story remains firmly anchored in the sharply defined reality of the fashionable world it describes.

In "The Diner Out," from *The Partners*, Auchincloss takes the basic situation of Wharton's "After Holbein" and grafts it onto a story about an aging attorney, Burrill Hume, who faces the bleak prospect of
retirement from practice. The grafting is not quite successful — and perhaps few if any of the young attorneys
who first read the story in *Juris Doctor* would have
caught the allusion. But the final lines, in which Hume
recognizes his approaching death, acquire added reso-
nance by their direct reference to the ending of Wharton's story, in which the senile, dying protagonist, leaving a dinner party given by an even more senile old lady,
takes a "step forward, to where a moment before the
pavement had been — and where now there was nothing." Auchincloss has transmuted Wharton's mordant
comedy into sympathetic humor tinged by pathos.

Auchincloss renders his most elaborate and subtle
tribute to Henry James in "The Ambassadress." In this
story from *The Injustice Collectors*, he reenvisions the
main characters of James's late novel *The Ambassadors*
from the perspective of Chad Newsome, the young man
who must be rescued from the clutches of Europe, rather
than through the consciousness of Lambert Strether, the
middle-aged protagonist and rescuer in the novel. Auchincloss's central character and narrator, Tony Rives,
is a somewhat older Chad Newsome endowed with a
good deal of Lambert Strether's sensibility. The rescue
mission in the story is carried out by Tony's older sister
Edith MacLean, who parallels Sarah Pocock in James's

version, but who also reflects some aspects of Strether's experience. Edith not only manages to bring her brother home but also gets him to marry her husband's niece — something her counterpart in the novel had been ordered to do but does not accomplish. In Auchincloss's ironic version of the tale, Edith's triumph is even greater, for it also includes taking away Gwladys Kane, the older woman to whom Tony had been attached, and making her one of her own friends. Edith's deepening relationship with Gwladys excludes Tony, which throws him into renewed acquaintance with the niece and eventually leads to his marriage. Strether's respect for the older woman in the novel (Madame de Vionnet) is transformed in Auchincloss's story into something that appears to be an instance of successful social manipulation by a powerful woman. And yet, in the concluding scene of the story, which takes place at his wedding, Tony still does not know whether his sister consciously plotted to draw Gwladys away from him or things merely worked out to her advantage by a lucky coincidence.

"The Ambassadress" is not merely a witty reworking of a Jamesian situation but a finely articulated tale of complex relationships in a closely knit group of people. As might be expected in a short story rather than a novel, Tony is a more limited character than Strether. In Tony's appreciation of his expatriate life, one finds none of Strether's luminous vision of European culture. Tony's reeducation, unlike Strether's, teaches him the power of strong family ties, which can even reach across the Atlantic. Tony returns to New York to be married, not with Strether's sense of renunciation and all it entails, but with a sense of how life is determined — albeit for the best — by forces we do not understand. Auchincloss is finally more interested in the complex psychological dynamics at work in a given situation than in James's theme of enlightenment and renunciation. The result is more realistic; though not so richly resonant, nonetheless subtle: a sharper, brisker story, but still a work worthy of the master.

The three stories that focus directly upon professional writers, "The Question of the Existence of Waring Stohl," "The Novelist of Manners," and "The Arbiter," show the aggressive or hostile impulses in writers who make use of people around them as material for their art. Auchincloss, a writer who himself draws much of the material for his fiction from life, shows a decided tendency to stress this exploitive side of the artist. In the earliest of the three tales, "The Question of the Existence of Waring Stohl," reprinted in *Tales of Manhattan*, a distinguished professor of English befriends one of his students, a young novelist with very little talent and an obnoxious personality. No one understands why he goes out of his way to cultivate the young man's acquaintance until the novelist dies and leaves him his unpublished journal. The journal becomes the central piece of evidence in the professor's last and greatest work: a literary history in which the young writer becomes the embodiment of the superficiality and vacuousness of his era, a "non-author" whose novel is called a "non-book." The professor wins a Pulitzer prize, and the young novelist receives a negative sort of immortality. In "The Arbiter," one of the stories in *The Winthrop Covenant*, the novelist Ada Guest bases one of the characters in her best novel, "a sterile dilettante, who is trying to hide his business failure in a drawing room success," on her longtime friend Adam Winthrop, and she seems likely to make similar use of her husband later. Though Auchincloss's primary interest in this fine story is the relationship that develops between the two men, Ada shows the same voracity in using material from life for her art.

Why this strange voracity in appropriating other people's lives? For the novelist of manners, as for the historian or journalist, it may be inevitable. Discussing class distinctions in an essay on Marquand and O'Hara,

Auchincloss has observed that the novelist of manners
"has two points of view about the society in which he
lives: that of a citizen and that of an artist. The latter
is concerned only with the suitability of society as material for his art. Just as a liberal journalist may secretly
rejoice at the rise of a Senator McCarthy because of the
opportunity it affords him to write brilliant and scathing
denunciations of demogogues, so will the eye of the novelist of manners light up at the first glimpse of social injustice." So too, within the limits of human decency or
the libel laws, the novelist of manners may exploit the
human material he finds around him, often in a seemingly amoral fashion.

"The Novelist of Manners" looks most directly at
this exploitive tendency and suggests it may also be a
weapon for striking back when the author is wounded.
Published in *The Partners*, the story describes the relationship between a young lawyer and the novelist Dana
Clyde. It is at once an interesting psychological study
and an oblique defense of the novel of manners in the
late twentieth century. The hero of the story, Leslie
Carter, a junior partner in Shepard, Putney & Cox, has
been sent abroad to take charge of the firm's Paris office. A frustrated novelist who unsuccessfully tried to
write his own *Great Gatsby* in college, he eagerly makes
his way into French society, much like the young Proust.
He is delighted to find that his firm must represent Dana
Clyde, whose society novels he has admired since college,
in a libel suit brought by someone maligned in his latest
book. After the suit is settled, he attaches himself to
Clyde as a kind of disciple, urging him to write "the last
great novel of manners of the western world" — the great
work he himself could never write. His life takes on new
meaning, for he now has a mission: "to save Dana Clyde
and make him compose his masterpiece."

When, however, after some urging, Clyde retires
to a hillside in Malaga to write the great book, he myste-

riously breaks off all connection with the younger man. The reason for the break is revealed only when Leslie reads the manuscript of the new novel. One of the main characters is a wickedly satiric potrait of himself as an absurd young lawyer who becomes the fifth husband of the novel's heroine, but who proves impotent on his wedding night and commits suicide. On his return to Paris, Clyde avoids Leslie entirely, and Leslie must seek an explanation for the malevolence of the portrait from the novelist's wife. Quite aware of what might happen all along, Mrs. Clyde had tried to warn Leslie, but he would not listen. Instead, his badgering has forced Clyde to recognize that he is an irrevocably second-rate writer. As Leslie admits, the new novel is "Dana Clyde at his best," but it is hardly the "last great novel of manners" he had predicted. In creating the character of the young lawyer, Clyde has gotten revenge against Leslie for destroying the saving illusion on which he has operated for many years — the idea that, if only he had worked harder, he could have written another *Madame Bovary*. At the end of the story Leslie recognizes that he has been a fool. The novel of manners "*does* still have a function," he says, "if only to prove to a poor thing like Leslie Carter that he doesn't want to write one any more."

Considered as a whole, the story recalls a pattern found in several of James's stories, in which a second-rate artist is protected by a wife who clearly sees her husband's lack of genius and the complication and interest of the plot arise from the entry of some third person who upsets the equilibrium achieved by the couple. In Auchincloss's variation of the pattern, however, Leslie is innocent of any intention to denigrate Dana Clyde's work. After having been attacked in the novel, he learns several lessons. He recognizes the folly of his own hidden aspirations to be a novelist and the ridiculousness of trying to live out those aspirations in someone else's career, and he is presumably a bit wiser about rushing in to meddle in someone else's life. Under Auchincloss's scrutiny, a seemingly casual relationship turns out to have multiple, ramifying effects.

Viewed in its biographical and historical context, however, "The Novelist of Manners" gains further interest. The story takes place in 1972, in a period when, as Dana Clyde is well aware, the novel of manners is in eclipse. "Oh, I have a following yet, I grant," he says to Leslie. "There are plenty of old girls and boys who still take me to the hospital for their hysterectomies and prostates. But the trend is against me. The young don't read me. The literary establishment scorns me." Clyde's plaint is heard frequently in Auchincloss's writings of the late 1960s and 1970s: "I have always dealt with the great world. The top of the heap. How people climbed up and what they found when they got there. That was perfectly valid when the bright young people were ambitious for money and social position. But now they don't care for such things. They care about stopping wars and saving the environment and cleaning up the ghettos. And they're right too. When the world's going to pieces, who has time to talk about good form and good taste?" Leslie suspects that Clyde's endorsement of social activism is not quite sincere, but the general question remains valid and pertains to Auchincloss's work as well.

Though much of the passage sounds as though it might fit Auchincloss himself, James Tuttleton is right to maintain that Dana Clyde is not Auchincloss.[5] As is true of many of his characters, there are elements of Auchincloss in Clyde, but there are also details from Auchincloss's personal history in Leslie Carter as well. Like Leslie, Auchincloss was impelled on his way to law school by the failure of a novel he had written in his last year at college. Though Dana Clyde is not Auchincloss, it is nevertheless correct to see the story in the context of Auchincloss's own work and the tradition of the novel of manners in the 1970s. As usual, Auchincloss keeps his claims for what he and others like him are doing quite modest and somewhat sardonic. Leslie's final words about the function of the novel of manners do not constitute a ringing general defense. But, as the story itself suggests, this sort of fiction is certain to endure in some form. Wherever human folly displays itself in faulty behavior, there is a need for the novel of manners, and, whether or not it is in current critical favor, fiction that evokes a particular time and place always seems to find an audience.

Obviously, however, even the most faithful rendering of the manners and customs of a given era will not necessarily yield great art. In a story from his most recent collection, Auchincloss carefully distinguishes between life and art and takes a more sanguine view of the writer in his role as an artist. Worthington Whitson, the absurd Mauve Decade dandy who is the protagonist in "The Artistic Personality," has, like the characters in the other stories, been wronged by a novelist, Alistair Temple. But Auchincloss varies the pattern. Rather than exploiting Whitson as a character in his fiction, Temple had staged an elaborate drama in real life that led to Whitson's downfall as "the acknowledged *arbiter elegantarium* of Fifth Avenue and Newport" at the end of the nineteenth century. The reader sees Temple obliquely, through Whitson's indignant remarks almost twenty-five years later in a conversation with Bernard Berenson, who admires one of Temple's novels and wants to know more about him.

As he questions Whitson about Temple, Berenson speculates about the artistic personality. Temple had cleverly engineered a situation in which the prominent hostess with whom Whitson was allied was tempted, against Whitson's advice, into attending a ball given by an unacceptable new family. This event effectively destroyed Whitson's authority as a social arbiter and put an end to his grandiose scheme to set standards for entry into New York society. For Whitson, Temple's actions represent betrayal — a betrayal all the more perfidious because the novelist arranged the episode deliberately "to divert himself by creating a drama in New York society." But for Berenson his actions are those of an artist. "You mean he constructed a scenario for his own inspiration? He modeled a plot out of real life? And then never used it?" he asks. "Perhaps," he suggests to Whitson, "you provided the scaffolding, my friend, which he had later to remove" when he wrote his greatest novel. Berenson toys with Whitson throughout the dialogue, however, and when the absurd Whitson decides at the end of the story that perhaps he can claim some renown for having helped a great novelist, Berenson laughingly rejects his own speculation.

In the course of the conversation one learns that Temple not only has played a clever trick on Whitson but that he himself was the most ardent of social climbers, in no way removed from the society he set out to satirize. Temple's actions and his character in life finally do not matter, for according to Berenson one "must distinguish . . . between an artist's individual personality and his artistic one." In the light of his masterpiece, Temple's personal failings are irrelevant: "The artistic personality is the creator. And that is something totally detached from the vulgar appetites, from greed, from Mammon, from snobbishness and social ambition. Alistair Temple the man may have been everything you think. But Alistair Temple the artist had not the smallest ounce of worldliness. Of that I am convinced." Though there is much else going on in the story — in his conversation with Whitson, for example, Berenson himself may be constructing a "scenario" not unlike Temple — Auchincloss provides, in the distinction between the two personalities, a final line of defense for all the voracious novelists in his fiction. Though it is presented in a complicated, oblique fashion and hedged about by ironies and qualifications, Auchincloss's view of the writer in "The Artistic Personality" is essentially Romantic. Art, especially great art, works in a mysterious way its wonders to perform; by some unfathomable process, the work of art, if it is worthy, transcends its creator. Like Henry James, Auchincloss accepts only the highest view of the writer's art.

Chronicles of Our Time

"But why is the artist whose subject is society any better than that society?" Whitson asks Berenson in the story just discussed. "Because he must see it in a different light. He illuminates it," Berenson replies. At their best, Auchincloss's stories about contemporary life do indeed manage to illuminate society and thereby illuminate the lives of everyone.

Since the beginning of his career as a writer, Auchincloss has kept careful watch on what was going on in the various worlds he has inhabited. In his first novel, *The Indifferent Children*, he captures the essential futility of the military bureaucracy, and in *The Great World and Timothy Colt* he presents a definitive account of life among young associates in the large corporate law firms during the early 1950s. Because of their smaller scope, however, the short stories have provided him with an especially useful medium for observing particular changes in business, society, and the professions. Indeed, in the last decade and a half, as his novels have tended to be increasingly concerned with the past, Auchincloss's keenest observations in contemporary life have most often been found in his stories.

In the stories in his four most recent collections, published from 1970 to 1983, Auchincloss notes many of the changes in sex roles, relations between generations, and behavior at the office witnessed in the 1960s and 1970s. Sometimes, as in "The Marriage Contract," pub-

lished in *The Partners* (1974), Auchincloss simply looks
at the enduring problems of marriage as they are manifested in a new situation. Marcus and Felicia Currier are
both lawyers, representatives of the sort of two-career
couple that was becoming more common in the early
seventies. The stresses on their marriage come from new
sources — managing two careers, including a temporary
move to another city by Felicia, competing for professional success, and simultaneously raising two children —
but the fundamental conflict for control between Marc
and Felicia is not radically different from the conflicts
between husbands and wives that one encounters in the
novels Auchincloss wrote in the 1950s.

At times, however, from his basically conservative
perspective Auchincloss can be amazingly prescient about
trends in American society. "The Double Gap," which
appeared in 1970, for instance, nicely predicts the disillusionment and grim professionalism that set in during
the early 1980s among those who had been the idealistic
young people of the sixties. Cast in the form of a series
of memos between a young law student and his grandfather, who is the senior partner in a large law firm, the
story vividly states the case for both sides of the debate
between generations during the era of the "generation
gap." Neither advocate persuades the other, but, after
the grandson has refused for the last time his grandfather's offer to join his firm and has totally rejected his
justification for practicing corporate law, the grandfather writes one more memo. Warning his grandson that
in his zeal for representing the downtrodden he too may
become "a one-client man" not unlike a dishonest former
member of his firm, he wishes him good luck.

I'm glad that I've made you independent so you won't be compelled, like your breadwinner friends, to go to work for a firm
in whose "mystique" you cannot believe. I am convinced,
sincerely convinced, that you will do big things. I am only
disappointed that you will not be doing them with me. And

I cannot help but wonder a bit, when you and your contemporaries have scraped all the gilt off the statue of life (gilt which I call passion and you call sentimentality), whether you will not be a bit disappointed at the dull gray skeleton that you find beneath. (*Second Chance*, p. 171)

By the end of the decade in which this story appeared, not only had the idealists of the sixties come face to face with the dull gray skeleton, but their younger brothers and sisters were rushing cynically into law and medical school without even the passion that justified the grandfather's career.

Though "The Marriage Contract" and "The Double Gap" accurately illustrate Auchincloss's responses to social change, neither represents his short fiction at its best. Another story of the 1970s, "Second Chance" is richer, more finely wrought, and characteristic of its author's unique strengths. In this, the title story of Auchincloss's 1970 collection, Gilbert Van Ness divorces his wife of more than twenty years, takes an entirely new job, and marries a younger woman — a common enough occurrence in recent years and a topic of much discussion when the story appeared. Auchincloss approaches this central situation from a fresh perspective, however. We see Gilbert's midlife transformation through the eyes of his brother-in-law Joe, who has known him since college and who handles the divorce for the family. Before he leaves his first wife, Gilbert seems a failure, "a Confederate officer returning to his ruined plantation after Appomattox." After the divorce he becomes an almost instant success in a flashy Madison Avenue advertising agency, quickly rising to president and ultimately marrying the daughter of the founder. Joe is blamed by his wife's family, the Kilpatricks, for letting his old friend off with a one-time financial settlement rather than a percentage of Gilbert's future earnings.

The central drama in the story is not Gilbert's amazing luck but rather his more stable brother-in-law's un-

easy response to his success, which Auchincloss depicts
with great sublety and tact. When the Kilpatricks start
complaining about the settlement, Joe finds that he would
rather have them believe that he was swayed by his longtime friendship than that Gilbert's "stronger personality had put it over my weaker one. Or that I had been
dazzled — even envious — at the prospect of his liberty."
Later in the story Gilbert accuses him of fearing the idea
that one can "start again and win" and argues that his
moral indignation is merely a convenient way of avoiding an opportunity to change his own life. "You hate me
because I remind you in your indolence that you could
do it, too. That it's *not* too late." It is this "demon of the
second chance" that Joe must confront in himself.

After he gets home from the party at which he
talked to Gilbert, he carefully considers his indictment.
He is reasonably certain that it is not valid, but a small
doubt remains. When he attends an impressive dinner
party at Gilbert's apartment, he is almost convinced
again that Gilbert has been right all along — until he
notices a very small detail. Gilbert hands a fork to his
butler without even pausing in conversation. Obviously there was a speck on it, but the fact that the butler
knows just what to do with the fork reveals "the enormous amount of domestic machinery that must have
been hid behind that simple gesture." Rather than being the free soul that he claims to be, Gilbert is a fraud.
"I had exorcised the demon of the second chance," Joe
comments at the end of the story. "I had saved my marriage, not from dissolution, but from the cloying idea
that I wanted its dissolution. Or that I had wanted to
be like Gilbert. Or that I had thought it might be un-
manly *not* to be like Gilbert. Now he could go on hand-
ing spotted spoons to his butler for eternity. I simply did
not care."

That the major psychological insight of the story
should turn upon this small detail of manners is thorough-

ly characteristic of Auchincloss's approach. The lawyer-protagonist is also typical of Auchincloss's reserved and invariably decent heroes; both his dilemma and its resolution seem fitting. Yet, in spite of the rather specialized elements present in "Second Chance," the story describes and offers surprisingly immediate and generally accessible commentary upon an ordinary experience shared by many men of the protagonist's age. In addition to this, Joe is expertly placed in the context of his marriage and his relations with his wife's family. We are given just the right amount of psychological and social background, and Auchincloss's tone, faintly ironic but generally sympathetic, achieves sufficient distance to permit us to see the humor in the narrator's situation. In "Second Chance" and in several other stories like it, we see what makes Auchincloss's short fiction entertaining and valuable.

8

▚▚▚▚▚▚▚▚▚▚▚▚▚▚▚▚▚▚▚▚▚▚▚▚▚▚▚▚▚▚▚▚▚▚

The Novelist as
Man of Letters:
The Nonfiction

"I have called myself a Jacobite because so much of my lifetime's reading has been over the shoulder of Henry James," Auchincloss writes in the foreword to his first collection of essays, *Reflections of a Jacobite*. In his own essays, memoirs, and historical writings, Auchincloss invites us to read over his shoulder, too. Under his guidance, one encounters the literary works and historical personalities that have meant the most to him as a writer. To read his nonfiction is to see again the central preoccupations of his fiction and to understand some of the sources of his art. Auchincloss is an amateur in the original sense of the word. His method as a critic and historian is appreciative; he is always personal, sometimes opinionated, and never narrowly academic. Like a Victorian man of letters, he eschews the jargon of the specialist and writes for a general audience of educated readers. At his best he is a charming essayist and a shrewd practical critic.

The body of Auchincloss's nonfiction — much of it written since 1970 — is substantial: two collections of literary and historical essays, *Reflections of a Jacobite* and *Life, Law and Letters*; a study of American women writers, *Pioneers and Caretakers*; a book of Shakespearean criticism, *Motiveless Malignity*; a study of Henry

James; biographies of Edith Wharton and Cardinal Richelieu; books on the court of Queen Victoria and women in the age of Louis XIV; an edition of an 1890s diary, *Maverick in Mauve*; and his own autobiographical memoir, *A Writer's Capital*. Almost every interest suggested in this long list of titles is picked up in some way in Auchincloss's novels and stories, not just in frequent allusions and references, but more fundamentally in the subject matter and themes of almost all his work. The influence of Wharton and James is of course pervasive in Auchincloss's writing, but the concern with things Victorian displayed in *Persons of Consequence* and in his numerous essays on nineteenth-century novelists also shapes the rest of his work. The historical studies of seventeenth- and eighteenth-century France are reflected not only in repeated references throughout his work but also in two novels set in the age of Louis XIV. And most of all, Auchincloss's own family history and personal experiences are refined and reconstituted at every turn in his novels.

Auchincloss's nonfictional writings, then, repay consideration for their intrinsic value as well as for the insights they provide about the rest of his work. They demonstrate the fundamental unity of their author's oeuvre. Although not all of the nonfiction is distinguished, Auchincloss's significant achievements in autobiography, history, and literary criticism mark him as an accomplished man of letters for our times.

A Writer's Capital

A Writer's Capital, published in 1974, is Auchincloss's finest nonfictional work. Only 126 pages long and accompanied by three brief recollections of literary "influences and experiments," this graceful autobiography "tells the story of what led up to his becoming a writer." A seemingly informal but carefully shaped memoir, it offers a witty and entertaining narrative of its author's life while also presenting an apologia for his dual career as writer and lawyer and a defense of his art. For readers of his novels it also provides a revealing account of their biographical sources. As Auchincloss has observed, "an author is always writing and rewriting his own name. For better or worse, he is essentially limited, in subject matter, to himself."[1] *A Writer's Capital* reminds one of how often Auchincloss has drawn upon his own experiences in creating his fiction. The book demonstrates the truth of its epigraph: "his childhood is a writer's entire capital."

As Gore Vidal once suggested, perhaps the most remarkable thing about Auchincloss's life is the fact that, with his background, he became a writer at all.[2] Progression from a childhood on the Upper East Side to Groton, Yale, and the University of Virginia Law School, and then to a New York law firm and Naval service in World War II, and finally back to Wall Street would not, in the normal course of events, lead to a career as a novelist. Auchincloss is aware of this oddity. At one point he refers to himself as "a kind of duck-bill platypus" at the literary gatherings he attended in the early 1950s. And from the very beginning of *A Writer's Capital*, he carefully places his family background in context. He recognizes that wealth and social position can engender hostility, but without apologizing or minimizing the advantages he has had in life he neutralizes criticism. "Snobbery about ancestors varies with the generations," he states at the outset, and goes on to tell how his grandfather's generation sought knighthoods and royal grants in their family tree, whereas his father liked to brag that he was descended from sheep stealers. The reader discovers that the Auchinclosses' ancestors in Scotland were pretty much what they became in nineteenth-century New York — prosperous merchants. Ancestry is plainly important to Auchincloss, but he makes the point in the

least offensive way. Though he feels that his background
has counted against him as a writer and says so at several
points, the tone of his memoir is never bitter.

Like several of his early novels, *A Writer's Capital*
is a narrative in which a shy, sensitive protagonist who
is closely tied to his or her family finally achieves a secure
sense of identity. At times the Louis Auchincloss of the
memoir reminds one of the timid heroines of such novels
as *Sybil* and *A Law for the Lion*, and his unhappy first
experiences at Groton are reminiscent of those of boys
like Michael Farish in *Venus in Sparta* or David Griscam
in *The Rector of Justin*. Auchincloss cheerfully acknowledges the feminine side of his nature and the crucial influence of his mother. Indeed, as a boy he envied his
mother's freedom from the drudgery and pressure of the
conventional masculine world of school and downtown
work. His bookishness and lack of athletic skills made
him an outsider in prep school, even as his social connections would later make him an outsider in literary
and intellectual circles. He freely admits a certain seriousness, a kind of fussiness, and an unappealing conservatism in his boyish personality.

Auchincloss's development in *A Writer's Capital*
may best be described as a kind of dialectical process in
which he moves between two poles represented by the
opposing worlds of his mother and his father. Though
closely attached to his mother with one side of his nature,
Auchincloss also accepted the demand to succeed in the
conventional masculine world, represented by his father,
of law and finance. Indeed, despite the "deep congeniali-
ty" between them, his mother would worry whenever
Louis became too serious about his studies or too wrapped
up in the world of art or parties, and "her nagging sense
of a responsibility to turn me into a man like the other
men in her world" would reassert itself. Looking back
on his life, Auchincloss observes a series of shifts between two extremes. Whenever things were going well

in the conventional course of the masculine career, he was able to write. But failure in his literary projects sent him back to a renewed attempt to satisfy the conventional expectations. His years at Yale were successful and happy, and he completed the manuscript of a novel. Yet when he received a polite rejection, he left Yale a year early and went directly to law school. After acquitting himself well in the traditional male ordeals of law school and the Navy, however, he felt confident enough to return to writing. Yet his first novel was published under a pseudonym, and he continued to work at the law firm he had joined before the war. The final step in the process was, of course, the two years he spent writing full-time, after which he returned to the practice of law but at the same time continued to write prolifically.

The title of the last chapter of *A Writer's Capital* suggests Auchincloss's final resolution: "Compromise." Partly through psychoanalysis, he was able to accept the competing claims represented by his mother and father and to understand that demands that appeared to come from his family and social background were in large measure demands he had created in his own mind. The "compromise" he reached was really more an acceptance of the influence of both his parents, who in their own ways had supported him all along. At the same time, the central insight Auchincloss achieved in his psychoanalysis — "that a man's background is largely of his own creating" — forms the basis for a defense of his novels against class-bound criticism. Auchincloss points out that the things he considered important in his past may well have been very different from what his siblings and cousins found important. "This may seem obvious enough," he says, but he ruefully observes that critics of his work do not seem to share his insight:

American critics still place a great emphasis on the effect of background on character, and by background they mean something absolute which is the same for all those in the foreground.

Furthermore, they tend to assume that the effect of any class privilege in a background must be deleterious to a character and that the author has introduced such a background only to explain the harm done. Now the truth is that the background of most of my characters has been selected simply because it is a familiar one to me and is hence more available as a model. In most cases, the problems of the characters are personal, or psychological, and would have existed in a multitude of other geographical areas and other social strata. (*A Writer's Capital*, p. 122)

Here the story of Auchincloss's life merges with a defense of his art.

Yet Auchincloss's balanced acceptance of both parents' examples may also explain a certain equanimity and distance in his fiction. Raised by loving parents in a tightly knit family, Auchincloss made his peace with his background. *A Writer's Capital* is filled with affection for both parents. He remains fascinated by, rather than resentful of, his family and its history. And he regards himself as part of a continuing tradition rather than a rebel. While he sees the flaws in the world he often depicts in his fiction — and he sees them quite clearly — he is not filled with savage indignation. And whereas his life has been touched at times by anguish and suffering, he is content with the compromise he has fashioned and does not write from the depths of despair. Auchincloss's reconciliation with both aspects of his nature implied in the examples of his parents yields the fundamentally conservative and balanced fiction that he gives us.

On a more basic level, too, *A Writer's Capital* also shows the sources of recurring characters and situations in Auchincloss's fiction. Not only do the large New York families depicted in *The House of Five Talents* and *Portrait in Brownstone* have their origins in branches of Auchincloss's own family, but the shy heroines and the timid young men who recoil from the threatening cityscape of the financial district and live in fear of failure

in the masculine world also reflect aspects of Auchincloss's self, as do the elegant bachelors and extra men.
Events from every period of Auchincloss's life permeate
the novels, early and late: Groton, Yale, Charlottesville,
Wall Street, and the Navy. Auchincloss's naval experiences figure prominently, for example, in both *The Indifferent Children*, his first novel, and his latest, *Honorable Men*, published thirty-eight years later. *A Writer's
Capital* is therefore an essential text for anyone who
wishes to understand Auchincloss's art.

At the same time, *A Writer's Capital* remains an
elegant and shapely memoir. Unified by Auchincloss's
quest for identity and by the contrasts between mother
and father, home and downtown, the inner life and the
outer life, and literature and law, the autobiography is
nicely rounded out by Auchincloss's return to Wall
Street, where paradoxically he tells us at last "I felt that
I had come home." At the end of the memoir he calls the
career he finds "a peculiar shell that over the years I have
managed to manufacture for myself." Yet in his graceful
final paragraph, he steps back and asks whether the pattern of his life had not been there all along waiting for
his discovery:

Was it not merely a question of clearing away the cobwebs of
fears that had obsessed me? And when they were cleared away,
was the shell not there, already made? I think that is the more
plausible answer. So often men are born with all the tools they
need, but are blocked by the simple fear of using them. Yet
I suppose that the very act of overcoming that fear may in itself
be an indispensable educative process toward using those tools
in certain ways. So one never really knows. All a writer can
do is tell the story of what led up to his becoming a writer. And
that is what I have tried to do. (*A Writer's Capital*, pp. 125–26)

The pattern that shapes his autobiography is the very
pattern that Auchincloss found latent in his own life. *A
Writer's Capital* is not only a revealing memoir but also

one of Auchincloss's finest narratives. It leaves one wishing that he had written more of his autobiography.

The Biographies and Popular Histories

Like *A Writer's Capital*, Auchincloss's five biographies and historical studies are, above all, narratives. Not for him are the painstaking analyses of bits of data undertaken by modern professional historians. Nor does he wish to construct large historical or biographical theories. Auchincloss is a popular historian, resolutely non-academic in his approach. Though he knows a great deal about his subjects, his histories are usually based upon secondary sources and the works of the authors he considers. He does not trouble his readers with discussions of previous research, footnotes, or extensive bibliographies. Even in his biographical works he does not press too hard to demonstrate a particular thesis. He is a genial, often shrewd twentieth-century observer who seeks to bring the past alive to a general audience. As a novelist looking at the past, he is capable of striking insights into individual character and social institutions, but his popular approach often leads to superficiality.

Maverick in Mauve, Auchincloss's 1983 edition of the diary of Florence Adele Sloane, stands midway between his autobiography and his other historical works. The diarist, whose mother was a grandchild of Commodore Vanderbilt, was also the grandmother of Auchincloss's wife. Because of this family connection and because Adele Sloane lived until 1960, she was very much a part of Auchincloss's own life. Yet, on the other hand, she is a link to the New York of the 1890s, the "mauve decade" suggested by the book's title. Auchincloss prints generous selections from her diary from 1893 to the time of her marriage in 1895, and a few entries from 1896. Intrinsically interesting and always lively, Adele's writing reveals the daily life and aspirations of an independent though ultimately obedient young woman who had her own listing among the famous "Four Hundred" of New York high society. Auchincloss's extensive commentary, which alternates with selections from the diary, makes up about a third of the book. Excellent social history in their own right, his observations give the book greater unity and shape. Adele's diary is useful family history and a social document well worth publishing, but in Auchincloss's hands *Maverick in Mauve* becomes a fine narrative of romance and courtship in the 1890s. Adele Sloane could well have stepped out of the pages of one of Auchincloss's own New York novels, such as *The House of Five Talents*.

Auchincloss's two biographies, *Edith Wharton: A Woman in Her Time* (1971) and *Richelieu* (1972), were published as Studio Books by the Viking Press. Though they are decidedly more than "coffee-table books," both are oversize volumes with numerous illustrations. As its subtitle suggests, *Edith Wharton* is not a full-scale biography but rather a study of the novelist in her time and place. Auchincloss does a good job of depicting the nineteenth-century New York society in which Wharton grew up and the Paris in which she lived as a mature writer, but his criticism of her novels remains somewhat superficial. Indeed, most of his discussion of the novels in the book repeats material from his previously published work on Wharton in the Minnesota Pamphlets on American Literature series. Nonetheless, taken together, the excellent illustrations and Auchincloss's graceful and astute observations on her background convey a vivid sense of Wharton's personal world, and the volume provides a sound introduction to Wharton for the ordinary reader. *Richelieu*, also a very handsome book, is a good example of popular history. Though he apparently does not break new ground, Auchincloss makes the rather forbidding figure of Cardinal Richelieu come alive and shrewdly analyzes the personalities and power struggles

of early seventeenth-century France. To treat complicated and often dry material in an interesting fashion is
an accomplishment that should not be scorned.

Persons of Consequence (1979) and Auchincloss's
latest historical work, *False Dawn* (1984), are both studies of groups of figures whose lives revolve around a monarch. Both display Auchincloss's abiding interest in wom-
en who are closely connected with power.

Persons of Consequence is the more successful work
because it is more detailed and better unified. Beauti-
fully illustrated with contemporary portraits and photographs, the book is a study of Queen Victoria and her
circle. Auchincloss sketches the Queen's life and character by considering her relationships with those around
her: her governess Baroness Lehzen, her husband Prince
Albert, her personal secretary, the various prime ministers who served her, and her children. Each of the chapters is a fine portrait in its own right — the discussions of
Gladstone and Sir Henry Ponsonby are especially pene-
trating — and they are arranged in roughly chronological
order so that the reader has a sense of Victoria's development as princess and queen. Auchincloss's insights into
the psychology of the young queen, his sense of how the
administrative machinery of government is affected by
the personalities of rulers and officials, and his skillful
use of the Queen's letters and diaries make this an entertaining and useful history. Though almost all the members of her "circle" in the book are male, Auchincloss is
plainly intrigued by the personality of the Queen, at once
a domestic and rather plain woman and at the same time
the most powerful ruler of her time.

False Dawn: Women in the Age of the Sun includes
portraits of fourteen figures in the courts of France and
England, ranging from the letter writer Madame de
Sevigny to Louis XIV's mistress Madame de Maintenon
and Queen Anne herself. Much more loosely organized
than *Persons of Consequence*, the book tentatively ex-

plores the idea that the period from 1650 to 1715 was a sort of "false dawn" for women, an age when women at court exercised some modicum of power only to have their successors in the eighteenth century "harness their force and genius to the chariot of charm," thereby losing much of their power and becoming merely decorative. All of the portraits are brief. Although some of them are lively, others read like exercises and the book as a whole never quite lives up to the promise of its title.

Literary Criticism

Auchincloss's diverse interests as a literary critic have found expression in three book-length studies and in the essays collected in *Reflections of a Jacobite* and *Life, Law and Letters*. Like his historical writing, his literary criticism is sprightly and never ponderously academic. It shares some of the defects of the histories — occasional glibness or superficiality, a lack of systematic rigor — but Auchincloss is blessed with unique strengths as a critic. Not only does he write from the experience of a practicing novelist; he is also, as would be expected, extraordinarily familiar with the works of Henry James and Edith Wharton, and because he was seriously reading Wharton and several Victorian novelists — Anthony Trollope, for example — well before it was fashionable to do so, he often writes with special authority. Though he maintains the tone of the man of letters addressing his peers, his best literary criticism is worthy of respect even in a more scholarly context.

As has been suggested at the beginning of this chapter, the topics of Auchincloss's criticism reveal the important influences upon his writing as well as his abiding interests as a reader. James and Wharton are obvious examples. But when one turns to the figures discussed in the two collections of essays, one gets an even clearer impression of Auchincloss's essential character as

a novelist. Not surprisingly, there are five essays on
James, Wharton, and the novel of manners in America,
and two pieces on nineteenth-century New York society. Yet there are also three considerations of Proust,
reminding one of the importance of recollection as well
as observation of elegant society in Auchincloss's work.
Essays on Trollope, Thackerary, George Eliot, Meredith, and Jane Austen bring to mind not only Auchincloss's interest in the nineteenth century, but more significantly the essentially moral cast of his novels. Like his
Victorian predecessors, Auchincloss delights in detailed
analysis of complicated ethical and social problems. The
presence of Emily Dickinson, along with George Eliot
and Jane Austen, also invokes his preoccupation with
shy, isolated heroines. Five essays on the Court of Versailles complete the picture of Auchincloss's art as it is
reflected in his two collections.

Only a sampling of Auchincloss's most important
essays is possible here, but his three book-length studies
are all worthy of brief description. *Pioneers and Caretakers*, published in 1965, considers nine female writers
ranging from Sarah Orne Jewett and Edith Wharton to
Carson McCullers and Mary McCarthy. In a short preface, Auchincloss argues that these women writers are
both pioneers, striking out on their own on new paths,
and caretakers "responsible for the packing and preser-
vation of the household gods." Unfortunately, this intriguing thesis is not followed out in the studies of individual
authors. Like *False Dawn*, *Pioneers and Caretakers* may
best be regarded as a loosely connected set of essays of
varying quality. Auchincloss is at his most perceptive in
discussing the work of Edith Wharton and Mary McCarthy, figures for whom he feels considerable affinity; his
discussions of several other authors are simply too brief
to be of much value.

Auchincloss took the title for his collection of Shakespearean criticism, *Motiveless Malignity* (1969), from

Coleridge's phrase about Iago: "the motive hunting of a motiveless malignity." As he explains in the preface, the fifteen essays that make up the collection are "connected only in their tendency to speculate on the lack of apparent motivation in some of Shakespeare's principal characters." Some of Auchincloss's speculations, as, for example, in his discussion of Falstaff and Prince Hal, are wrong-headed; others are right on target and offer fresh views of Shakespeare from, as usual, the perspective of an intelligent general reader. The essays on Coriolanus's self-destructiveness, on Bertram and Helena in *All's Well that Ends Well*, and on Antony and Cleopatra as very "human" lovers show Auchincloss's fine grasp of the complexities of character. The insights Auchincloss gained in creating shy and self-destructive characters in his own works enrich his consideration of Shakespeare.

Reading Henry James (1975) is Auchincloss's most successful critical study precisely because it draws upon his own practical experiences as a novelist, as well as his lifelong immersion in the works of James. Here the critic and his subject merge. As T. K. Meier has observed, "rather than come to grips with the significance of James's novels by reference to what James actually wrote, Auchincloss prefers to consider the feasibility and effect of other alternatives James might have chosen and to infer interpretations by contrast. Carried out by an author as conscious of his craft and a reader as sensitive to nuance as Auchincloss, this approach gives a new perspective on James."[3] Because of his writer's viewpoint, Auchincloss is particularly effective in assessing flawed works such as *The Princess Casamassima*. His lifelong reading yields a fine appreciative discussion of *The Ambassadors*, and he also has new things to say about Americans abroad in James. Though it is brief, *Reading Henry James* deals with early and late novels and discusses James's notebooks and criticism. Auchincloss's authorial voice (a lighter version of James's own) and the chronological arrange-

ment of chapters give the work unity. Even though this
is Auchincloss's most satisfying critical work, the short-
ness and suggestiveness of some essays are frustrating.
One might wish, for example, that he had developed his
ideas on the artist and writer in James's fiction more fully.

Besides being sensible criticism, *Reading Henry
James* also reveals Auchincloss's own theories as a novelist. Like *A Writer's Capital*, it is an implicit defense of
Auchincloss's own art. This is particularly true in the
chapter on James's notebooks, where Auchincloss eloquently defends James's technique. Many readers of the
notebooks have been "shocked by the seeming triviality
of the themes which appealed to James," Auchincloss
says. Not only are there no socially relevant entries, but
there is little "mention of such general topics as science,
religion, labor, industry, politics, or war." Of necessity, the entries are "confined to those sparks which James
knew from experience could be kindled into his particular brand of fiction." According to Auchincloss, non-
writers often find it difficult to comprehend an essential
fact:

The writer can use only his own spark or germ or *donnée* or
whatever he chooses to call it. The friend may possibly suggest one to the writer in the course of his chatter, but this will
usually be in some odd, irrelevant part of his story. The writer,
however, learns to recognize his spark when it flashes before
his eyes . . . and without questioning its importance to the rest
of the world he seizes it for his very own. Why should he care
if it seems trivial to others? Only *he* knows what he can make
of it. (*Reading Henry James*, p. 17)

Although one suspects that Auchincloss may often have
rather detailed ideas of his settings in mind before he
writes, this explication of James's practice remains an excellent defense for his own methods as a novelist.

Ultimately, then, Auchincloss is best as a critic when
his own world and work overlap the subject he considers.
This is nowhere more true than in the considerations of

James and the novel of manners in his two collections of essays. As academic criticism, such essays as "Edith Wharton and Her Two New Yorks," "The Novel of Manners Today: Marquand and O'Hara," and "Proust's Picture of Society" are permanent contributions to the literature. Equally authoritative are his discussions of old New York. Here Auchincloss cannot be bettered.

To conclude with Auchincloss's contributions to scholarship, however, would be highly misleading. Auchincloss remains a man of letters, and his practice of the art of criticism in a variety of fields adds to his stature.

9

~~~~~~

The Uses of the Past:
Recent Novels

Since the appearance of *The Winthrop Covenant* in 1976, Auchincloss has published eight novels, a collection of essays, and a collection of stories, as well as three historical works. Always a prolific writer, he has, if anything, increased his pace in the past several years, publishing a novel every year since 1980. Two of the novels, *The House of the Prophet* and *Watchfires*, are significant additions to Auchincloss's canon. Because of their importance, they will be discussed in a separate chapter. The two most recent novels, *The Book Class* and *Honorable Men*, make interesting use of Auchincloss's past, whereas the other lesser novels of the late 1970s and early 1980s demonstrate the variety and range he has achieved in his mature work. Despite their variety, all the recent novels, along with *The Winthrop Covenant*, reflect a growing historical consciousness in their author.

This increasingly obvious historical cast is hardly surprising when one considers Auchincloss's career. For one thing, most novels of manners, even when set in the present, are historical in some sense. If nothing else, they seek to preserve the customs and behavior of one era for transmission to another, and they must inevitably interpret the manners of one generation in the context of what has gone before. Moreover, the underlying consciousness in much of Auchincloss's work is conservative; that is to say, Auchincloss is keenly concerned with describing and evoking a vanishing past. The impulse behind the novels of old New York published around 1960, *The House of Five Talents* and *Portrait in Brownstone*, with their emphasis upon continuity and change over several generations in a particular social and geographical setting, is certainly historical, and *Reflections of a Jacobite*, published at about the same time, contains two historical studies — both of them, significantly, on subjects that Auchincloss has used as the bases for recent novels. Finally, of course, there are the popular histories Auchincloss has written, which have been discussed in chapter 8: his biography of Cardinal Richelieu, *Persons of Consequence*, and *False Dawn*, as well as his edition of the diary of Florence Adele Sloane, *Maverick in Mauve*.

Despite this strong historical tendency, Auchincloss cannot be said to be a historical novelist in the strictest sense of the term. The historical content of his recent novels varies greatly, and even in the most explicitly historical his primary goal is not accurate reproduction of historical detail or total fidelity in his plots or characterization to the events and behavior of another era. He is more interested in universal problems of human nature and often approaches individual characters and social institutions in his novels psychologically, from a distinctly twentieth-century point of view. Nonetheless, one cannot help observing that almost all of Auchincloss's fiction from *The Winthrop Covenant* onward has looked to earlier times for its inspiration, that all the novels except the most recent contain actual historical events or figures, and that three of them are based directly upon the lives of important historical figures. Indeed, the stories in *The Winthrop Covenant*, in their considerations of various aspects of puritanism in American history, establish the themes for much of Auchincloss's fiction during the past decade.

If all these novels take a backward glance at the

past, they are also retrospective in another sense. In each book, Auchincloss returns in some way to a previous work. Three novels are recast and expanded versions of short stories (two from *The Winthrop Covenant*, a third from Auchincloss's earliest collection). Others return to episodes or figures from his own life as related in *A Writer's Capital*. Still others are fictional explorations of historical topics that had already engaged his interest in essays, and *The House of the Prophet* marks a return to the narrative technique employed in *The Rector of Justin*. Though Auchincloss has always been an author who tends to consider a particular problem more than once, this proclivity has been even more evident in his recent work.

As might be expected in so prolific an author, Auchincloss's recent novels vary in quality. If in some of them he seems to repeat himself, in others his various uses of the past are fruitful and creative. Although they do not rank with his best work, the six less-important novels of the last decade — *The Dark Lady*, *The Country Cousin*, *The Cat and the King*, *Exit Lady Masham*, *The Book Class*, and *Honorable Men* — are all worthy of attention. Even in minor or flawed works, Auchincloss writes intelligently on the basis of interesting ideas. Each novel attempts something different or presents a new variation on a recurring theme. Together, the six novels reveal Auchincloss's continued growth as a writer.

The Dark Lady and *The Country Cousin*

The Dark Lady, published in 1977, draws upon Auchincloss's research for his book on Shakespeare, *Motiveless Malignity*. Like the "dark lady" of Shakespeare's sonnets, Elesina Dart, the heroine of the novel, betrays her older lover for a younger man. The novel also returns to the world of fashion-magazine publishing, a milieu that

Auchincloss had described in *Pursuit of the Prodigal* in
1959. Like Gilda Doremus of *A Woman's World* in the
earlier novel, one of the main characters, Ivy Trask, edits
the fashion section of a woman's magazine called *Tone*.

The novel begins on the eve of World War II.
Coached by her mentor Ivy, Elesina pulls herself up
from a failed career as an actress and from incipient
alcoholism in order to capture the love of Irving Stein,
a wealthy investment banker and former judge about
thirty years older than she. Ivy urges her protégé to settle for nothing less than marriage, and forces Irving to
divorce his wife. Once married to Irving, Elesina has an
affair with his son David, who is only nine years her
junior. Irving dies, leaving Elesina his estate and extensive art collection, which David urges her to renounce
in order to marry him. When she refuses to do so, David
enlists in the Canadian army and is killed on the beach
at Dunkirk.

After the war, Elesina uses the Stein fortune to run
for a seat in Congress as a Republican from Westchester
County. Ever the actress, she finds "her ultimate role"
in politics. Having used Judge Stein and taken her pleasure with his son, she finally abandons Ivy Trask, who
had urged her to use smear tactics against her McCarthy-
ite opponent in the primary. No longer able to play a
central role in Elesina's career, Ivy commits suicide as
Elesina, having won the election, is about to take office
in Washington.

Since Judge Stein is a sophisticated collector, *The
Dark Lady*, like several other Auchincloss novels, is filled
with beautiful paintings that are given symbolic significance. Two of the minor characters are a Shakespearean scholar and a lesbian poet, and several crucial scenes
turn upon debates over vexed issues in Shakespearean
criticism, which later become ironically relevant to the
actions of the main characters. Not only does Elesina reflect the dark lady of the sonnets, but references to

Shakespeare's other works abound. Furthermore, the main action of the novel — the affair between Elesina and her stepson — reflects the Hippolytus–Phaedra story treated by Euripides and by Racine, whose *Phedre* is frequently alluded to in Auchincloss's fiction. Though all the literary references are clever and many of the ironies that spring from them are intriguing, *The Dark Lady* is an unappealing work. None of the characters is particularly sympathetic, and while the plot is briskly paced, the sometimes lurid action of the novel has little of interest to recommend it. Despite its elegant literary trappings, *The Dark Lady* remains rather too sensationalistic.

Auchincloss's next novel, *The Country Cousin*, published in 1978, is considerably more effective. Though its major characters are involved at the end in covering up a crime, there is something "light, and bright, and sparkling" (to use Jane Austen's words in another context) about the novel. The champagne is very dry, almost to the point of acerbity, but it is champagne rather than stale wine.

In *The Country Cousin* Auchincloss opens up and expands an early short story, "The Unholy Three." In the story, a young woman from Maine serving as a paid companion to her wealthy aunt in New York is taken, out of kindness, to the theater and a nightclub by the aunt's only son. When the son's jealous wife discovers who is the object of his attentions, she angrily confronts the young niece. Urged on by her aunt, who dislikes the wife, and driven by a penchant for self-dramatization and a romantic desire to make herself exciting in some way, the niece loftily announces that she and the husband have fallen deeply in love. The husband disavows this love, and the niece is taken home from the nightclub where the scene has occurred by the middle-aged "extra man" who has accompanied her. After her big scene, she tells her aunt that she has decided to go back home to Maine. "Yet," Auchincloss writes at the end of the story, "there was still a remnant of her earlier exhilaration that had survived the end of the piece, and she wondered, with a strange new bound of her heart, as she walked down the long corridor to her own bedroom, whether it might not take her further than simply to her home in Maine."

In place of the niece, he introduces Amy Hunt, the country cousin of the title. Amy's outburst at the nightclub, rather than closing the action of the story, causes the husband, Herman Fidler, to leave his ill-tempered wife, become a painter, and live with Amy in Greenwich Village. Realizing that she was never in love with Herman at all, Amy returns to her elderly cousin, Dolly Chadbourne, in exchange for her promise to destroy a codicil to her will that would have disinherited Herman. Dolly suffers a stroke before fulfilling the bargain, however, and Amy gets her to tear up the codicil only after there is serious doubt about the old lady's mental capacity. After Dolly's death, Amy marries Jamey Coates, the family friend who had taken her home after her outburst. A shadowy figure named Mr. Delancey in the story, Jamey in the novel is a successful lawyer from a wealthy family. He finds out about the questionable destruction of the codicil, but in his romantic avowal of his love offers to keep it a secret.

The second and somewhat shorter portion of the novel involves the discovery of the secret by Fred Stiles, an unsavory partner in Jamey's firm who has helped a client bribe a judge. Stiles, who is married to Herman Fidler's ex-wife Naomi, tells Amy that he knows about the codicil, and in a weak moment she agrees to make love to him in order to keep him quiet. When Jamey finds out about the bribe, however, he insists upon reporting Stiles to the bar association, even though that will lead to his own punishment. Amy initially goes along with this grand gesture of honesty, but, at the end of the novel, she agrees to let Herman Fidler put his improperly gained inheritance in trust for his daughters (who would have received it under the lost codicil to the will), and she and Jamey remain silent about Fred Stiles's conduct.

When it first appeared, some reviewers saw *The Country Cousin* as a kind of commentary on misconduct in high places.[1] That, however, is not the novel's point at all. Indeed, the work is flawed by the convoluted plotting connected with Dolly's will, and the resolution achieved in the final chapter is too hasty and contrived. *The Country Cousin* is most successful insofar as it is a witty novel of manners. The fine satiric portraits of Cousin Dolly, Herman and Naomi Fidler, and even Jamey Coates, are the best parts of the novel. In them, Auchincloss offers the same sort of sardonic scrutiny of characters that he had attempted in such early novels as *Sybil*, but with a far lighter touch, and he manages to show Amy's naiveté without making her seem silly. The first two-thirds of the novel, in sum, fulfill the promise held out in the early novels of manners, whereas the final chapters slide rather too quickly into the world explored in early law-firm novels such as *The Great World and Timothy Colt*.

The Country Cousin is noteworthy in another respect — as a playful redaction of the nineteenth-century romantic novel. Amy sees her life as a Victorian novel. Like a Brontë heroine, she is a penniless clergyman's daughter reduced to household service. She longs for the drama and love suddenly discovered by such a heroine, and wonders if, by rejecting Jamey's initial proposal, she has become "a Jane Eyre who had missed her Rochester." She later compares Jamey to the proud Darcy in *Pride and Prejudice*. When she and Jamey decide to share the punishment that would be connected with revealing the truth about Dolly's will, she thinks she has finally found her Rochester. But, as the novel works out, they decide not to reveal the secret and therefore never get to bear the punishment. Ultimately the possibility of living out a romantic novel is lost in the compromises of ordinary life. The uniquely exciting patterns of fiction must ultimately yield to the ordinary world of real life. As Amy realizes at the end of the novel, her marriage "would not now be individualized from the rest by any particular passion or any particular idealism." Though this realization seems bleak, it reflects the sort of adjustment to the limitations of existence that most of Auchincloss's characters must make sooner or later.

Though explicitly set in the 1930s, *The Country Cousin* is less historical in a rigorous sense than any of the novels Auchincloss has published in the last decade, with the possible exception of *The Book Class*. It is a period piece, and the numerous references to Victorian novels serve to heighten our awareness of this fact.

The Cat and the King and Exit Lady Masham

At the other extreme from *The Country Cousin* stand two novels that are explicitly historical: *The Cat and the King* and *Exit Lady Masham*, published in 1981 and 1983, respectively.

Set in the Court of Versailles during the reign of Louis XIV, *The Cat and the King* is based directly on the *Memoirs* of Louis Rouvroy, the second duc de St. Simon. Though seventeenth-century Versailles may seem a long way from the settings of most of his other novels, it is a logical environment for Auchincloss to work in: a carefully circumscribed and stratified world in which manners assume an exaggerated importance and in which members of the nobility jockey for power and place with all the energy and ruthlessness of partners in large law firms or matrons in fashionable summer resorts.

Making St. Simon himself the narrator and central character, Auchincloss bases his novel upon three episodes from the *Memoirs* that, according to St. Simon, had an important bearing upon the writing of his masterpiece. Each episode displays St. Simon's obsessive concern with rank and precedence. In the first, St. Simon attempts to prevent his friend the duc de Chartres from marrying an illegitimate daughter of the King. In the second, he is involved in the unsuccessful candidacy of the prince de Conti for the Polish crown. In the third, he promotes the marriage of Chartres' daughter to the duc de Berry in order to prevent his rivals from controlling the succession to the throne on the death of Louis XIV. All three schemes are, in a sense, failures. In the first two episodes, St. Simon's hopes are not realized and he gets into serious trouble with the king. In the final one, he accomplishes his goal, only to discover that Chartres' daughter is a libertine and that the king has deftly maneuvered Madame de St. Simon into close association with her as a lady of honor. Like other Auchincloss heroes, St. Simon discovers the limitations of his ideal — ironically at the very point at which he achieves his goals. St. Simon's supreme goal was Virtue, but at the conclusion of the novel he questions his "lifetime involvement with rules and precedents" as means to this end. Even when, after the death of the king, St. Simon and his friend Chartres, now the regent, strip the illegitimate sons of Louis XIV of their titles as princes of the blood, he realizes that morality has not triumphed. All that is left as "a hedge against chaos" is style. But perhaps that is enough. St. Simon finally realizes that his destiny is literary, not political. He will write the classic account of his age.

The theme of discovering oneself as a writer recurs in Auchincloss's fiction — its major statement is in *The Rector of Justin*. But there is another notable development in *The Cat and the King*. Auchincloss takes the role of St. Simon's wife, Gabrielle — already an important one in the *Memoirs* — and heightens it. Gabrielle is at once the practical and seemingly amoral wife of an idealistic husband (a figure that goes back at least to Ann Colt in *The Great World and Timothy Colt*) and something more: an equal partner in her husband's endeavors, free to use her own strategies to achieve their mutual ends. Auchincloss's interest in Gabrielle points ahead to the new view of marriage that emerges more fully in *Watch-fires*.

Though *The Cat and the King* is a minor novel, it is a delightful and lively recreation of life at Versailles. Auchincloss's interest in St. Simon and his era, already evident in an essay on the great memoirist published in 1961 in *Reflections of a Jacobite*, is manifested with greater sympathy and warmth, and in some instances Auchincloss's thumbnail sketches of figures at court improve upon those of his model. *The Cat and the King* succeeds admirably as historical fiction in the conventional sense of the term.

Like *The Cat and the King*, *Exit Lady Masham* is a memoir of life at court, here the English Court of Queen Anne. The first-person narrator is Abigail Hill, later Lady Masham, the poor relation of Sarah Churchill, Duchess of Marlborough, who rises to a position of influence as attendant to the Queen. A shy, homely woman who gains in confidence as she becomes intimate with the Queen, Abigail Hill plays an important role behind the scenes, helping the Tory cause and working to end the War of the Spanish Succession. By her personal loyalty and modesty, she vanquishes her imperious cousin the Duchess of Marlborough as Queen Anne's favorite. She is befriended by three notable political and literary figures on the Tory side — Robert Harley, Earl of Oxford; Henry St. John, Viscount Bolingbroke; and Jonathan Swift — all of whom figure prominently in the action of the novel.

Unlike the vain and often self-destructive men around her, Lady Masham gives her first loyalty always to the Queen, whom she loves more than her own husband, and her great goal is always peace. She is an interesting example of one of Auchincloss's favorite types: the apparently weak, self-effacing woman who ultimately acquires considerable power and triumphs over her more glamorous and famous rivals. Lady Masham's very self-effacement makes her a relatively unappealing heroine, however. Though the novel briskly presents the politics and intrigue leading up to the Peace of Utrecht, none of the characters ever really comes alive. The world it evokes remains distant rather than compelling.

Exit Lady Masham is less successful than *The Cat and the King*. Nonetheless, by taking Lady Masham's point of view, Auchincloss manages to convey a sense of the sadness that comes from exercising political power. Lady Masham may have prevented further bloodshed by urging Queen Anne to end the War of the Spanish Succession, but in doing so she destroys her personal relationship with the monarch. Though she participates in affairs of state, the question always remains whether she has been manipulated by the powerful men around her. Like the Duchess of Marlborough and Queen Anne, Lady Masham is the subject of one of the essays in *False Dawn*. In that work, Auchincloss as historian treats her somewhat less sympathetically. The Lady Masham of the novel, like Queen Victoria in another of his historical studies, plainly catches Auchincloss's imagination because of the collision between her strong domestic nature and the political power that touches her life. *Exit Lady Masham*, like its predecessor *The Cat and the King*, shows the continuity between Auchincloss's histories and his fiction. In both novels, an exploration of the past becomes the occasion for meditation on some of the author's most characteristic themes.

Living Off Capital: *The Book Class* and *Honorable Men*

Auchincloss's most recent novels, *The Book Class* (1984) and *Honorable Men* (1985), are both strong perform-ances. They are remarkable for the extensive use they make of what Auchincloss calls "a writer's capital," the experiences of childhood and youth that he invokes so eloquently in his autobiographical memoir of the same title. In these two novels more than in any of his other works of the past decade, Auchincloss is living off his capital — not in the usual negative sense of frittering away one's capital, but in the sense of making very crea-tive use of one's heritage. Readers of *A Writer's Capital* will recognize many of the sources for characters and situations in the two recent novels, but they will also see that Auchincloss is making more skillful and more re-laxed use of aspects of his own personality and experi-ence. Both works also carry on the consideration of the puritan strain in American life begun in *The Winthrop Covenant*. Though they lack the substance and complex-ity of Auchincloss's major works, *The Book Class* and *Honorable Men* are somehow pleasanter and less obvi-ously flawed than his novels of the late 1970s.

In discussing Edith Wharton's *The Age of Inno-cence*, Auchincloss remarks that it was "the habit of Vic-torian novelists to set their stories in the era of their childhood" and notes the tendency of the novelist of manners since then "to revert to a usually recent past where social distinctions, which make up so much of his subject matter, were more sharply defined, or at least where he thinks they were." He points out the "Prous-tian mood of remembered things" that produced Whar-ton's "tribute to her own background" in *The Age of Innocence*.[2] In many ways, *The Book Class* is Auchin-closs's tribute to his own background, to the world of his mother as he was growing up. Though his attitude toward this world is warm, the novel is also comic, and recollections of the past are filtered through a first-person narrator who both is and is not Auchincloss.

As in several other Auchincloss novels, the first-person narrator, Christopher Gates, is both a character in the novel and someone who is collecting the stories of others for publication. In fact, with its episodic plot and chapters by or about nine members of Christopher's mother's literary discussion group, *The Book Class* borders on the sort of unified short-story collection Auchincloss created in *Powers of Attorney* and *The Partners*. Nonetheless, the novel is held together by the question Christopher raises at the outset: What sort of "power" did the apparently unliberated women of his mother's generation possess? Having been goaded into claiming on a television talk show that women actually lost power when they "got sidetracked in the dreary *cul-de-sac* of men's jobs," Christopher feels obliged to ponder the nature of the power that impressed him so much in his mother and her contemporaries and to ask "what it contributed to or subtracted from their own welfare."

An interior decorator with a fashionable clientele and a waspish sense of humor, Christopher Gates is at least partly a comic figure. The scrape that starts him writing is humorous, and the conclusion to the novel, in which members of the book class comment on Christopher's portraits of them from beyond the grave, is whimsical, but almost all the details from which Christopher's character is constructed come straight from Auchincloss's own life. A shy boy with an ironic appreciation for the vulgar side of the rich, Christopher is close to his mother, who shares many of the attributes of Auchincloss's mother. Unathletic and initially unpopular with other boys, he goes reluctantly to Chelton School, where he finally achieves happiness as editor of the literary magazine. At Yale he knows a young radical not unlike the suspected communist Bill Remington described in the chapter on Auchincloss's college years in *A Writer's Capital*. With her interest in Moral Rearmament, one of the book-class members resembles a great aunt in Auchincloss's wife's family. Another member of the class, who spends her youth as companion to an elderly jurist, is reminiscent of Auchincloss's family friend Aileen Tone, who lived with Henry Adams during the last years of his life. These and numerous other similarities suggest, not so much that Auchincloss drew from life as that writing *The Book Class* served him as an occasion to explore the enigma of his mother. The comic distance he establishes between himself and Christopher Gates merely gives him further freedom to consider the role of his mother and women like her.

The first two chapters of the novel, in which Christopher quickly delineates the book class and places its members and his own family in their social setting, contain some of Auchincloss's finest portraits of upper-class life in New York between the two World Wars. The opening chapter concludes with a delightful comic sketch of the ladies of the class at a typical luncheon meeting. The next chapter introduces the first of a series of crises in the lives of members of the class. Christopher's mother, Cornelia Gates, is made to perjure herself slightly to save her husband from being convicted of income tax evasion. She does this against the advice of Christopher, who vehemently opposes his father. Rather than proving Christopher's point about the power of women, this example seems initially to demonstrate the opposite: "Father decided what was right and wrong in the eyes of his own dark, inscrutable god, and he made mother his puppet in placating this deity." But such a literal conclusion does not account for the multiple ironies in the aftermath of the episode. Despite his acquittal on the charges, the whole world "knew" Christopher's father was guilty, and Mrs. Gates loses her admiration for her husband, who no longer feels able to reproach her for

her conduct. The effect on Mrs. Gates, however, provides the final — and most telling — irony. Though she
was deeply ashamed of perjuring herself, Christopher's
mother felt she had been right. "She would have done
it all over again, she insisted stoutly — but she was nonetheless convinced that this did not make her morally
right," Christopher observes. "Such was the puritan in
Mother!"

This puritanism tinges the moral natures of almost
all the women in the book class. When another member
of the class, Justine Bannard, prevents her husband's ap-
pointment as headmaster of the Chelton School because
she is convinced that he will embarrass himself by having extramarital affairs with young faculty wives, she
earnestly examines her motives in protecting her husband. Was she trying to preserve his reputation and the
welfare of the school, or was she merely trying to get
back at him for his past infidelities? Where the women
of the book class seem to have most power is in preventing divorces among their children. Even Polly Travers,
the idealistic "political" member of the class, works
against the desires of her daughter who wants to marry
Mrs. Bannard's son Chuck. Together, she and Justine
Bannard protect the interests, not of their own children
but of Chuck's wife.

The members of the book class are more various
than these two episodes may suggest. One is an unmarried woman with exquisite literary taste, another a
French marquise, and another an unhappy divorcée who
kills herself with an overdose of sleeping pills. When
Christopher has written up the lives of the other members, he shows his manuscript to Mrs. Erskine, the one
remaining member, who had been the wife of a diplo-
mat. He asks her whether she thinks the women in the
class would have been happier if they had been born fifty years later. She replies that "they were so much of
their era that I can't visualize them out of it," yet she con-

cludes that "they accepted the status quo. But they accepted it critically. It was, after all, a men's status quo, and I think every one of them believed, deep down, that, given the opportunity, she could have made a better job of it" (*The Book Class*, p. 203). When Christopher asks how he can sum them up, she tells him to repeat what he said earlier: "that they were serious." "Oh you can laugh at them, but they didn't waste their lives. They didn't throw away that precious gift, as so many people do. They knew they were supposed to be privileged, and they thought that placed them under some kind of duty"—a duty, she adds, "to be good."

Though Mrs. Erskine's words do not answer the question Christopher posed when he started to write, perhaps they point the way to Auchincloss's own conclusions about the women of his mother's generation. Behind the comic exterior of the novel is admiration for the seriousness of the women in the book class and respect —especially in the case of Mrs. Erskine, who confesses to Christopher that her marriage was never consummated—for an era where sexual freedom was not a positive good. Behind the comic coda in which each departed member of the book class is allowed her chance to comment on Christopher's book lies Auchincloss's abiding affection for his own mother. Cornelia Gates, is, of course, not Priscilla Stanton Auchincloss, but is difficult not to hear Auchincloss's own voice as Christopher replies to her complaint that he has made a goose of her in the book:

But surely, dearest Mother, if you have another life it is one where such things are understood. I couldn't bear even to think of this little book if that were not the case. For everything I have said has been said with love. There are those, I suppose, who will not believe that I know what love is. They are wrong. Everyone knows what love is. It is life. (*The Book Class*, p. 212)

Sometimes *The Book Class* seems contrived, and certainly the material might have been given more focus.

But the almost palpable affection behind the portrayal of many of the women gives the novel its own life and charm, and Auchincloss's unerring eye for social details and the manners of a past era gives it unique authority. In its relaxed series of narratives, *The Book Class* shows us its author's lighter side.

Though more unified in its structure, Auchincloss's most recent novel, *Honorable Men*, is somewhat less satisfying because it lacks the comic touch of *The Book Class* without wholly succeeding in more serious ways. Like the earlier novel, it explores the strain of puritanism embedded in the character of upper-class Easterners of Auchincloss's generation. This time, however, the puritanism is on the male side of the family. Once again, Auchincloss returns to his past and to ground covered in some of his earlier fiction. The opening chapters of the novel introduce one to familiar territory — the summer resort world of Bar Harbor and the small society of St. Luke's, an Episcopal boarding school not unlike the Groton School described in *A Writer's Capital*. But Auchincloss makes even greater use of settings from a slightly later period in his life: the University of Virginia Law School and naval service in the Caribbean, off Normandy, and in the Pacific Theater during World War II. The wartime episodes recall events in his autobiography and, more especially, the action of his first novel, *The Indifferent Children*. In addition, Auchincloss takes the main characters and basic situation of the novel from a story in *The Winthrop Covenant* entitled "The Penultimate Puritan,"[3] and he again picks up themes explored in that work and in *Watchfires* as well. Despite all these reversions to familiar territory, however, Auchincloss provides fresh views in *Honorable Men*, both of his protagonist, Chip Benedict, and of his dilemma.

The narrative point of view in the novel alternates between the perspectives of Chip Benedict and Alida Struthers, the young woman he marries. The older daughter of a New York family whose fortune has almost been exhausted, Alida turns herself into the debutante of the year through an elaborate publicity campaign run by a friend. Her marriage to Chip, the scion of a Connecticut family whose glass business is the mainstay of the town that bears their name, is a social triumph.

After sketching their childhoods, Auchincloss follows Chip and Alida's lives from 1937, the year of their marriage, to their divorce a little more than thirty years later. They live happily in Charlottesville, Virginia, after their marriage while he attends law school. Then Chip reenlists in the Navy at the outbreak of World War II. After the war, he returns to Benedict and enters the family firm, rising to president and greatly expanding the business during the 1950s. In the midst of a bitter corporate takeover attempt, he unexpectedly sells the firm and moves to New York, depriving Alida of the settled place she has come to enjoy. When Chip moves to Washington to accept a post in the State Department during the Johnson administration, their marriage is already in trouble. Along with their two children, Alida vehemently opposes the Vietnam War, and this disagreement puts another barrier between them. Though Chip later becomes disillusioned with the war and decides to resign his post, he still leaves Alida to marry his secretary at the end of the novel.

Chip's unbending sense of duty is the thematic and psychological focus of the novel. Like Michael Farish in *Venus in Sparta*, he is heir both to the family business and to the high expectations of his parents. Though he does not share Farish's compulsion to destroy himself, Chip also feels that behind his successful façade he is a fraud. Imbued since childhood with the idea that "people like us" born with privileges are "bound to contribute more than the average to their fellow men," Chip tries repeatedly to break free of his family. Even as a boy he tells his father that he envies the ex-convicts who work on the family's estate because no one expects anything from them. At Yale he threatens to reject a bid to join Bulldog, the prestigious secret society to which his father had belonged, but he is talked out of his rebellion by his mother. His marriage to Alida is similarly intended to annoy his family, but during his law-school years Alida manages a reconciliation with the Benedict family against his wishes. World War II comes as a welcome escape from the burdens of his family. Defusing a German bomb on the deck of his LST off Normandy, he feels a curious sense of void, followed by strange euphoric happiness. As he later tells his college roommate, war is the only occasion where "I don't have to be concerned with Mummie and Daddy and Benedict and love, love, love. All I have to do is kill rats. . . . And maybe in killing them I can get rid of some of the rottenness in myself."

The war against the Germans and even the atomic bomb, with its demonstration that "perhaps it had become true that the process of destruction was futile," have a paradoxical liberating effect upon Chip. He returns home with the hope that there may be a chance for redemption both from the evil he sees in himself and from the evil around him. He plunges into modernizing the family glass works and becomes a model executive and civic leader in Benedict. Yet even this sense of well-being is temporary. In converting the Benedict company into a modern, highly profitable corporation, he has destroyed all vestiges of the family firm with pride in its products that he had inherited. When he realizes that his own position in fighting the takeover is not a whit more noble than the position of the conglomerate that seeks to acquire his company, he quickly sells out. In the episode of the takeover, Auchincloss puts his finger on the corruption of modern institutions. When Chip moves to New York City and joins the boards of various cultural and educational institutions, he realizes that they too have become corrupt. With the "vulgarization in the arts and sciences," he begins "to feel that he might as well be back in the glass business, making shabbier products for higher prices" under "the disapproving eye" of his father, who had stood for the former, higher standards.[4]

As Auchincloss reveals in this implicit critique of cultural institutions, Chip is motivated by a sort of desperate Manichaeism. Like the twelfth-century Albigensian heretics alluded to several times in the novel with whom he felt a keen sympathy as a boy when he visited southern France, he believes that man and the universe were created out of evil. His stern conscience and repeated attempts to strike out against the evil around him are products of his sense of the evil in himself. Perhaps the final manifestation of his Manichaeism in the novel is his support for the Vietnam War. Though partly motivated by anger at his children's self-indulgent criticism of the war, Chip's decision to work for the State Department stems also from a perverse idealism. He thinks of the Vietnam War as "the first real moral challenge that we've had since Pearl Harbor," a duel fought against evil in which America nobly abstains from crushing its enemy by excessive force. With the reports of massacres of civilians by US soldiers, however, Chip realizes that his idealism has been misplaced. This crusade, like his campaign to modernize the Benedict glass business, turns to ashes in his mouth.

The sort of guilty Manichaeism that underlies Chip's behavior is something that Auchincloss had explored in the title character of his 1956 novel *The Great World and Timothy Colt*, yet there are significant new dimensions to Chip's character. For one thing, his sense of evil is nowhere nearly so self-destructive as that of Timothy Colt. His unrelenting conscience, rather than always turning upon himself, often drives him harshly to criticize others, such as his corrupt schoolmate Chessy Bogart, with whom he is involved at several points in his life. With his mild and almost irreproachable father and moralistic mother, Chip Benedict is also an interesting study in what turned some members of the East Coast Establishment into early architects of the Vietnam War. Auchincloss, who attended school with such prominent figures as William and McGeorge Bundy, is at any rate in a good position to speculate upon the mixed motives and miscalculations that can, for what seem the most idealistic reasons, lead a nation into difficulties; and his examination of the problems of being a male member of a family like the Benedicts gives *Honorable Men* much of its interest.

The concluding episode of the novel also marks a significant departure from Auchincloss's previous patterns. When Chip moves to Washington and falls in love with his secretary, Violet Crane, his mother leases a house in Georgetown. In earlier novels the sort of mother represented by Mrs. Benedict might well have intervened to thwart Chip's affair with Violet and patch up his marriage. In a surprising turnaround, Mrs. Benedict encourages the affair and confesses her failure in raising Chip and his sisters. She realizes that her constant worry about Chip's struggles with evil had not helped and that Mr. Benedict's parental philosophy that it was best to love but never intervene in his son's life merely created distance. In this crisis, all she tries to offer is unconditional love. Finally aware that both she and Chip are "puritans without a god," she recants her earlier criticism of his behavior.

With the prospect of a happy marriage to Violet, Chip seems to have been granted a second chance at the end of the novel. But the final situation is ambiguous. Chip can learn from his experiences, but Alida, who now realizes that she does not want to lose her husband, seems to be a victim of her marriage and Chip's successful escape. Chip has apparently broken free, but the last words in the novel belong to Alida: "It would be just my luck," she says, "to see puritanism take its last twisted stand in both my children." *Honorable Men* offers at once the hope that one can escape his past and a reminder of the enduring power of the puritan character over several generations.

In this respect, then, *Honorable Men* is a successful extended exploration of the puritanism depicted among the various members of the Winthrop family in Auchincloss's 1976 collection, *The Winthrop Covenant*. Unfortunately, however, the novel is flawed somewhat by its hasty ending. Chip's attitudes toward the war are not sufficiently developed in the three short chapters Auchincloss devotes to them. Nor is Alida's career as an impecunious debutante sufficiently related to Chip's life in the novel. Nonetheless, *Honorable Men* contains some of Auchincloss's best writing on the experience of war, amply fulfilling the promise held out in his first novel, *The Indifferent Children*. Insofar as it demonstrates Auchincloss's ability to work creative variations on the patterns of his previous fiction and the experiences of his youth, *Honorable Men* represents a most fruitful use of a writer's capital.

10

◊◊◊

The Historical Imagination: *The House of the Prophet* and *Watchfires*

The House of the Prophet and *Watchfires* are the best novels Auchincloss has written since the appearance of *The Rector of Justin* and *The Embezzler* in the mid-1960s. Though both works reflect their author's growing historical consciousness, each stands out for a different reason, and each displays a different side of his artistry. *The House of the Prophet* shows his strengths as fictional biographer and psychologist, as historian of the self. *Watchfires* demonstrates his ability to relate changes that occur in the lives of individuals to larger patterns of change in society—his skill as historian of society. More conventionally historical, *Watchfires* is a particularly appealing book that suggests that Auchincloss may be at his best when he writes about the past. Both novels, however, are good examples of a mature craftsman at the top of his form. As Auchincloss has moved into the 1980s, he has gained renewed vigor and assurance as a novelist.

The House of the Prophet

When *The House of the Prophet* appeared in 1980, several reviewers compared it with *The Rector of Justin*, and Christopher Lehmann-Haupt of the *New York*

Times called it perhaps "the most accomplished book [Auchincloss] has written to date."[1] Not every critic greeted it with such praise: but *The House of the Prophet* is a more significant work than any of the novels Auchincloss published in the 1970s by virtue of the rigorous analysis it presents of its central character, the journalist and commentator Felix Leitner, and because it brings together, in a novelistic *tour de force*, a wide variety of settings, motifs, and images from Auchincloss's previous works.

Because of its narrative method *The House of the Prophet* invites comparison with *The Rector of Justin*. Like the earlier novel, it presents segments of the protagonist's life from the vantage points of various people who have known him — the young admirer and research assistant who plans to write his biography, Leitner's college classmate and best friend, his two wives, a former law partner, the daughter of his second wife. These individual narratives — and two chapters of memoirs by Leitner himself — are held together by the presence of the main narrator, Roger Cutter, the would-be biographer, who has arranged them in chronological order and provides a general frame for the action of the novel in his own narratives. Like Brian Aspinwall in *The Rector of Justin*, Roger Cutter serves as a foil to the older, more eminent central figure. Where Felix Leitner is strong, Roger is weak. Like Brian Aspinwall, Roger is indebted to the older man for what amounts to his personal salvation. Having been hurt as well as rescued by Felix, Roger is a good deal more ambivalent about his subject, and unlike Brian he seems to possess very little independent existence apart from his relationship with his subject.

Felix Leitner is based in many respects upon the late Walter Lippmann, whom Auchincloss and members of his family knew, and who, in his later years, was one of Auchincloss's legal clients.[2] In no other Auchincloss novel perhaps is the connection between the real-life model and the fictional character so close. *The House*

of the Prophet may therefore be said to be an exploration of the enigma presented by the personality and
career of Walter Lippmann. Yet reference to the well-
known public figure on which he is based never really
explains Felix Leitner. In *The Rector of Justin*, even
though one sees the protagonist Francis Prescott from
conflicting perspectives, one achieves some general sense
of his personality. In *The House of the Prophet* Felix
Leitner's true character remains elusive. As Auchincloss
probes the mystery of Felix Leitner, he makes one keenly
aware of the distinction between the private life of the
individual and the public identity of the writer.

The novel begins at a party organized for Leitner's
eighty-third birthday by Roger Cutter. Leitner, now
senile and in ill health, has been placed in a small private
nursing home, but he still tries to write articles, which
Roger must intercept in order to prevent the embarrassment their publication might cause to Leitner's reputation. When Leitner suffers a stroke a few days later,
Roger begins to assemble the materials for his biography.

The events of Felix's life cover the period of American history from Teddy Roosevelt to the Vietnam War.
Born into a wealthy German-Jewish family on Riverside
Drive, Felix attends Yale College at the urging of his
closest friend, Heyward Satterlee, the son of a socially
prominent New York family. Even in college there are
puzzling shifts in Felix's opinions and actions. He seeks
Heyward's support in joining an exclusive social club,
but then becomes an idealistic socialist. Closely attached
to his mother, a former English actress, Felix rebels
against his father and in his last year of college refuses
to accept any support from him because most of the
family's money has been made from rents on slum ten-
ements. Though interested at first in becoming an art
historian, he decides to go to law school, impelled as
much by a fascination with power as by youthful
idealism.

After law school and a year clerking for a Supreme

Court justice, Felix marries Frances Ward, the plain but idealistic daughter of the editor of a small literary magazine. A lawyer herself and a sort of Eleanor Roosevelt figure from an old New York family, Frances is a shy, dependent woman very different from her husband. As she becomes more and more annoyed with Felix's apparent desertion of his former liberal principles, the couple move further and further apart in their marriage.

The same intellectual brilliance and puzzling shifts of opinion that marked Felix in college characterize his public career. At the time of his marriage, he is caught up in the Bull Moose campaign and writes an enthusiastic biography of Teddy Roosevelt. After World War I, he joins the American staff at the Versailles Treaty negotiations. His experiences in France precipitate the first major crisis in his life. Disillusioned with the terms of the treaty, he loses all his idealistic faith in the future and suffers what he later refers to as "a kind of a nervous breakdown." He is nursed back to health by his French mistress and an aunt who is in Europe purchasing works for her art collection. After his recovery, he returns to New York and writes a trenchant analysis of the treaty that establishes his fame as an author.

After a decade as professor of government and constitutional law at New York University, Felix becomes part of FDR's "brain trust." Disappointed by the increase in government regulations brought about by the New Deal, he soon breaks with Roosevelt and joins a large corporate law firm in New York. He writes a book criticizing the New Deal, and continues to write and publish while practicing law. When one of his books conflicts with the position he must argue on behalf of an important client, he resigns from the firm. Shortly thereafter, he falls in love with Gladys Satterlee, the wife of his college friend. His affair with Gladys and ensuing divorce from Frances constitute the second major crisis of his life. Many of his old friends desert him, and he and Gladys move to Washington, where he becomes famous as a political columnist. The pattern of his subsequent life is set: his column in the morning, some reading or research in the afternoon, and a carefully managed round of dinner parties and receptions in the evening.

Felix's second marriage breaks up in a dispute with Gladys over their social life. She thrives on Washington parties, but Felix's refusal to defend the State Department at the time of the Alger Hiss case puts an end to most of their invitations from the White House and high government officials. Felix, who could not abide his wife's increasingly hysterical arguments, is alone again. In the final episode of the novel, his daughter Felicia comes to live with him and persuades him to address a rally against the Vietnam War organized by friends of her daughter. When Felix's uncompromisingly independent speech annoys the young radicals in his audience, Felicia berates him, and Felix banishes her from his house. At the end of his life he is alone once again, separated from family even as he has been solitary in spirit throughout his life.

The House of the Prophet takes its title from Auchincloss's epigraph, the well-known verse from Matthew 13: "A prophet is not without honor, save in his own country, and in his own house." Though we see enough of Felix Leitner the influential commentator and public figure to get a general idea of his career, the emphasis, as the title suggests, is upon the last phrase of the scriptural quotation. The novel is emphatically a portrait of the prophet in his own house — a search for some pattern in the personality that lies behind the shifts in Leitner's public positions as he responds to sixty years of American political history. Roger Cutter mentions early in the novel that he intends to write two books about his hero: one, "a university press kind of thing, a history of his thinking," the other, "much more personal, a picture of Felix Leitner, the man." In *The House of the Prophet*, Auchincloss gives us the second book.

The ways in which Auchincloss both adopts and changes details from Walter Lippmann's life in creating the novel give a good sense of his artistry and suggest his fundamental character as a novelist. For the general structure of Felix's life, he follows the pattern of Lippmann's life set forth in Marquis Childs's biographical sketch in *Walter Lippman and his Times*. Writing in 1959, Childs divides the life into three phases, separated by two major crises: Versailles and Lippmann's divorce and remarriage in 1938.[3] Though the Versailles episode is given its due, Auchincloss is plainly more interested in Felix's divorce and remarriage, which form the central episodes of the novel. As Roger Cutter points out, "leaving Frances and his family" to marry Gladys was "the single most important moral and emotional event of his lifetime."

This emphasis upon major personal events is reflected time and again in similar shifts from the public to the domestic sphere in the novel. As he charts the various ideological turnings of Felix's career, Auchincloss usually focuses upon the personal conflicts raised by his ideas rather than the ideas themselves. Felix's early political idealism, for example, is seen in the novel as growing out of intense oedipal resentment at his father. According to his most recent biographer, however, Lippmann resented his mother's indifference far more than his father's.[4] Felix's own account of his disillusionment at Versailles focuses not so much on the failure of the treaty as on his affair with the French translator assigned to his staff, Mireille de Voe. Similarly, an argument between Frances and Felix about the New Deal is the first rift leading to the breakup of their marriage, and Felix's second marriage founders in a dispute that begins with an argument he gets into with a high State Department official at a Georgetown dinner party. *The House of the Prophet*, then, is not so much a novel of ideas as a novel of character that explores the effects of ideas on human relationships. Given these limitations, Auchincloss is remarkably faithful in reflecting Lippmann's positions on political issues at each point in his life. He is less successful, however, in analyzing Lippmann's ideas or placing them in their intellectual setting.

When Auchincloss does diverge from the facts of Lippmann's life, the changes he makes are revealing. In several instances, Felix or other characters are fitted into patterns that one encounters elsewhere in Auchincloss's fiction. Felix's mother, unlike Daisy Lippmann, for example, but very much like the mothers in *Venus in Sparta* and *The Pursuit of the Prodigal*, is a cloying, over-protective figure with whom her son identifies closely. The motif of the betrayal of a best friend, though obviously present in Lippmann's life, is heightened by added details from one of Auchincloss's earlier novels. Like Rex Geer in *The Embezzler*, Felix Leitner steals the wife of someone who is not only his best friend but also a college classmate and schoolmate who has helped introduce him to respectable society. When he finds it useful, Auchincloss falls back upon his own sense of the primary patterns in human behavior to explain Felix Leitner's psychological development. Though there is no other Auchincloss protagonist quite like Felix, the novel in which he appears bears many of the distinctive traits of Auchincloss's work in general.

To say that Auchincloss falls back at points in *The House of the Prophet* upon familiar patterns from his previous novels is not necessarily to minimize his achievement. In many ways, Walter Lippmann's life almost invited a novel of manners by someone like Auchincloss. This is especially true when one examines the settings in the novel. Choosing a man who was intimately involved with the rich and powerful, a molder of public opinion, an advisor to presidents, and a well-to-do writer who annually visited Europe to talk with world leaders provides Auchincloss with an opportunity to describe settings he knows well. Walter and Helen Lippmann summered on Mount Desert Island in Maine, and Lippmann had often visited friends there with his first wife.[5] Not surprisingly, Auchincloss's finely drawn descriptions of life in the two contrasting summer communities on the island — the artistic and academic enclave of Seal Cove and the fashionable resort of Butterfield Bay — are some of the chief delights in the novel. Similarly, when Auchincloss explains crucial moments in Felix's life by set pieces describing famous paintings — works of El Greco in Toledo, Phillipe Champaigne's portrait of Richelieu at the Louvre, portraits of French revolutionary leaders at the less well-known Carnavalet Museum in Paris — the device becomes quite credible when one realizes that Lippmann wanted to be an art historian at one point in his life and was a friend of Isabella Stewart Gardner and Bernard Berenson. All this material is handled quite skillfully.

Auchincloss's most significant departure from the biographical facts is his portrayal of Felix's first wife, Frances Ward Leitner. Though her family is not rich, Auchincloss gives them a network of "old New York" connections. This change (Lippmann's first wife, Faye Albertson, was the daughter of a Congregational minister with few, if any East Coast social connections) is effective, for it raises the possibility that Leitner may have been a social climber. More importantly, Frances Ward's fundamental seriousness and social awkwardness make her almost totally unlike Lippmann's first wife, who according to one observer at the time of their marriage, would have been far better matched "with some dancing playmate."[6] Frances reflects a female character type one encounters often in Auchincloss, but the decision to draw a sharp contrast between her and Gladys (who does resemble Helen Byrne, Lippmann's second wife,

whom Auchincloss undoubtedly knew) is a sound, novelistic one. Not only does the vivacious and socially adept
Gladys provide a foil to the shy, earnest Frances, but
Felix's inability to remain married to either of two very
different women throws into bold relief the inscrutabil-
ity and isolation of his character. Though Helen Lippmann was a difficult woman, Walter remained devoted
to her until her death less than a year before his own.
The contrast between life and novel in this case again
shows how Auchincloss underscores Felix's fundamental
isolation.

In conceiving the central episode of the novel, however, Auchincloss did not need to heighten or embellish
the facts from Lippmann's life. Auchincloss's account of
Felix Leitner's affair with the wife of his best friend is
actually less romantic than the events leading up to Lippmann's divorce.[7] In the novel Gladys Satterlee is bored
with her marriage to Heyward. Searching for the "great
passion" she thinks she has missed in life, she first sets
her sights on a liberal millionaire and yachtsman named
Mark Truro, but Truro, who has been married five times
and in his world-weary way is not interested in serious
romance, suggests that Felix may be attracted to her.
Gladys pursues Felix, and their mutual attraction leads
to an affair, which is discovered by Heyward, who immediately sues for divorce. After an awkward confron-
tation with Frances, in which he leaves the impression
that he might continue to accept a marriage in name
only, Felix writes her to request a divorce. He also tries
to explain his actions to Heyward, again in a letter, but
Heyward refuses to open the letter and sends it back with
a bitter response.

The equivalent episode in Lippmann's life was much
stranger and marked at several points by coincidences
that one might expect to see only in cheap popular fiction. Walter declared his love to Helen Byrne Armstrong
over dinner at the Rainbow Room, then newly opened

in Rockefeller Center. He had been asked, oddly enough, to take Helen to dinner by Armstrong himself, who had been called to an unexpected meeting. The affair continued for several months, with romantic trysts in an apartment Helen had rented for the purpose, while Lippmann would talk almost daily with Armstrong by telephone and meet him at least once a week for lunch. The affair was finally revealed when four letters that Walter had addressed to Helen while she was on vacation in Austria were mistakenly forwarded to Armstrong's office in New York. Helen and Walter had arranged to meet in Paris after Armstrong had returned to New York, but the day Walter was to land in France was the very day Armstrong received the letters. Expecting a call from Walter, Helen excitedly picked up the phone in her hotel room, saying "darling, at last," only to discover that it was Armstrong on the line and he had found out about the affair. Lippmann was even more indirect in his treatment of his wife than Felix is. He never confronted Faye directly, relying instead upon his father-in-law, to whom he had loaned considerable sums of money, to break the news to her and prepare the way for the letter he wrote later requesting a divorce. Like Heyward Satterlee in the novel, Armstrong refused to read or accept Walter's letter of explanation.

The real-life affair, however, had a remarkable, if belated sequel. Armstrong remained bitter, and for the thirty-five years after the divorce during which he continued to edit *Foreign Affairs* magazine, he never permitted Lippmann's name to be mentioned in its pages. Yet at his death the four letters from Walter to Helen (three of them still unopened) were found in a packet among his papers with instructions that they be given to Helen. Inside was a note: "I only read the first three lines of one of these."[8]

Though the truth of this episode from Lippmann's life is stranger and more vivid that the fiction made from it, *The House of the Prophet* deserves ultimately to be considered on its own as a novel. Auchincloss is working with rich material, but he makes it more vivid and shapelier, not merely through the addition of the sorts of settings and characters that he is known for, but also by providing psychological motivation for the major actors in the drama and by adding depth to the enigma of Felix's character by placing it in a complex web of human relationships. The central episode of the novel provides a good example of Auchincloss at work on his own as a novelist. The Maine resort setting for the affair between Felix and Gladys is more than merely another opportunity to sketch manners. The contrast between Butterfield Bay and Seal Cove underlines the contrast between the characters of Gladys and Frances. Moreover, in the six chapters that make up the central portion of the novel, one sees the breakdown of Felix's first marriage from four distinct viewpoints — those of Frances, Gladys, and Roger Cutter as well as Felix's own. Each person — even the ostensibly objective Roger — is emotionally involved in the events. Frances's motives are more complex than might initially appear. Not only does she want to hold onto Felix as her husband, but she also wants to retain him in the ranks of New Deal liberal politics. Paradoxically, she, who appears to others to be an independent woman with her own career, is willing to give up all of her rights to maintain her marriage. Gladys is passionately in love, but is at the same time motivated by somewhat questionable needs for romantic fulfillment and a desire to acquire Felix as a sort of possession. Roger, through whose observant eyes we see the two summer colonies, adores Felix as a substitute father and unconsciously betrays the affair because he thinks that Gladys's affection is what Felix needs to continue his work. At the same time, the episode of the divorce marks Roger's coming of age. His support for Felix's side in the scandal gets him into a serious argument with his father that forces him belatedly to leave home and live on his own as an adult.

Felix's account of the divorce is characteristically rational. Though he stresses his sexual attraction to Gladys, he carefully assesses his various responsibilities and sums up the significance of his decision at the end of his narrative. "I always knew that the real weakness, the real cowardice," he writes, "would have been to preserve a stale union to avoid a short pain, to abandon what I then believed to be a passionately loving woman for what I then considered an essentially passive one, to turn my back on a life that offered the finest fruition of heart and mind." After the divorce, he and Gladys take a tour of the great cathedrals of France. He looks back on the trip as "the most serene period of my life." Rather than reminding him of his infidelity, the spires and stained glass of the cathedrals lead him to a historical analysis of his situation. Medieval society presented man with not only duties but also rewards. Felix claims, rewards that twentieth-century man no longer has, "I had to live in my own time, under my own moral law. Each man must find it for himself." Once he comes to this decision, Felix is "not to be thwarted by sentiment."

So it always is with Felix, and the question finally becomes what to make of his repeatedly asserted independence. His erstwhile law partner Grant Stowe sees him as "a kind of monster of self," someone "incapable of conforming to any pattern, noble or ignoble," whose pleasure in "separating himself from the team" far outweighs any other consideration. Felix himself admits that he "doesn't want to be on anyone's team," but he sees his independence in noble terms. Roger echoes this view several times. Felix, he thinks, "belonged only to his concept of human liberty." Yet at the end of the novel he remains profoundly ambivalent about Felix. Was he a monster, "a cold-hearted egotist who wanted all the good things in life for himself," or was he an idealist single-mindedly devoted to the pursuit of truth? The novel as a whole is a monument to Roger's indecision on this issue. After a sleepless night, Roger decides to put aside his personal debate about Felix and simply assemble the documents relating to his life. "The point was to make the record." Before doing so, however, he turns for relief to Felix's writings.

In reading *The House of the Prophet*, one senses that Auchincloss had many of the same doubts about Lippmann as Roger had about Felix. If one regards the novel simply as a roman à clef about the character of Walter Lippmann, Auchincloss succeeds admirably in his attempt to "make the record." Indeed, the appearance of *The House of the Prophet* within a few months of the publication of Ronald Steel's biography of Lippmann invites this sort of reading. Two of the best discussions of the novel confirm the validity of Auchincloss's portrait of Lippmann. A reviewer who had known the Lippmanns praises Auchincloss, for example, for aptly depicting Lippmann's overpowering self-confidence and extraordinary rationality.[9] In comparing the novel with Steel's biography, Kenneth Lynn is even more adulatory. Because Auchincloss "has a profound understanding of the man he is writing about," he comments, *"The House of the Prophet* gives us more insight into Lippmann in 275 pages than *Walter Lippmann and the American Century* does in 600."[10]

Even if one takes into account his neo-conservative dislike for Steel's liberal viewpoints, Lynn is right about Steel's failure to take a definite stand on Lippmann's personal flaws or directly confront the contradictions in his character. This Auchincloss plainly does, without, as Lynn reminds one, denying the greatness of his subject. Auchincloss's tributes to Lippmann's writing are also important achievements in the novel. Indeed, the virtues of the novel are its economy, its clarity, and the unflinching honesty of its portrait of Leitner — all virtues that

Lippmann would have valued highly. *The House of the Prophet* is an excellent fictionalized biography.

When one considers the work purely as fiction, however, a few flaws are evident. In his attempt to show the contradictions of Leitner's personality, Auchincloss does not quite do justice to his ideas. He asserts the great man's intellectual brilliance repeatedly, but he never manages to show it in action. Often the elaborate intellectual dialogues in which Felix participates seem both stilted and superficial. Yet Auchincloss set himself a difficult task in the novel: to explore the character of a great man who is not finally a very appealing person and much of whose life involves ideas rather than people. As in *The Rector of Justin*, Auchincloss shows us how the costs of idealism are often paid, not by the idealist himself but by those around him. Indeed, the final answer to Roger's questions about Felix is that he may well be both a monster and a hero. With admirable economy, precision, and energy, *The House of the Prophet* reminds one of this central truth. This is the major achievement of the work, whether one considers it as fiction or history. In *The House of the Prophet* Auchincloss's historical sensibility merges with his acute psychological vision. The result is a compelling and interesting study of the intellectual personality, in all of its uneasy relations to the worlds in which it must dwell.

Watchfires

Even more than *The House of the Prophet*, Auchincloss's 1982 novel *Watchfires* indicates renewed strength. As one reviewer aptly commented when the book appeared, "If there is for long-distance writers what runners call a second wind, Louis Auchincloss seems to have found it."[11] Ostensibly a novel about the Civil War, *Watchfires* is really a novel about marriage, duty, and personal liberation. To be sure, the historical background is always there: the events of mid nineteenth-century history and the Civil War constantly interpenetrate individual characters' actions, but the Civil War also becomes a metaphor that is creatively invoked throughout the novel. In *Watchfires* Auchincloss takes a new, mellower look at the institution of marriage.

Watchfires is divided into three sections, each dealing with a major episode in the lives of a New York lawyer, Dexter Fairchild, and his family. It closes with a brief epilogue in which Auchincloss brings events up to 1895 and clarifies and offers ironic commentary on the preceding episodes. The novel and its three sections take their titles from words or phrases in Julia Ward Howe's "Battle Hymn of the Republic." In fact, Auchincloss seems to have found ideas for some details of plot and character in the lives of Mrs. Howe and her husband.[12]

In part 1, entitled "A Fiery Gospel" and set in 1860, Dexter Fairchild, the senior partner in a family law firm, sets out to break up a romantic affair between the wife of his partner and cousin, Charley Fairchild, and a journalist, Jules Bleeker. Using his own social connections and those of his father-in-law, Mr. Handy, he succeeds in driving Bleeker out of the city, but himself succumbs to the charms of his partner's errant wife, Annie Fairchild, who is also the youngest sister of his own wife, Rosalie. Dexter's affair liberates him from some of the strictures of his background, but at the same time it threatens his own marriage of more than fifteen years. Dexter's wife Rosalie, encouraged by a large, no-questions-asked donation from him, occupies herself almost totally with her work as an ardent abolitionist and supporter of the Underground Railway. At the end of part 1, when Dexter's affair with Annie breaks up, he returns contritely to Rosalie and commits himself to the cause of preserving the Union and freeing the slaves. Shortly thereafter Annie leaves Charley and moves permanently to France.

Part 2, "His Terrible Swift Sword," recounts the involvement of the Handy and Fairchild families in the Civil War. Though it is the shortest section of the novel, it is the most important, for these activities change each member of the family and crucially affect Dexter and Rosalie's marriage. Along with Mr. Handy, Dexter works to organize and equip the New York regiments for Lincoln's army. Rosalie and her unmarried sister Joanna, who has kept house for their father, leave home to serve as nurses on a hospital ship. For the first time each woman acquires an independent sense of identity, and their experiences radically change their perceptions of the role and condition of women. At the end of the section, however, both Rosalie and Joanna must bow to social convention and the pressing needs of their families. They return home, Joanna to care for her rapidly aging father and Rosalie to support Dexter in his efforts to build and maintain hospitals for Union soldiers in his role as Sanitary Commissioner. Rosalie's sacrifice enables Dexter to achieve modest fame for his work.

The third part, "In the Beauty of the Lilies," takes place in 1868, at the time of the impeachment trial of President Andrew Johnson. Dexter, who had initially favored impeachment, agrees to help defend the President because of his devotion to the higher cause of preserving the Constitution. Influenced by her wartime experiences, Rosalie has become an ardent suffragette. Her political activity disturbs Dexter, and she in turn is disappointed by his failure to support her fully. Mr. Handy has grown noticeably older and begins to fail, but a new generation has grown to adulthood. Rosalie and Dexter's older son, Fred, a veteran of the Wilderness Campaign under General Grant, works for a brokerage firm that is helping Cornelius Vanderbilt in his attempt to gain control of the Erie Railway. He is engaged to his employer's daughter, Ellie Bristow. His younger brother, Selby, who has decided to give up an unsuccessful career as an artist, also accepts a job with Fred's employer, riding the Erie trains in order to gather evidence of mismanagement against the company. When Commodore Vanderbilt makes a deal with his rivals Fisk and Gould, however, Fred loses his naive faith in capitalism and quits his job. Immediately thereafter, Selby, the darling of both his parents, is killed in a railroad accident. Fred is tortured by guilt at the loss of Selby, but with the firm guidance of his wife, he decides to study law and join his father's firm. Dexter and Rosalie are also shattered by the loss, but go on with their work because Selby had encouraged them to do so. Dexter comes to share Rosalie's opinions on women's suffrage, and she admires his work in defense of the presidency. After years of disagreement, anger, and loss, they finally appreciate and accept each other.

In the brief epilogue, set at a lawn party given by Mrs. William K. Vanderbilt at Newport, the reader learns that Rosalie died four years after Selby and that Fred has become a successful corporation lawyer. At seventy-seven, Dexter looks back upon the last four years of his marriage as the happiest of his life and faces the prospect of his own death with equanimity.

As this summary suggests, the plot of *Watchfires* is complex. Auchincloss himself speculated that the novel might not find wide popular approval. "I think it's probably difficult to follow," he commented before its publication, "because it is so totally divided in its sympathies and interests."[13] Like such earlier novels as *Portrait in Brownstone* and *The House of Five Talents*, *Watchfires* covers three generations in the life of a family. Yet, despite the complexity and divided sympathies of the novel, what one reviewer has called Auchincloss's "clockwork plotting" ensures that this mass of disparate material is elegantly put together. More importantly, the very multiplicity of interests in the novel is one of its greatest strengths. Auchincloss interweaves a variety of themes, characters, and historical events in such a way that each individual aspect of the novel illuminates other, often seemingly unrelated aspects.

The complexity of *Watchfires* may also be related to its long gestation period. As Auchincloss points out in a brief foreward, he got the germ of the novel — Dexter's attempt to break up the affair between his cousin's wife Annie and Jules Bleeker — from an unpublished section of the diary of George Templeton Strong, a nineteenth-century New York lawyer. Auchincloss developed the episode into an article that first appeared in his 1961 collection of essays, *Reflections of a Jacobite*. In 1976, he returned to the situation from another perspective in one of the best stories in *The Winthrop Covenant*, "In the Beauty of the Lilies." Thus *Watchfires* is the product of more than twenty years of meditation on a particular domestic theme and historical moment.

Watchfires closely reflects the main outlines of the relationship between Strong's own cousin Charley and his errant wife, Eleanor, and Dexter's elaborate campaign to ostracize Bleeker from New York society, which may seem incredible to twentieth-century readers, is precisely the sort of crusade Strong carried on in 1857. In the fictionalized version of the story, Auchincloss deftly suggests a romantic interest on the protagonist's part in his cousin's wife. The story ends, however, with his troubled night thoughts after he has succeeded in driving his opponent from the city. There is no subsequent affair. In his mind, and in the story as a whole, his attraction to Annie is subtly connected with his feelings about the Civil War. He recognizes that one of his motives in the campaign against her lover was jealousy, but then he thinks about the South — associated already with the journalist-lover, who has taken a job in Richmond — and images of war, vengeance, and rape flare up in his mind. Only lightly sketched in "In the

Beauty of the Lilies," the connection between marriage and the union of the States is drawn repeatedly in *Watchfires*.

That Dexter in the novel goes on to have an affair with Annie and the action of the plot continues well beyond the end of the affair underlines Auchincloss's central concern. *Watchfires* is, above all, a novel about marriage: a marriage almost destroyed by Dexter's affair, patched up again but threatened by Rosalie's need for independence and Dexter's failure of sympathy, and finally reconstituted on a higher plane by new understanding between husband and wife. In this novel, Auchincloss presents by far his most hopeful view of the institution. Auchincloss has always drawn sympathetic portraits of wives who were hemmed in by marriage or unappreciated by their husbands, but in his earlier novels such wives achieve whatever peace they can by accepting their married state as a sort of tribal convention; or, in the case of Ida Trask in *Portrait in Brownstone*, Auchincloss shows how an initially shy wife can achieve a sort of personal triumph by outlasting her husband. Even in a novel such as *The Great World and Timothy Colt*, in which the protagonist's marriage is threatened and then restored, the comic ending only hints at the possibility of a happy marriage to follow. In *Watchfires*, Auchincloss shows for the first time the process by which a troubled marriage is maintained and repaired. This, as one reviewer suggested, is a rare sight in fiction.[14]

In depicting Dexter and Rosalie Fairchild, moreover, Auchincloss sets himself another difficult challenge. Both husband and wife are unflamboyant, morally earnest characters, latter-day Puritans who examine their motives carefully. Dexter is even a bit of a prig: in the first scene of the novel, he pompously announces at the breakfast table, "I cannot allow disunion to be advocated in my house." He is the man in the middle who dislikes the South but fears the zeal of the Abolitionists. Although he gets swept up in the fervor of the Northern cause once the war begins, he parts company with the radical Republicans after the war in order to defend President Johnson. Rosalie is more overtly idealistic, both in her expectations for marriage and in her espousal of abolition and women's suffrage, yet she is equally earnest.

Dexter decides to marry Rosalie as much out of rational calculation as out of love. Brought up under the shadow of a scandal connected with his father, a Rector of Trinity Church who had deserted his wife and run off with another woman to Paris, "Dexter was determined that his marriage should replace in the eyes of New York society the image of his father's shattered one." Making his choice of the perfect bride "equally by heart and head," he would consider "beauty, character, social position, health and fortune." In fact, he had selected his father-in-law, Mr. Handy, an influential banker and powerful civic leader, even before he met Rosalie. Yet, despite his calculation, Dexter falls in love with Rosalie. She is powerfully attracted to him, even though she dislikes his eager acceptance of her family's respectability and his enthusiasm for Newport social life. And she marries him even though he does not live up to the heroic expectations for a husband set by her dying mother in a letter given to her when she turned eighteen: "Do not marry unless you are fully convinced that you will be able to love your husband with all your heart and revere him with all your mind."

Dexter's admiration for Mr. Handy presents a sort of double burden for Rosalie, since she had wanted badly to escape the domineering control of her powerful and egotistical father. It is in this context that Dexter's affair with Annie takes place — and that Rosalie begins her work on the Underground Railway. Rosalie desires somehow to establish an independent relation to her family background and her role as wife and mother, and her vague knowledge of Dexter's affair simply makes her involvement in antislavery work more intense. At one point, she entertains romantic fantasies about Frank Halstead, the minister in charge of the Underground Railway in New York, but, true to the serious tenor of her character, she realizes that she would reject any sexual advances from him. "Even if the old puritanism of the Handys and the Howlands had been diluted in her to the point of excluding the sin that existed only in the mind, the ancient sense of guilt had been replaced by an equally sharp horror of seeming ridiculous." As Auchincloss observes, "she was the victim, even in fantasy, of her own sense of what was fitting." Here, again, Rosalie is not a conventional romantic figure.

After his affair has run its course and he finds that Annie had been physically involved with Bleeker, Dexter confesses to Rosalie. Acting partly out of his repulsion at Jules Bleeker, he has already changed his political opinions and announced his support for Abraham Lincoln, in the hope that he might retrieve himself in Rosalie's opinion by sharing her beliefs. In the first of a series of fine scenes between husband and wife in the novel, however, Rosalie tells Dexter that she can forgive his intrigue with Annie, but cannot forgive his "exultation" over his redemption. She distrusts his newfound opinions: "You're like so many abolitionists. You don't love the slave. You hate the slaveholder. There's only death and destruction in your heart." When Dexter points out that her father Mr. Handy has welcomed him gladly to the fold, Rosalie brusquely replies, "It's easy for *him* . . . he owns you."

In this the final scene of part 1, Auchincloss skillfully brings together Dexter's mixed motives, Rosalie's frustration in her roles as daughter and wife, and the political issues on the eve of the Civil War. Rosalie's questions about Dexter's feelings apply equally to his own personal situation and to the self-righteous idealism with which the North entered the war — as well as the violent righteousness that characterizes any "just war." Nonetheless, Dexter is not left totally without hope. Rosalie proposes that they "just go on" with their marriage and see what happens.

With the advent of the war, in the second part of the novel, almost everyone finds new purpose in life. As they both participate in the war effort, Rosalie and Dexter begin to come more closely together. They saw much less of each other, "but when they did talk, it was with a mutual interest in what each was doing that was novel in their relationship." Rosalie remains unhappy about Dexter's enthusiasm for war, however, and when she announces that she will leave home to work as a nurse, he is upset both because she is leaving him and because she will be closer than he is to actual combat. The scene in which Rosalie tells Dexter about her new job begins as a conventional argument between husband and wife about the wife's deserting her domestic duties, but Auchincloss suddenly shifts our attention to another, less predictable plane. Dexter reveals to Rosalie that he has accepted the post of Sanitary Commissioner. In that capacity, he will be able to help many more soldiers than she. Rosalie is reminded again of her relative insignificance as a woman: "Oh, he still had his old power of turning the tables on her! She, who had yearned for the high seriousness of a role of her own in the war, basing the shedding of domestic duties on the seemingly solid ground of his inconsequence, was now faced with a situation where the sacrifice was all on his part and her mission turned into a kind of joy ride."

Rosalie's experiences as a nurse are, of course, no joy ride, and they affect her life significantly, but, in keeping with the realities of nineteenth-century marriage and her own sense of duty, she leaves them behind and returns home to care for Dexter and her sons. Before Rosalie gives up her job, Auchincloss shows the extent to which her relationship with Dexter has advanced.

After her husband has collapsed from overwork, she nurses him back to health on the hospital ship. For Dexter, the experience is a sort of idyll; in the isolation of the ship, he feels euphorically content. Auchincloss captures the moment admirably. But for Rosalie, who must after all do the nursing, the experience is less satisfying. Nonetheless, she realizes that she too has been a prig, "so sure of my sincerity, my honesty, my deep, *deep* heart." She has learned that she is only as useful as she is competent, not a bit more. When she kisses Dexter on the forehead, he realizes that "it was more than the kiss of a devoted nurse, if perhaps less than that of a devoted wife."

Rosalie's decision to return home to care for Dexter is spurred on by an odd encounter with Dexter's mother, who has always seemed to reflect the conventional proprieties of the wifely role, but who bitterly urges her to return to the hospital ship. "If I'd had what you have," she says, "I wouldn't have given it up for any man under the sun!" Rosalie realizes that Dexter has been included in his mother's general wrath against men and that, as his wife, she is the only person who has promised to love him. She has, in effect, no choice. This sacrifice comes to her mind again when Dexter fails to vote in favor of a women's suffrage resolution she has introduced at a meeting of the Equal Rights Association. She reminds Dexter that she left the hospital ship for him and forgave his affair with Annie. "I've been a good brownstone wife. And now that at fifty I begin to see at last how to work for a cause in which I passionately believe, now that I want this *one* thing for Rosalie Fairchild, all you can talk about is your domestic peace!" Though her words have a slightly anachronistic ring — and are meant to remind the reader of women in our own century — they do express her situation precisely. Dexter's response, rather than being a caricature, is complex. He is disturbed by the strident political tone of the suffragists, but he has abstained rather than vote against Rosalie's resolution, and he is tempted to join Rosalie rather than engage in self-pity because of the disruption of his orderly life.

Full reconciliation between husband and wife only comes after Dexter has observed the pro-impeachment forces at Johnson's trial and realizes that "a congress of women would have been incapable of such behavior." Rosalie, who has also been watching the proceedings, joins Dexter as he leaves the Capitol. As he expresses his support for women's suffrage, she expresses her misgivings about her work. While Dexter helps to save a president, all she can do is "orate in some dingy hall to five snorers and one heckler." But Dexter points out to her that "the reason I'm in a position to accomplish more than you is that men have had things their own way so long." Rosalie now sees that Dexter does understand her position, but she is still honest enough to question her own motives. "There may be as much anger as idealism in my stand," she says, "anger at Papa, at you, at that horrible Mr. Cranberry." And she worries that she may be a "wrecker" rather than a "builder." Dexter reassures her that she is trying to preserve society, not destroy it. "I've accepted enough sacrifices from you," he concludes. "I don't wish to accept any more."

This is the final scene between them and, except for the brief epilogue, the last scene in the novel. The mutual acceptance that Dexter and Rosalie have attained is not remarkable in the late twentieth century, though it might have been unusual in 1868. Nor are Dexter's political opinions striking today. But that is not the point. Auchincloss's achievement is to show the process by which two people have changed. This is the first Auchincloss novel in which a husband and wife both engage in significant work in the wider world and both are able to accept the frustrations as well as the satisfactions in such work, without begrudging the other his or her independence. Although Auchincloss does not show more of this new phase in the Fairchilds' marriage, his decision is sound: Marriages are like families, and as Tolstoy writes at the beginning of *Anna Karenina*, "All happy families resemble one another, but each unhappy family is unhappy in its own way."

The gradual metamorphosis of Dexter and Rosalie's relationship is the central focus of *Watchfires*, but closely related to the progress of their marriage is the theme of liberation, which Auchincloss considers from a rich variety of viewpoints. Throughout the novel, Auchincloss reminds one of the interconnectedness of the various senses of the term. At one point, for example, after Dexter's affair with Annie has become public knowledge, Mr. Handy calls Rosalie a heroine for enduring her fate without complaining. She rejects the compliment but tells him that she knows what a heroine is: "every female slave who flees her master." In their dialogue, as elsewhere in the novel, political liberation — the emancipation of the slaves — is tied to domestic and personal liberation.

The process of personal liberation is most evident in the lives of Rosalie and her sister Joanna. Their work on behalf of escaped slaves is the first step toward their growing independence from socially imposed roles. Their service on the hospital ship completes the process of breaking away from their old lives. Paradoxically, Rosalie's upper-class background helps rather than hinders her work as a nurse. "The habit of deference" instilled in her as a child makes it easier for her to accept military hierarchy, and a secure social position enables her and Joanna to take on "demeaning" tasks without complaints. They "would cheerfully help the black boys in the galley when the other matrons wouldn't." In the world of the hospital ship Rosalie begins to experience "that elusive 'life of her own' that she had so long assumed would be provided, if at all, only by a husband."

Joanna's "fussiness and nervousness" now seem focused in a "steady flurry of hard work," and the soldiers like her rather than condescend to her. Above all, the relationship between the sisters changes. Rosalie respects Joanna's competence and realizes how unhappy she has been at home. A deep sense of solidarity develops between the two women.

Only after Rosalie returns from the war, however, does the full meaning of her liberation become plain. Not only does she follow out the political implications of her own work — and the logical implications of a war to free slaves — by campaigning for women's suffrage, but she also has freed herself from her excessive deference to her father. Dexter notes this and is "startled to hear Rosalie, for the first time, refer to her father's general philosophy simply by his address. Did this represent some ultimate step in her long emancipation from the paternal authority?" The word "emancipation" is obviously significant in the context of the Civil War, and it comes to mind again in a slightly different sense when Rosalie advises Ellie Bristow to sleep with Fred before they are married. Though Rosalie remains too much of a Puritan to be "emancipated" in her own sexual conduct, her attitudes on the subject have changed. For Auchincloss, however, Rosalie is finally free only at the point of her reconciliation with Dexter. Only then is she capable not merely of acting independently but also of understanding the anger and inevitably mixed motives that impel most human actions.

Because she does not participate in the redemptive work of the war, Annie Fairchild does not share in the sort of liberation her older sisters experience. Like Jules Bleeker, she is associated with a certain decadence that Dexter and others see in the South. Nevertheless, she finds her own identity in escape from the earnest world of New York, and her decision to leave Charley and live in Paris is also related to the war. "Rebellion is in the air," she tells Dexter, "I've seceded at last."

It is, of course, not only the women in the novel who are liberated. Dexter experiences his own liberation on several levels. His affair with Annie frees him of certain naive romantic preconceptions, and, more importantly, it frees him of a kind of guilty subordination to his mother: "All his life he had been afraid of disappointing her, as if her image of him had been a kind of ideal that he could only live by constantly aspiring to." After he recognizes his attraction to Annie, he is immune to his mother's reproaches, and he sees his father and the impossible project of making up for that parent's actions in a more realistic light. Though Dexter remains moralistic, he is no longer so self-righteous.

Liberation in its widest sense comes to Dexter after the affair with Annie. Both his participation in the impeachment defense and the changes in his relationship with Rosalie contribute to the process. In rejecting the arguments of the radical Republicans and defending the moderate principle of constitutional law, Dexter frees himself of the vestiges of Northern fanaticism. The changes in Rosalie force him to reevaluate his marriage and to see his wife, and women in general, in a new way. That Dexter's liberation is most fully realized at the same moment as his wife's and that the moment coincides with their reconciliation affirms Auchincloss's opinion that personal and social liberation are related and that true freedom is possible only within some sort of social structure. This is the vision of liberation that informs the novel.

With its overlapping interest in personal liberation and the social institution of marriage, *Watchfires* is both a novel of character and a novel of manners. Although Rosalie and Dexter live at a particular time and in a particular place, their problems seem at once contemporary and universal. In what sense, then, is *Watchfires* historical? Advertised on its dust jacket as "a novel of the Civil War," the book has puzzled some readers because it seems to have so little to do with the actual events of the war. Admittedly, the reader never sees an actual battle and Dexter Fairchild's participation in the war is purely administrative, but *Watchfires* is indeed a novel about the war. On one level, as has been suggested, Auchincloss draws attention to historical issues by repeated metaphorical connections between the lives of his characters and the events of the war. Not only is Annie said to have seceded from her marriage and Rosalie to have been emancipated from her father, but Dexter's earlier, frantic attempts to patch up Charley and Annie's marriage are related to his opinion that the Union must be maintained at all costs. In the third section of the novel Dexter's efforts to reconstruct his marriage with Rosalie parallel the nation's own awkward attempts at reconstruction.

More than a metaphoric image connecting public and private realms, the Civil War is a reflection of a certain spirit present in mid-nineteenth-century America, and this spirit is the true historical subject of the novel. Auchincloss has commented: "The Civil War always seemed to me the one war that was worth fighting. It also seemed to me, through what I've read, that the scene on both sides was filled with all the hysteria and violence that cause unnecessary wars — but in this case happened to be causing a war that perhaps was necessary. That sort of thing is the difficulty of the novel."[15] More than any other character, Dexter becomes an embodiment of the Northern mind and the "difficulty" presented by the war. At the outset of the novel, he suffers from "a violent perturbation of spirits" brought on by reading Harriet Beecher Stowe's *Uncle Tom's Cabin*. One result of this inner turmoil is his affair with Annie, but even before the affair has ended, the experience of reading Southern editorials on the execution of John Brown triggers in his mind "a sudden surge of hate so strong as to make him actually giddy."

After he realizes that he has shared Annie with him,

his hatred for Bleeker (a figure already associated with the South) contributes to his desire for war, as expressed in the prayer that ended the short story and ends the chapter of the novel in which Dexter breaks with Annie: "Dear God, I know we should allow our Southern states to live in peace. But if in your infinite wisdom, and through the mediation of your servant, Abraham Lincoln, you should see fit to permit *them* to strike the first blow, . . . will it be wrong if we leap to arms with joy and jubilation? If we bring the devastation of your anger to their fair land? If we burn their plantations with cleansing fire and chastise their rebel people with the sword? Or even worse? Will you blame us if their women are raped by the very slaves we have freed, if . . . " The imagery of divine vengeance in the prayer is important, for it echoes the imagery of the day of wrath in the "Battle Hymn of the Republic," the poem that, as Edmund Wilson and others have observed, reflects the predominant myth under which the North fought the war. Dexter's language reflects not only the poem but also his puritanism; and the sexual imagery at the end of the prayer also suggests that he is motivated not only by jealousy at Bleeker but also by a desire to root out all the Bleeker-like tendencies in his own soul. Bleeker not only personifies the South, but he is also the other man who has shared Annie's favors, and, as revealed when the two men first meet, an art collector who shares Dexter's tastes. Dexter's motives in joining the crusade to free the slaves are muddied by these connections with his rival. That a decent and otherwise moderate man like him can be so carried away suggests the problematic nature of the Northern responses to the Civil War. From a wider perspective, Auchincloss also seems to be suggesting that war in general is primarily a male activity. Neither Rosalie nor Joanna ever shares the violence of Dexter's enthusiasm, but, significantly, Mr. Handy does.

As Auchincloss places Dexter's affair with Annie in

the wider context of Dexter's marriage, so he also places the Civil War in a larger historical context. As has been suggested, Dexter's participation in the defense of Johnson is an attempt to heal some of the wounds caused by the war. But the war, which technically did free the slaves and which (in the novel at least) leads to the possibility of women's suffrage, is finally part of a larger cycle that Auchincloss discerns in American history. One sees this cycle in the careers of Dexter's two sons. Fred, the hero of the Wilderness Campaign, returns home to New York to participate, with all the warlike enthusiasm of the crusade the free the slaves, in Commodore Vanderbilt's raid on the Erie Railway. He even enlists his gentler, artistic brother Selby in the cause. Ironically, it is Selby who loses his life in the dubious cause of capitalistic acquisition. When Vanderbilt makes a deal with his even more corrupt opponents Jay Gould and Jim Fisk, Fred likens it to an agreement between Grant and Lee in which Grant permits slavery to continue in the South. Even after "possibly the one war that was worth fighting," there is a rapid fall from the innocent, idealistic state that had been reflected in the best motives of the best men who fought. This inevitable decline from an ideal that itself may have been partly illusory is a theme one encounters more than once in Auchincloss. In *Watchfires* it fits in well with the essentially mixed motivations and results of America's perhaps most idealistic war.

After a period of despair, Fred goes on to become a lawyer and to turn his father's firm into one of the first large corporate law firms in the country. This result may suggest that despite the abolitionist fervor the triumph of the North in the Civil War was ultimately the triumph of the large industrial corporation. At the heart of Auchincloss's view of the historical results of the war, at any rate, is a clear-sighted and ironic vision of the way American society works. This finally emerges in the epilogue to the novel, in which Auchincloss also offers one last view of Dexter and his family. The scene is a garden party on the grounds of Marble House, one of the ostentatious mansions erected on Bellevue Avenue in Newport at the end of the nineteenth century. As Dexter observes, Commodore Vanderbilt had never been accepted socially by Mr. Handy and his contemporaries, but now the wives of his two grandsons "were practically running the summer community," while families like the Handys had receded into the background. "Such was social history," he thinks. As if to confirm his train of thought, he soon meets Rosalie's sister, Lily Van Rensselaer, at eighty-four very much a representative of the older New York. In the midst of the domestic difficulties and divorces of the Vanderbilts, Lily still thinks of Dexter's own marriage as irretrievably ruined by his affair. Dexter aggressively affirms the happiness of the last years of his marriage.

Elsewhere at the gathering, Dexter encounters his son Fred, who asks him to give up his large corner office at the law firm. Fred's embarrassment clearly indicates that he has been put up to making the request by his ambitious wife, but Dexter accedes gracefully and avoids saying anything about the real source of the request. Now at peace with himself, Dexter is capable of a self-restraint and forbearance that he was unable to muster earlier. In a burst of emotion, however, Fred withdraws the request. Both this encounter and the previous conversation with Lily confirm the validity and the significance of the changes in Dexter's personality.

The special attraction at the party, however, is a concert featuring a performance of the "Battle Hymn of the Republic" with Julia Ward Howe in attendance. By 1895, public renditions of the hymn on ceremonial occasions had become a common custom, though Auchincloss's setting for the performance may be an invention.[16] As the soloist sings the verses of the hymn and the audience joins in the chorus, Dexter is stirred with some of his old fervor. Yet he catches himself, and, in the novel's final commentary on the spirit of the Civil War, he thinks back upon an episode in his own life in which he and Mr. Handy had joined a crowd of fashionable Northerners expecting to witness a Union victory at Bull Run:

And then he suddenly recalled what Mrs. Vanderbilt had said about the conception of the poem. In a carriage riding back to Washington, had it not been? He thought now, less comfortably, of his own ride to the capital after the disaster at Bull Run. Looking around him, in altered mood, at the splendor of the house and its gardens, at all the fine clothes and shiny baubles, he had an eerie sense of that old retreat somehow turned into a victory march, a rush over a prostrated enemy, a stampede from Atlanta to the sea, with the parasols, the floppy hats, the Irish lace, the cutaways, the gray waistcoats, the gleaming canes, the pearls and the diamonds, no longer abandoned by the wayside, but brandished in triumphant, upstretched hands like the banners of conquering legions. Christ might have died to make men holy, but had not Mrs. Vanderbilt and God won the war? (*Watchfires*, p. 347)

The final sentence with its allusion to the fourth verse of Mrs. Howe's poem ("As he died to make men holy, let us die to make men free") ironically reminds one that the real victors in American society were not the forces of mercy or the gentle Christ who was born "in the beauty of the lilies," far away, "across the sea," and that modern American society may have become free but it has not succeeded in becoming holy, either in fashionable Newport in 1895 or since. The brilliant epilogue to *Watchfires* shows that Auchincloss can excel in evoking the rituals of fashionable society of the past, while at the same time offering trenchant moral criticism of the very scene he describes.

Watchfires may be divided in its sympathies and interests, but it is a rich and lively novel. It is also the work of a highly skilled practitioner of the craft of fiction. Some of its richness comes from the variety of sharply defined characters that Auchincloss manages to present in the relatively short span of 348 pages. Such minor figures as Fred's fiancée Ellie Bristow and Commodore Vanderbilt, whom we glimpse briefly in two small scenes, reveal in their very economy of presentation Auchincloss's special gifts for characterization. Perhaps the most striking thing that *Watchfires* reveals about Auchincloss's mature art is his ability to construct a certain sort of old-fashioned scene — almost a set piece but at the same time a significant element in the meaning of the novel as a whole. The epilogue is a fine example of this scene-making ability, but the previous chapter to which the epilogue alludes is perhaps the most telling example of Auchincloss's unique gift, an inheritance finally from the great moral novelists of Victorian England, Thackeray and George Eliot. The shade of Thackeray's *Vanity Fair* hovers over the chapter in which we witness the retreat from Bull Run.

Perhaps *Watchfires* is too complex, too divided in its loyalties, but it is one of Auchincloss's finest novels precisely because of the various things it manages to do. It presents an optimistic view of marriage, a fresh look at human liberation, and a serious analysis of the passions that resulted in the Civil War and the effects of that war as they have shaped and continue to shape the American character. It is truly a work of the historical imagination. Along with *The House of the Prophet*, it offers abundant testimony to Auchincloss's continued creative power and growing range as a novelist.

Afterword

In a recent study of the American novel since 1940, labeled on its title page "a comprehensive history and critical evaluation," Louis Auchincloss is mentioned only twice in 595 pages of text; once in a footnote that links him with Gore Vidal as a writer who "has made literary choices that — despite trendy themes — look back, not forward," and then in a comment on another writer whose style is criticized as "pseudo-James, a kind of religious version of Louis Auchincloss."[1] Admittedly Auchincloss often does look back in terms of both style and subject matter, yet the novels and stories he has written over the past forty years are worthy of more sustained and careful critical attention than they have received. Auchincloss richly repays reading, and in this age of rampant criticism when a university library may contain more than a dozen book-length studies of John Updike, and a half-dozen or more on John Cheever, James Gould Cozzens, or even Gore Vidal, Auchincloss deserves notice.

This is not, of course, to say that Auchincloss is destined to become one of the major figures of twentieth-century American literature. He is not: but what he does, he does well. As a novelist, he has chosen to go his own way, largely ignoring the predominant trends of literary modernism. For much of his career he has worked in a genre, the novel of manners, that does not encourage technical experimentation, and he has written psychological novels in the tradition of such great nineteenth-century predecessors as Jane Austen and

243

George Eliot, as well as his acknowledged masters, Henry James and Edith Wharton. Yet even in his novels set in the past, he displays a twentieth-century sensibility, skeptical, ironic, and thoroughly modern in its psychological point of view.

Auchincloss's great strength as a novelist is not invention. He does not create strange new worlds but remains, as Henry James once advised Edith Wharton to be, "tethered in native pastures." He writes about the worlds he knows best. Though not all his characters are White Anglo-Saxon Protestants and not all his novels take place in New York City and environs, Auchincloss is usually concerned with upper-class characters or members of the high bourgeoisie. As a reading of his autobiography *A Writer's Capital* will reveal, much of Auchincloss's fiction grows directly out of his own life and experiences. The autobiographical aspects of his work are often ignored; indeed, his career may be seen as a series of creative reinvestments of the capital of his early experiences. Despite the particular choices he has made, however, it is unfair to overemphasize the limitations of Auchincloss's world. Within an apparently small compass, there is great variety of character and situation.

As a stylist, Auchincloss inherits a certain formality and evenness of tone from James. He never insists: "cool and straightforward are the correct labels" for his style, as one critic has observed.[2] As a self-proclaimed "Jacobite" he often follows the example of James in starting from a central problem or "germ" in creating his novels. Yet, more than is often noticed, many of his novels are also based fairly directly on the detailed examples of particular lives: the career of Walter Lippmann in *House of the Prophet*, the Richard Whitney scandal in *The Embezzler*, the failure of Edward Gilbert in *A World of Profit*. He is "Jamesian" in the way he carefully works out a particular *donnée*. Yet he is also autobiographical, and at other times his fictional technique approaches that of a documentary novelist. Here again there is more variety to Auchincloss than initially meets the eye.

As Benjamin DeMott and others have pointed out, it is also a mistake merely to regard Auchincloss as a novelist who "does" the life and manners of New York, much as Marquand "did" Boston or O'Hara Pennsylvania. Though he is an accurate historian of manners, he is almost invariably concerned with psychological problems that extend well beyond a particular class or locale — with guilt and feelings of inadequacy in his characters, with a sort of bleak netherworld where people caught between a vanishing past and an unfriendly present exist in a personal void. As DeMott observes, "his writing is subtlest when it inquires into the moment-by-moment complications of self-regard — especially self-regard under pressure."[3]

Louis Auchincloss is finally a novelist whose work is both popular and profoundly literary, designed to entertain a general audience but at the same time self-consciously allusive and often based upon previous literary models. As a popular novelist, he is above all prolific — perhaps too prolific for his own good. Like Anthony Trollope he often relies on what appear to be formulas. Yet he has been able to change over time, and even those novels that return to previous themes or situations do so in new ways. Clearly Auchincloss has continued to develop and grow as a writer over the years. In each of the past three decades he has produced major additions to his canon.

In addition to the large quantity of his fiction — twenty novels and eight collections of stories — Auchincloss has also made significant contributions as a critic and popular historian. Perhaps his finest work of non-fiction is *A Writer's Capital*, a memoir of considerable charm and grace. As a practicing novelist, he writes authoritatively on James and Wharton. His knowledge of, and sympathy for, the tradition of the novel of manners make his essays on O'Hara and Marquand, Proust, and Edith Wharton permanent contributions of scholarship. Yet, as his popular histories as well as most of his literary essays reveal, Auchincloss is essentially a generalist addressing a non-scholarly audience. At its best his criticism and historical writing introduces the average reader to the pleasures of the past while providing shrewd insights into characters and events. Auchincloss's achievements in nonfiction mark him as a true man of letters for our times.

Despite these achievements, Auchincloss will ultimately be judged by his fiction. Here the sheer body of his work is impressive, a sustained examination of what might be called the Auchincloss world: men in Wall Street law firms and investment houses, shy heroines and powerful matrons who must come to terms with the values of the tribe, insecure young men who must come to terms with familial expectations and the terrors of success. Yet the quality of Auchincloss's individual novels and stories varies widely. His finest novels, however, are all historical in some significant sense. *Watchfires* and *The House of Five Talents* look back to eras before Auchincloss was born. *The Rector of Justin* and *The Embezzler* evoke the world in which he grew up. For Auchincloss's most acute commentaries on contemporary life, one must turn to his short stories.

As one considers Auchincloss's development as a novelist, one observes, as has been suggested, a growing historical consciousness. Yet throughout his work Auchincloss is also a moralist. He is able, as James Tuttleton has argued, to evoke nostalgia for the lost elegance of the past without romanticizing the society that produced it. At points, too, especially in *The Rector of Justin* and the flawed but significant *I Come as a Thief*, his moral analysis includes religious themes. This is still further testimony to his variety.

By the enduring standards of criticism, Auchincloss remains a minor novelist. Reviewing *The Embezzler* some years ago, R. W. B. Lewis, the biographer of Edith Wharton, observed that "Auchincloss's historical world is, or is becoming, a minor one; and the task he has set himself, as its chronicler, is inevitably to be a minor novelist." Yet he also pointed out that Auchincloss's chosen task is more difficult, in some significant respects, "than the effort to become a major writer. It is the minor writers, both masculine and feminine, on whom we must always count to preserve the best in our culture. We have never had enough of them, mainly because we have not honored them enough; in the absence of a Melville, we settle for the pretentious hack. But Louis Auchincloss is as responsible, as craftsmanlike and honorable a representative of this crucial literary species as any one can think of."[4]

This tribute to Louis Auchincloss remains true today. Tactful, intelligent, and perceptive, Auchincloss's best works seem destined to endure as permanent contributions to the tradition of American letters.

Notes

1. A Life in Law and Letters: A Biographical Sketch

1. Louis Auchincloss, *A Writer's Capital* (Minneapolis: University of Minnesota Press, 1974), p. 125. Unless otherwise indicated, all quotations in this chapter are taken from *A Writer's Capital*. In the following chapters extended quotations from Auchincloss's novels and stories are identified by short title and page number in the body of the text. All such citations refer to the editions of Auchincloss's works that are listed in the bibliography at the end of this volume.

2. There is no full-scale biography of Auchincloss. My account of his life is based upon his memoir, *A Writer's Capital*, such standard sources as *Contemporary Authors* and *Who's Who in America*, and the interviews and brief biographical articles listed in the bibliography at the end of this volume.

3. William McFee, "Another Newcomer Writes an Impressive First Novel," *New York Sun*, 27 May 1947; quoted in *A Writer's Capital*, p. 115.

4. For summaries of virtually every review of Auchincloss's work from 1947 to 1976, see Jackson R. Bryer, *Louis Auchincloss and His Critics: A Bibliographical Record* (Boston: G. K. Hall, 1977).

5. Elizabeth Bowen, "Outspoken Grief," *The Tatler and Bystander* (London), 124 (19 June 1957):641.

6. J. Donald Adams, "Speaking of Books," *New York Times Book Review*, 29 September 1963, p. 2.

7. Kenneth S. Lynn, "Versions of Walter Lippmann," *Com-*

mentary, October 1980; repr. in *The Air-Line to Seattle* (Chicago and London: University of Chicago Press, 1983), p. 177.

8. James W. Tuttleton, *The Novel of Manners in America* (Chapel Hill: University of North Carolina Press, 1972), pp. 246 and 261.

9. Gore Vidal, "Real Class," *The New York Review of Books*, 21 (18 July 1974); repr. in *Matters of Fact and Fiction* (New York: Random House, 1977), pp. 27–38.

10. Benjamin DeMott, "In Praise of Louis Auchincloss," *New York Times Book Review*, 29 September 1979, p. 7.

11. Susan Cheever, "The Most Underrated Writer in America," *Vanity Fair*, October 1985, pp. 104–7, 119–20.

12. James Tuttleton, "Louis Auchincloss," in *American Novelists Since World War II*, ed. Jeffrey Helterman and Richard Layman (Detroit: Gale Research, 1978), p. 11.

2.   The Complexities of Character: *The Rector of Justin*:

1. Granville Hicks, *Literary Horizons* (New York: New York University Press, 1970), p. 185. Hicks's doubts have been echoed by numerous other reviewers, especially during the 1960s.

2. In a note to the revised edition of *Peabody of Groton* (Cambridge, MA: Riverside Press, 1967), p. 320, Frank D. Ashburn comments: "No book about Groton or by a Grotonian occasioned as much discussion as Auchincloss's *The Rector of Justin*, which, in spite of the author's disclaimers, was generally considered to be a portrait of Endicott Peabody. . . . The result was confusion and much unhappiness. Many felt it a pity that such an important work of fiction should be popularly considered as an authoritative picture of a man, his school, and his family."

3. For Auchincloss's discussion of the biographical sources of the novel, see *A Writer's Capital*, pp. 35–61, and his essay, "Origin of a Hero," in *Life, Law, and Letters*, pp. 21–29. Auchincloss states that aspects of Prescott's character were based also on the jurist Learned Hand and

makes it clear that Brian Aspinwall was in no way intended as a portrait of the young Groton English master,
Malcolm Strachan. Endicott Peabody's life is detailed in
Frank Asburn's *Peabody of Groton* (cited above), which
was written in 1944.

4. "Origin of a Hero," p. 29.
5. "Louis Auchincloss: The Image of Lost Elegance and Virtue," *American Literature* 43 (1972): 619.
6. Paul Pickrel, "Manners of Mammon," *Harper's Magazine*, 229 (1964): 98.

3. Quests for a Limited Identity: The Early Novels

1. Henry James, *The Letters of Henry James*, ed. Percy
   Lubbock (New York: Scribner's, 1920), 1: 396.
2. This and subsequent quotations in the paragraph are
   from the Foreword to *The Indifferent Children* (Engle-
   wood Cliffs, NJ: Prentice-Hall, 1964), p. v. For a further account of Auchincloss's feelings about his first novel,
   see *A Writer's Capital*, pp. 107–08 and 113–15.

4. New York Then and Now: *The House of Five Talents* and *Portrait in Brownstone*

1. For an excellent discussion of this problem see James Tuttleton, *The Novel of Manners in America* (Chapel Hill:
   University of North Carolina Press, 1972), especially
   Chapter 1, "The Sociological Matrix of the Novel." I am
   indebted to Tuttleton's insights about the novel of manners and Auchincloss's place in the tradition of the genre
   throughout this chapter.
2. C. Hugh Holman, *John P. Marquand*, University of Minnesota Pamphlets on American Writers, No. 46 (Minneapolis: University of Minnesota Press, 1964), p. 7.
3. Robie Macaulay, "Let Me Tell You about the Rich . . . ,"
   Kenyon Review 27 (1964):655. The Millinders in *The*

House of Five Talents resemble some of the members of the Vanderbilt and Whitney families to whom Auchincloss's wife is related. However strange the events of Gussie's late-nineteenth-century girlhood may seem to a contemporary reader, they realistically reflect the world portrayed in the diary of Mrs. Auchincloss's grandmother, Florence Adele Sloane, *Maverick in Mauve*. As suggested later in this chapter, the Denisons in *Portrait in-Brownstone* are based in part on the Dixons, the family from which Auchincloss's mother came.

4. Auchincloss makes this point in an interview accompanying Granville Hicks's review of *Portrait in Brownstone*. See Iola Haverstick, "The Author," *Saturday Review*, 14 July 1962, p. 21.

5. For a photograph of Palmer's statue, see Curtis Dahl, "Sculpture in Victorian Fiction," *Nineteenth Century* 7, no. 2 (Summer 1981):20. Dahl discusses the tradition in nineteenth-century American fiction that Auchincloss revives in *The House of Five Talents*.

6. Macaulay, "Let Me Tell You about the Rich . . . ," p. 654.

7. Haverstick, "The Author," p. 21.

8. Tuttleton, *The Novel of Manners in America*, p. 251.

9. William Barrett, "Once Affluent Society," *Atlantic* 210 (August 1962): 143.

5. Novels of the Great World

1. Gore Vidal, "The Great World and Louis Auchincloss," repr. in *Matters of Fact and of Fiction* (New York: Random House, 1977), p. 38.

2. Wayne W. Westbrook, "Louis Auchincloss' Vision of Wall Street," *Critique* 15 (1973): 57–66; and *Wall Street in the American Novel* (New York University Press, 1980), pp. 182–96.

3. For a more detailed discussion of the hierarchy of lawyers in Auchincloss's fiction and Auchincloss's attitude to law-

ricia Kane, "Lawyers at the Top: The Fic-
Auchincloss," *Critique* 7 (1964–65):36–46.

story, "The Trial of Mr. M.," published in
per's Magazine in 1956, served as the source for the
conclusion to *The Rector of Justin*. The headmaster in
the story, whose experiences are virtually identical to the
events in the final episode in Francis Prescott's life in *The
Rector*, is named Minturn.

5. Marcel Proust, *Remembrance of Things Past*, trans. C.
K. Scott Moncrieff and Terence Kilmartin (New York:
Random House, 1981), 2:629–36. In this important episode, found at the beginning of the "Cities of the Plain"
section, the narrator first learns of Charlus's homosexuali-
ty. Michael's intense relationship with Peter Teriot also
raises the question of homosexual tendencies. In any event,
Auchincloss's reference to the scene in Proust, whether
conscious or unconscious, shows how thoroughly his imagination was permeated by the works of the great French
novelist. Auchincloss was obviously familiar with the
scene, which was criticized by Edith Wharton. He mentions it in a recent article: "Marcel at the Transom: Something Is Wrong With Proust's Narrator," *New York Times
Book Review*, 4 August 1985, p. 15.

6. James Tuttleton, *The Novel of Manners in America*
(Chapel Hill: University of North Carolina Press, 1972),
p. 250.

7. Benjamin DeMott, "Monge and Other Destinations,"
Hudson Review 12 (1959–60):623.

8. For a very brief discussion of the connection between Gil-
bert's career and Jay's downfall in the novel, see John
Brooks, "Fiction of the Managerial Class," *New York
Times Book Review*, 8 April 1984, p. 36.

9. I am indebted to Susan Cheever for drawing my attention to this connection in her article, "The Most Underrated Writer in America," *Vanity Fair*, October 1985,
p. 120. Auchincloss's use of *Renée Mauperin* along with
details from Gilbert's career in *A World of Profit* nicely
illustrates how he is at once literary *and* topical in his
fiction.

6. The Great World Revisited: *The Embezzler*

1. For a fuller account of Richard Whitney and his role in the downfall of the old order on Wall Street, see John Brooks, *Once in Golconda: A True Drama of Wall Street 1920–1938* (New York: Harper & Row, 1969). I have listed only a few of the parallels between the Whitney case and events in *The Embezzler*. For another discussion of the parallels, see Wayne W. Westbrook, *Wall Street in the American Novel* (New York University Press, 1980), pp. 186–88.

2. Brooks, *Once in Golconda*, pp. 134–35, 206–9.

3. As Westbrook points out, Thomas W. Lamont was the son of a country parson and published a memoir entitled *My Boyhood in a Parsonage* (New York: Harper & Brothers, 1946). Rex Geer is said to have written a similar book, *My Boyhood in a New England Rectory*. For the relationship between Richard Whitney and his brother George, see Brooks, *Once in Golconda*, pp. 134–35.

4. Even Brooks's lengthy examination of the case leaves one puzzled as to Richard Whitney's motives.

5. According to Brooks, Whitney asked Charles R. Gay, the President of the New York Stock Exchange, for special consideration after his misuse of customers' securities had been discovered. "After all, I'm Richard Whitney," he apparently told Gay. "I mean the Stock Exchange to millions of people" (*Once in Golconda*, p. 258).

6. Whitney's conduct was similar. When finally confronted, he did not plead but "assumed more of a reasoning attitude, as if he were discussing someone else than himself" (Brooks, *Once in Golconda*, p. 258).

7. R. W. B. Lewis, "Silver Spoons and Golden Bowls," *Book Week* (The Washington Post), 20 February 1966, p. 8.

7. The Stories

1. Gore Vidal, *Matters of Fact and Fiction* (New York: Random House, 1977), p. 32.

2. William Peden, *The American Short Story: Continuity and Change 1940-1975* (Boston: Houghton Mifflin, 1975), p. 55.

3. For a discussion of the shrinking market for short fiction in mass circulation magazines see Peden, *The American Short Story*, Chapter 2.

4. G. Edward White shows how Auchincloss's fiction reflects these changes in the organization of large New York firms in "Human Dimensions of Wall Street Fiction," *American Bar Association Journal* 58 (1972): 175-80.

5. James Tuttleton, "Louis Auchincloss," in *American Novelists Since World War II*, ed. Jeffrey Helterman and Richard Layman, (Detroit: Gale Research Co., 1978), 2: 11.

8. The Novelist as Man of Letters:
The Nonfiction

1. Louis Auchincloss, Preface to *Louis Auchincloss and his Critics*, by Jackson R. Bryer (Boston: G. K. Hall, 1977), p. ix.

2. Gore Vidal, "The Great World and Louis Auchincloss," in *Matters of Fact and Fiction* (New York: Random House, 1977), p. 34. Vidal writes: "Right after the war when I was told that a Louis Auchincloss had written a novel, I said: Not possible. No Auchincloss could write a book. Banking and law, power and money — that is their category."

3. T. K. Meier, rev. of *Reading Henry James* in *Modern Fiction Studies* 21(1975):648.

9. The Uses of the Past:
Recent Novels

1. Even so perceptive a reviewer as Abigail McCarthy in *The New York Times Book Review* (26 November 1978) mentions that "the moral question posed" in the novel "is currently relevant, related to bribery and chicanery among

those in whom society places its trust." A reviewer in the *Minneapolis Tribune* spoke of Auchincloss's "inner view of misconduct in high places."

2. Louis Auchincloss, *Pioneers and Caretakers* (Minneapolis: University of Minnesota Press, 1965), p. 42.

3. In *The Country Cousin* and *Watchfires* Auchincloss begins with the events described in the previously published short story and then extends the narrative of his novel beyond what had been the ending of the story. In *Honorable Men*, however, the conclusion of the novel closely resembles that of the story, and Auchincloss expands his account of the events leading up to it: Chip's boyhood, Alida's career as a debutante, Chip and Alida's courtship, and, above all, Chip's naval experiences. Chip, Alida, and their son and daughter all have their equivalents in "The Penultimate Puritan." If anything, Chip's puritanism is even more fully explored in the novel.

4. In a letter to the editor in the *New York Times* of 16 September 1981, Auchincloss commented sardonically on reports in the press that the management of the family-owned Corning Glass Works had sold their holdings in a subsidiary in such a way as to make a hostile takeover inevitable. This decision by members of the Houghton family may well have provided the germ for the episode in *Honorable Men* in which Chip decides to accept the takeover offer for Benedict Glass.

10. The Historical Imagination: *The House of the Prophet* and *Watchfires*

1. Christopher Lehmann-Haupt, "*The House of the Prophet*," *New York Times*, 4 March 1980, p. C10.

2. The Lippmann papers at Yale (Box 54, Folder 128) contain letters from Louis Auchincloss, his father J. Howland Auchincloss, and other members of the family written in the 1950s and 60s. For Auchincloss's role at the end of Lippmann's life, see Ronald Steel, *Walter Lippmann and the American Century* (Boston: Little, Brown, 1980), pp. 596–98. My comments on Lippmann's life are based upon Steele's biography.

3. Marquis Childs, "Introduction: The Conscience of the Critic," in *Walter Lippmann and his Times*, ed. Marquis Childs and James Reston (New York: Harcourt Brace, 1959), pp. 2–20.

4. Ronald Steel, *Walter Lippmann and the American Century*, p. 8.

5. Ibid., p. 251, p. 377, p. 497.

6. Ibid., p. 119. For an account of Lippmann's first marriage and Faye Albertson's family, see Steel, pp. 117–20 and pp. 30–31.

7. Indeed, Kenneth Lynn takes Steel to task for romanticizing the episode in his biography. "Steel's treatment of the parallel episode in Lippmann's life seems much more fictional, in a sense, than Auchincloss's," he complains, "for the romantic details he chooses to play up, and his lack of a critical attitude toward the 'hero' and the 'heroine', are the soggy stuff of which stories in magazines like *Woman's Home Companion* and *Good Housekeeping* are made." "Versions of Walter Lippmann," repr. in *The Air-Line to Seattle* (University of Chicago Press, 1983), p. 179.

8. Steel, *Walter Lippmann*, p. 363. See also pp. 342–66 for an account of the affair and Lippmann's second marriage.

9. Robert Yoakum, "The Importance of Being an Egoist," *Nieman Reports* 34, No. 3(1980):44–47.

10. Kenneth Lynn, "Versions of Walter Lippmann," in *The Air-Line to Seattle* (Chicago: University of Chicago Press, 1983), p. 177. Lynn's essay is a revised version of an article he published in *Commentary* in October 1980.

11. Peter S. Prescott, "Civil Strife," rev. of *Watchfires* in *Newsweek*, 26 April 1982, p. 78.

12. Julia Ward Howe was a member of an old New York family. Like Dexter and Annie, Julia and her husband Samuel Gridley Howe had a stormy relationship. He resented her independence during their marriage and at one point at least carried on an extramarital affair. During the Civil War, he served on a newly founded Federal Sanitary Commission. "The Battle Hymn of the Republic" was written after a trip to the front not unlike the outing that Dexter takes with Joanna and Mr. Handy to

watch the Battle of Bull Run. After the war, Mrs. Howe was also active in the woman-suffrage movement. For a lively account of her life, see Deborah Pickman Clifford, *Mine Eyes Have Seen the Glory* (Boston: Little, Brown, 1979). My account of the Howes is based on this source.

13. David Black, "Louis Auchincloss Reconciles His Two Worlds," *Saturday Review*, April 1982, p. 28.

14. Prescott, "Civil Strife," p. 78.

15. Black, "Louis Auchincloss Reconciles His Two Worlds," p. 28.

16. Public recitations and choral performances of the Hymn were common. Indeed, Julia Ward Howe attended many of them as an honored guest. See Clifford, pp. 3–5, 147, and 276.

Afterword

1. Frederick R. Karl, *American Fictions 1940/1980: A Comprehensive History and Critical Evaluation* (New York: Harper & Row, 1983), pp. 92 and 249. Leo Braudy treats Auchincloss more respectfully in his chapter, "Realists, Naturalists, and Novelists of Manners," in *The Harvard Guide to Contemporary American Writing*, ed. Daniel Hoffman (Cambridge, Mass.: The Belknap Press, 1979), pp. 136–38. Nonetheless, Karl's evaluation of Auchincloss does not misrepresent the prevailing attitude among academic critics.

2. Benjamin DeMott, "In Praise of Louis Auchincloss," *New York Times Book Review*, 29 September 1979, p. 7.

3. Ibid., p. 21.

4. R. W. B. Lewis, "Silver Spoons and Golden Bowls," *Book Week* (The Washington Post), 20 February 1966, p. 8.

Bibliography

I. Principal Works by Louis Auchincloss
Arranged chronologically

The Indifferent Children. New York: Prentice-Hall, 1947.
[Published under the pseudonym of "Andrew Lee."]
The Injustice Collectors. Boston: Houghton Mifflin, 1950.
Sybil. Boston: Houghton Mifflin, 1951.
A Law for the Lion. Boston: Houghton Mifflin, 1953.
The Romantic Egoists. Boston: Houghton Mifflin, 1954.
The Great World and Timothy Colt. Boston: Houghton Mifflin, 1956.
Venus in Sparta. Boston: Houghton Mifflin, 1958.
Pursuit of the Prodigal. Boston: Houghton Mifflin, 1959.
The House of Five Talents. Boston: Houghton Mifflin, 1960.
Reflections of a Jacobite. Boston: Houghton Mifflin, 1961.
Edith Wharton. Minneapolis: University of Minnesota Press, 1961.
Portrait in Brownstone. Boston: Houghton Mifflin, 1962.
Powers of Attorney. Boston: Houghton Mifflin, 1963.
The Rector of Justin. Boston: Houghton Mifflin, 1964.
Ellen Glasgow. Minneapolis: University of Minnesota Press, 1964.
Pioneers & Caretakers. Minneapolis: University of Minnesota Press, 1965.
Editor. *The Edith Wharton Reader*. New York: Charles Scribner's Sons, 1965.
The Embezzler. Boston: Houghton Mifflin, 1966.
Tales of Manhattan. Boston: Houghton Mifflin, 1967.

A World of Profit. Boston: Houghton Mifflin, 1968.

Motiveless Malignity. Boston: Houghton Mifflin, 1969.

Second Chance — Tales of Two Generations. Boston: Houghton Mifflin, 1970.

Henry Adams. Minneapolis: University of Minnesota Press, 1971.

Edith Wharton — A Woman in Her Time. New York: Viking Press, 1971.

I Come as a Thief. Boston: Houghton Mifflin, 1972.

Editor. *Fables of Wit and Elegance.* New York: Charles Scribner's Sons, 1972.

Richelieu. New York: Viking Press, 1972.

The Partners. Boston: Houghton Mifflin, 1974.

A Writer's Capital. Minneapolis: University of Minnesota Press, 1974.

Reading Henry James. Minneapolis: University of Minnesota Press, 1975.

The Winthrop Covenant. Boston: Houghton Mifflin, 1976.

The Dark Lady. Boston: Houghton Mifflin, 1977.

The Country Cousin. Boston: Houghton Mifflin, 1978.

Life, Law and Letters: Essays and Sketches. Boston: Houghton Mifflin, 1979.

Persons of Consequence: Queen Victoria and Her Circle. New York: Random House, 1979.

The House of the Prophet. Boston: Houghton Mifflin, 1980.

The Cat and the King. Boston: Houghton Mifflin, 1981.

Unseen Versailles. Garden City, New York: Doubleday & Company, 1981. [Text by Auchincloss; photographs by Deborah Turbeville.]

Watchfires. Boston: Houghton Mifflin, 1982.

Exit Lady Masham. Boston: Houghton Mifflin, 1983.

Narcissa and Other Fables. Boston: Houghton Mifflin, 1983.

Editor. *Maverick in Mauve: The Diary of a Romantic Age,* by Florence Adele Sloane. Garden City, New York: Doubleday & Company, 1983.

The Book Class. Boston: Houghton Mifflin, 1984.

False Dawn: Women in the Age of the Sun King. Garden City, New York: Doubleday & Company, 1984.

Honorable Men. Boston: Houghton Mifflin, 1985.

Editor. *Quotations from Henry James, Selected by Louis Auchincloss*. Charlottesville: The University Press of Virginia, 1985.

II. Works About Louis Auchincloss

Bibliographies

Bryer, Jackson R. *Louis Auchincloss and His Critics: A Bibliographical Record*. Boston: G. K. Hall, 1977.

Critical Studies and Major Reviews

Adams, J. Donald. "Louis Auchincloss and the Novel of Manners." In *Speaking of Books — and Life*. New York: Holt, Rinehart and Winston, 1965.

Adams, Robert M. "Saturday Night and Sunday Morning." *New York Review of Books* 2(9 July 1964):14–16.

Brooks, John. "Fiction of the Managerial Class." *New York Times Book Review*, 8 April 1984, pp. 1, 35–37.

DeMott, "In Praise of Louis Auchincloss." *New York Times Book Review*, 29 September 1979, pp. 7–8.

Galbraith, John Kenneth. "Reading About the Rich." *New York Times Book Review*, 21 October 1984, pp. 1, 54–55.

Hicks, Granville, "Louis Auchincloss." In *Literary Horizons — A Quarter Century of American Fiction*. New York: New York University Press, 1970.

Hoffman, C. Fenno. "Wise Folly and Pure Manners: The Distance Between *Herzog* and *The Rector of Justin*." *Church Review* 23(February–April 1965):3–9.

Hurley, Neil P. "Liberation Theology and New York City Fiction." *Thought* 48 (1973):338–59.

Kane, Patricia. "Lawyers at the Top: The Fiction of Louis Auchincloss." *Critique* 7(1964–65):36–46.

Lewis, R. W. B. "Silver Spoons and Golden Bowls." *Book Week* (The Washington Post), 20 February 1966, pp. 1, 8.

Long, Robert Emmet. "The Image of Gatsby in the Fiction of Louis Auchincloss and C. D. B. Bryan." *Fitzgerald/Hemingway Annual* 4(1972):325–28.

Lynn, Kenneth S. "Versions of Walter Lippmann." In *The Air-Line to Seattle: Studies in Literary and Historical Writing about America*. Chicago: University of Chicago Press, 1983.

Macauley, Robie. "'Let Me Tell You About the Rich. . . .'" *Kenyon Review* 27 (1965):645–71.

Tuttleton, James W. "Capital Investment." *Sewanee Review* 82(1974):xlvii–lii.

_____. "Cozzens and Auchincloss: The Legacy of Form." In *The Novel of Manners in America*. Chapel Hill: University of North Carolina Press, 1972.

_____. "Louis Auchincloss." In *American Novelists Since World War II*. Ed. Jeffrey Helterman and Richard Layman. Detroit: Gale Research, 1978.

_____. "Louis Auchincloss: The Image of Lost Elegance and Virtue." *American Literature* 43(1972):616–32.

Vidal, Gore. "The Great World and Louis Auchincloss." In *Matters of Fact and of Fiction*. New York: Random House, 1977.

Westbrook, Wayne. "Familiar as an Old Mistake." In *Wall Street in the American Novel*. New York: New York University Press, 1980.

_____. "Louis Auchincloss' Vision of Wall Street." *Critique* 15(1973):57–66.

White, G. Edward. "Human Dimensions of Wall Street Fiction." *American Bar Association Journal* 58(1972):175–80.

Yardley, Jonathan. "A Refreshing Conservatism." Rev. of *I Come as a Thief*, in *New Republic* 167(16 September 1972):30.

Yoakum, Robert H. "The Importance of Being an Egoist." *Nieman Reports* 34, No. 3(Autumn 1980), pp. 44–47.

Interviews and Biographical Sketches

Black, David. "Louis Auchincloss Reconciles His Two Worlds." *Saturday Review*, April 1982, pp. 24–28.

Bryan, C. D. B. "Under the Auchincloss Shell." *New York Times Magazine*, 11 February 1979, pp. 35–37.

Cheever, Susan. "The Most Underrated Writer in America." *Vanity Fair*, October 1985, pp. 104–7 and 119–20.

INDEX